Contemporary Political Theory

PHILOSOPHICAL TOPICS

PAUL EDWARDS, GENERAL EDITOR

Contemporary
Political Theory

Edited, with an Introduction,
Notes, and Bibliography by

PHILIP PETTIT

THE AUSTRALIAN NATIONAL UNIVERSITY

Macmillan Publishing Company
New York
Collier Macmillan Canada
Toronto
Maxwell Macmillan International
New York   Oxford   Singapore   Sydney

Editor: Helen McInnis
Production Supervisor: George Carr
Production Manager: Sandra Moore
Text and Cover Designer: Angela Foote

This book was set in Caledonia by Digitype, Inc., and printed and bound by Edwards Brothers, Inc. The cover was printed by Phoenix Color Corporation.

Macmillan Publishing Company
866 Third Avenue, New York, New York 10022

Collier Macmillan Canada, Inc.
1200 Eglinton Avenue East
Suite 200
Don Mills, Ontario M3C 3N1

Library of Congress Cataloging-in-Publication Data

Contemporary political theory / edited with an introduction, notes,
    and bibliography by Philip Pettit.
        p.   cm. — (Philosophical topics)
    ISBN 0-02-394955-4 (paper)
    1. Political science—Philosophy.   I. Pettit, Philip, 1945– .
II. Series.
JA71.C585 1991
320′.01—dc20   90-6278
                              CIP

Printing: 1 2 3 4 5 6 7   Year: 1 2 3 4 5 6 7

ACKNOWLEDGMENTS

I wish to thank Dr. David Bennett who provided invaluable assistance in preparing this volume; I could hardly have done it without him. I am also grateful for advice received, but alas not always heeded, from Professors Paul Edwards, Thomas McCarthy, and Frederic Schick. The following is a list of the original sources for the articles in this volume. I wish to thank the copyright holders for permitting me to draw upon this material and, in some cases, to abridge it:

Joel Feinberg, "The Nature and Value of Rights," *The Journal of Value Inquiry*, 1969, 4, pp. 243–257. Copyright Kluwer Academic Publishers. This paper is reprinted with a postscript in Joel Feinberg, *Rights, Justice and the Bounds of Liberty*. Princeton University Press, Princeton, N.J., 1980.

Quentin Skinner, "Two Views on the Maintenance of Liberty," *Politics*, 1983, 18, pp. 3–13. (Original title: "Machiavelli on the Maintenance of Liberty"; other changes were made to the text by Professor Skinner.) Copyright Australasian Political Studies Association.

Richard Wollheim, "A Paradox in the Theory of Democracy," in *Philosophy, Politics and Society*, Second Series, Peter Laslett and W.G. Runciman, eds. Basil Blackwell, Oxford, 1962, pp. 71–87. Copyright Basil Blackwell.

James Griffin, "Modern Utilitarianism" *Revue Internationale de Philosophie*, 1982, 36, pp. 331–375; sections 9, 10, 11, pp. 345–353 omitted here. Copyright Institute de Philosophie.

Amartya Sen, "Poor, Relatively Speaking," *Oxford Economic Papers*, 1983, **35**, pp. 153–168; section 8, pp. 165–167 omitted here. Copyright Oxford University Press.

Carole Pateman, "Feminist Critiques of the Public-Private Dichotomy," in *Public and Private in Social Life*, S.I. Benn and G.F. Gaus, eds. Croom Helm, London, 1983, pp. 281–300. Copyright S.I. Benn and G.F. Gaus.

John Rawls, "The Basic Structure as Subject," *American Philosophical Quarterly*, 1977, **14**, pp. 159–165. Copyright American Philosophical Quarterly. An expanded version of this paper appears in *Values and Morals*, Al Goldman and J. Kim, eds. Reidel, Dordrecht, 1978.

David Gauthier, "Bargaining Our Way Into Morality: A Do-It-Yourself Primer," *Philosophical Exchange*, 1979, **10**, 15–25. Copyright The Center for Philosophical Exchange.

Philip Pettit, "Habermas on Truth and Justice," in *Marx and Marxisms*, G.H.R. Parkinson, ed. Cambridge University Press, Cambridge, 1982, pp. 207–228. Copyright Cambridge University Press.

Jon Elster, "The Market and the Forum: Three Varieties of Political Theory," in *Foundations of Social Choice Theory*, J. Elster and A. Hilland, eds. Cambridge University Press, Cambridge, 1986, pp. 103–128. Copyright Cambridge University Press.

James Buchanan, "Politics Without Romance: A Sketch of Positive Public Choice Theory and Its Normative Implications," in *IHS Journal*, 1979, **3**, pp. B1–11. Copyright Physica-Verlag.

F.A. Hayek, "Competition as a Discovery Procedure," in *New Studies in Philosophy, Politics, Economics and the History of Ideas*, Routledge and Kegan Paul, London, 1978, pp. 179–190. Copyright F.A. Hayek.

CONTENTS

PART III
THE FEASIBLE: WHAT CAN WE GET?

Contemporary Political Theory

Political Theory: An Overview

1. Introduction

"By political theory," John Plamenatz wrote, "I do not mean explanations of how governments function; I mean systematic thinking about the purposes of government."[1] Political theory is a normative discipline, designed to let us evaluate rather than explain; in this it resembles moral or ethical theory. What distinguishes it among normative disciplines is that it is designed to facilitate in particular the evaluation of government or, if that is something more general, the state.[2] We are to identify the purposes of government — more strictly, the *proper* purposes of government — so that we can decide on the best political arrangements for society.

I work with Plamenatz's definition in this book. The readings offered here are all in one way or another relevant to the normative analysis of the state. I stress this point at the outset as readers interested in explanatory political theory — the sort of theory that ideally informs empirical research on the state — may otherwise be disappointed with what I provide. If such readers know at the beginning what they are getting, then they will have no reason later to complain. Indeed they may even be pleasantly surprised, when they discover that normative political theory, as the essays in this volume represent it — particularly

[1]John Plamenatz, "The Use of Political Theory" (*Political Studies*, Vol 8, 1960), p. 37.
[2]On the various ways of understanding the state see Alan Hamlin and Philip Pettit, "Normative Analysis of the State: Some Preliminaries," in Alan Hamlin and Philip Pettit, eds., *The Good Polity* (Oxford: Blackwells, 1989).

those in Part III—is more connected with explanatory theory than they might have expected.

As it has been practiced over the past quarter century or so, normative political theory involves three relatively distinct sorts of enterprise. The first is the study of the values relevant to assessing political arrangements; the second is the study of the sorts of arrangements that we would be likely to choose if we were able to make a social contract of some kind; and the third is the study of the sorts of arrangements that we can expect to remain firmly in place, once put in place. The essays in the volume are in three sections, corresponding to these three kinds of projects. The first project focuses on what is desirable, the second on what is eligible, and the third on what is feasible.

2. The Desirable

The study of the desirable, as I describe it, means the analysis and assessment of those properties for which we ought to look in political arrangements, according to different political philosophies. One such property is liberty, another equality, another happiness or utility. In the case of each such valuable property, each such value, two main questions arise. The first, the question of analysis, is what is required for the property to be realized; the second, the question of assessment, is what is to be said for or against the value, particularly in the context of other values.

Take a value like equality. The question of analysis ramifies here into a variety of different issues. What subjects are required to be equal: individuals, or just groups of some sort—racial groups, gender groups, social classes, and so on? In what regards are they required to be equal: in opportunities, in holdings, or in some other feature such as resources or capacities or satisfactions? If we cannot attain full equality, how do we rank degrees of inequality? Is it better in a group of one hundred to have ninety well off and equal, with ten miserable at various levels, than to have fewer than ninety well off and equal, with the others spread over an above-misery range?

But even when we have settled our minds on the appropriate analysis of equality, there remains the question of assessment. How important is equality? In particular, how important is it beside other values such as liberty and utility? Is it better to have an equal society with a lower average level of happiness than a slightly unequal society with a slightly higher happiness count? What is the trade-off function, as economists put it, between equality and utility or between equality and liberty? Is equality lexically prior, in the sense that we are allowed to concern ourselves with utility or liberty only after we have done all we can for equality: in effect, after we are looking at alternative arrangements that do equally well by equality? Or is the trade-off function more continuous, so that we can say that so many units of equality are worth so many of utility or liberty? Or is there no general function available? Have we to rely on intuition, as intuitionists claim, when weighing the importance to be attached to different values in any assessment of political arrangements?

But the question of assessment goes even deeper than these illustrative problems may suggest. There is one particularly important sort of problem that we have so far ignored, a problem that arises, at least in theory, with every putatively valuable property. It is also a problem of trade-off, but the elements in the trade derive from one and the same value.

Suppose that a liberal government comes to power in a traditionally oppressive society, a government that is devoted to the cause of liberty: in particular, the cause of liberty in the negative sense in which it means, roughly, exemption from interference by others. But suppose further that this government is threatened by a fascist movement that is likely to attain power. What should the liberty-concerned government do? Should it honor or respect the liberty of the fascists to advance their cause within the existing law, even though this means that in the long term liberty overall will suffer? Or should it be prepared to deny the liberty of fascists, suppressing their movement, for the sake of more efficiently promoting liberty overall?

In such a case, the trade to be decided is between honoring a value, as we might say, and promoting it, given that the best way to promote it in some cases is to offend against it. The trade is between the state's honoring liberty by letting the fascists carry on at least their legitimate activities and the state's promoting liberty by suppressing the fascist movement. The problem arises with values generally. Should the state honor equality by never itself treating parties unequally? Or should it promote equality, being prepared to treat parties unequally, if this reduces inequality overall? Should it honor the value of happiness, never allowing itself directly to make others unhappy? Or should it promote happiness, being prepared to cause unhappiness to some, if this means that others generally will create more happiness for others?

These issues are not just of abstract interest. Consider the judge who, acting in the name of the state, has to decide between giving an offender his justly deserved punishment, equal to what is given to relevantly similar others, and giving him an unequal, exemplary sentence in the hope of reducing crime, increasing the proportion of offenders convicted, and thereby increasing the overall equality of offenders in receiving their just deserts. Should the judge honor the value of equality in just deserts or should he seek to promote it, being prepared to give some offenders exemplary and strictly undeserved punishments?

The issue of assessment on which we have been focusing comes in general terms to this. Should an agent, in particular the state, treat every value recognized as an objective to be promoted? Or should it go to the other extreme and treat some values as constraints, as values that require to be honored, even if this makes for their lesser promotion overall? Those who say that all values have the status of objectives to be promoted are described as consequentialists or teleologists. Those who say that at least some values have the status of constraints are described as nonconsequentialists or deontologists.[3]

Most of the values proposed as relevant for the assessment of political arrangements can be regarded in a consequentialist or a nonconsequentialist light. Liberty is often regarded as a value that attracts a nonconsequentialist construal but there is nothing incoherent in the notion of a liberty-concerned government being prepared to ban fascist movements. Utility or happiness is taken invariably as a consequentialist objective, but again there is no strict incoherence in the notion of a state who motto is never to reduce the level of happiness by its own hands: to keep its own hands clean, so to speak, in the happiness stakes.

The one example of a political value that may seem to be tied to a nonconsequentialist reading is that of having certain rights satisfied. A right is usually regarded as a constraint in our sense, and indeed as a weighty constraint: a constraint that not only requires to be honored even if there is less of that right overall — others honor it less in their mutual dealings — but also requires to be honored even if other goals such as the society's economic performance or level of happiness are thereby compromised.[4] But if rights are constraints in this sense, then don't they call for a deontological response from the state? Not necessarily. The state may be regarded as privileged among other agents and its task may be described in "rights-consequentialist" terms as that of promoting the honoring of certain rights rather than necessarily honoring them itself.

To sum up then, the study of the desirable in political theory involves two tasks: the analysis of the various values proposed for the assessment of political arrangements and the assessment of those values in relation to one another. Questions of analysis vary from one value to another, but in the area of assessment the same sorts of issues arise. One of the most important of these is whether any value should be regarded as a constraint or whether, as consequentialists hold, all values have the status of objectives.

---

[3]I offer a more detailed characterization in "Consequentialism," in Peter Singer, ed., A Companion to Ethics (Oxford: Blackwells, forthcoming).
[4]This view of rights is particularly associated with two contemporary thinkers, Robert Nozick and Ronald Dworkin. I discuss it in "Rights, Constraints and Trumps" (Analysis, Vol 47, 1987).

3. The Eligible

It is a melancholy fact about the study of the desirable that it has not generated much consensus among political theorists. Among philosophers who focus their attention on this sort of project, we can distinguish two more or less pure positions—polar opposites, as it happens. One is the natural rights tradition, under which the only relevant value in the assessment of political arrangements is how far the state honors a few allegedly basic rights: the usual form is classical liberalism or libertarianism—strictly, deontological libertarianism. The other pure position is the utilitarian tradition, under which the only relevant value is how far the state promotes the happiness or utility—this may be variously construed—of the sentient creatures it affects, in particular its own members. But philosophers who have tried the way of the desirable are usually averse to either of these extremes and tend to languish in the uncertain territory between. They go for various mixes of values such as liberty and equality, unsure about how far they are constraints or objectives and unsure about how heavily they should be weighted against each other.

This feature of the study of the desirable is undoubtedly the reason why in recent years more and more political theorists have begun to explore the way of the eligible. Despairing of reaching consensus, even perhaps precision, through focusing directly on the analysis and assessment of candidate values, they have investigated an indirect strategy of political argument. The idea is to ask, not what is of value in political arrangements according to our actual view, but rather what arrangements we would choose to institute were we, counterfactually, put in the position of having to make a social contract.

The idea of the social contract has been familiar for centuries, since it figures in the work of classical authors such as Thomas Hobbes, John Locke, and Jean Jacques Rousseau. But most contemporary theorists put the idea to a sort of use quite different from what it has for these writers. They are not so much concerned, as those writers were, with the source of legitimacy of the state: the basis for the legitimacy of the state's claims on the citizen. They use the social contract device to identify what form the state should ideally take: whether it should be a minimal state, restricted to honoring and protecting natural rights, for example, or a state responsible in utilitarian fashion for the promotion of the welfare of its citizens.

Although he was not the first among contemporary authors to invoke the social contract in this role—John Harsanyi did so before him—John Rawls has been the most influential of contractarian political theorists. In his monumental work *A Theory of Justice*, Rawls asks us to imagine ourselves in a position—the original position, as he calls it—to choose between different sets of public rules for organizing social life: different basic structures for society.[5] In particular, we are to imagine that in that original position we are ignorant of our individual features — our color, our lack of intelligence, our gender, for example — and that we have to make our choice under this veil of ignorance. The question then is what would we choose. The assumption is that whatever we would choose is fair and so far as it is fair, just. Thus Rawls's contractarian procedure is designed as an indirect way of elucidating the requirements of justice as fairness. For the record, he argues that what is required is a basic structure involving two principles: first, and with a nearly absolute priority, a principle of equal, maximal liberty for all; second, a principle allowing that provided there is fair opportunity for all, some may be allowed to be richer than others if this inequality improves the lot of the worst off in the society.

Contractarian approaches have multiplied in the wake of A Theory of Justice, published in 1971. In the remainder of this section I shall try to situate Rawls in relation to other approaches, highlighting the differences between Rawls's contractarianism and approaches such as those of Robert Nozick, Jürgen Habermas, and David Gauthier. In doing so I draw on work done elsewhere.[6]

There are two important dimensions in which we find differences between political theorists who are or might be described as contractarian. First there are differences on the role of the contract invoked and second there are differences on the nature or kind of contract envisaged. I shall look in turn at Rawls's view of the role and the nature of the contract, contrasting them in each case with alternative views.

On the role of the contract, as it is envisaged by Rawls, there are two things to say. First, that the contract serves in an evaluative rather than a legitimizing role, and second, that it serves in a heuristic rather than a definitional one.

Suppose that someone wonders why it is legitimate, if indeed it is legitimate, for a state to claim authority over its citizens: say, for a state to claim the right to a monopoly of force or the right to tax. One answer, which picks up a long-standing tradition of thought, is to say that implicitly, if not explicitly, the citizens have contracted with one another to give those who occupy political positions such power over them. If a contract is invoked in this way, then we may say that it is given a legitimizing role. It serves to legitimize the existence of the state in question, providing it with a suitable pedigree.

Rawls quite clearly does not mean to accord such a role to his contract. He does not see the contract as something that people have actually undertaken, even if only implicitly. "The undertakings re-

---

[5]A Theory of Justice (Oxford: Oxford University Press, 1971).
[6]Chandran Kukathas and Philip Pettit, Rawls: A Theory of Justice and Its Critics (Oxford: Polity Press, Blackwells, 1990).

ferred to are purely hypothetical."[7] Thus the contract cannot serve to legitimize the status quo, in the manner of a founding covenant.

The role assigned to the contract in Rawls's approach is evaluative rather than legitimizing. The contract is envisaged as a test such that if a sociopolitical arrangement passes it, that is proof of the justice and thus far of the desirability of the arrangement. If we decide that among a range of sociopolitical options, one candidate would undoubtedly be chosen in the original position, that is meant to show under Rawls's approach that the candidate is to be highly valued.

But if we agree that the contract envisaged is a purely evaluative instrument, a further question about its role immediately arises. Suppose we decide that a candidate X possesses the contractarian property of being the one that would be chosen in the original position. In Plato's *Euthyphro* Socrates asks whether something is holy because the gods love it, or whether the gods love it because it is holy. And similarly here we may now ask whether X, under Rawls's picture of these matters, is just because it would be chosen in the original position or whether it would be chosen because it is just.

The question at issue is whether the contractarian property of being such as to be chosen in the original position is definitional of what it is to be just, or whether it is a property that merely signals the presence of the independent property of being just: a property that may provide a heuristic procedure for identifying just arrangements, but that does not definitionally mean that they are just.

For Rawls the contractarian property is meant to serve as something symptomatic rather than constitutive or definitional of justice. He conceives of the contract he envisages as having a heuristic role. It is meant to provide evidence on which among the arrangements under discussion is the most just but it is not supposed to define *ab initio* what it is to be just. If the argument goes through and people are persuaded to see justice the contractarian way, then they may come to define it in such terms.[8] But the contractarian account is not presented merely as a definitional exercise; it is offered as a way of explicating an antecedently identified notion of justice. The notion explicated, as we have seen, is that of justice as fairness.

The fact that Rawls sees the role of contract as evaluative rather than legitimizing, and heuristic rather than definitional, enables us to situate his approach relative to other contemporary contractarians. All such contractarians agree that the role is evaluative rather than legitimizing but they differ on the heuristic-definitional issue.

Contemporary heuristic contractarians will certainly include John Harsanyi, who looks to his contract to determine which candidate on

[7]*A Theory of Justice*, p. 16.
[8]See *A Theory of Justice*, p. 111.

offer promises to maximize overall utility; and James Buchanan, who sees unanimous agreement as the only test that an arrangement is Pareto-superior to alternatives: such superiority means that it is preferred by at least some relevant parties and no others prefer anything else.[9] Contemporary definitional contractarians include David Gauthier, who defines what is right in terms of what would be agreeable to rational parties under certain hypothetical circumstances; and Tim Scanlon, who defines what is right in terms of what no one could reasonably reject as a basis for informed unforced general agreement.[10] Someone like Jürgen Habermas, on the other hand, does not really come clean on the question of whether the contract he envisages relates heuristically or definitionally to justice.[11]

The variations possible in contractarian theory on the role of the contract invoked can be represented in a tree diagram. At each fork in the diagram Rawls's position lies to the right.

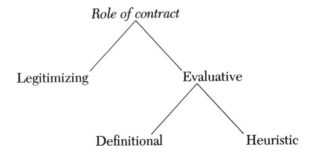

Role of contract

Legitimizing   Evaluative

Definitional   Heuristic

But the variations on the nature of the contract invoked are even more numerous in contractarian theory than variations on its role. We turn now to these. There are three questions that arise here and therefore three things to say in specification of Rawls's position: that he envisages, first, an intentional contract rather than any unintended quasicontractual arrangement; second, an economic contract rather than a political one; and third, a noninteractive rather than an interactive contract.

The first question is one on which Rawls's position, and indeed that of most contractarian thinkers, differs from that of Robert Nozick.[12] It

---

[9]See John Harsanyi, *Essays on Ethics, Social Behaviour and Scientific Explanation* (Dordrecht: Reidel, 1976) and Geoffrey Brennan, "The Buchanan Contribution" (*Finanzarchiv*, Vol 45, 1987, pp. 1–24). I assume here that for Buchanan choice does not necessarily reveal preference; otherwise he is a definitional contractarian.

[10]See David Gauthier, *Morals by Agreement* (Oxford: Oxford University Press, 1986) and T.M. Scanlon, "Contractualism and Utilitarianism," in A. Sen and B. Williams, eds., *Utilitarianism and Beyond* (Cambridge: Cambridge University Press, 1982).

[11]See my "Habermas on Truth and Justice," reprinted in this volume.

[12]*Anarchy, State and Utopia* (New York: Basic Books, 1974).

may not be quite right, and indeed it runs counter to his own intuitions, to describe Nozick as a contractarian.[13] But his approach is close enough to the contractarian tradition to warrant mention here. Nozick is a believer in certain libertarian rights, a position that forces him to explain how any state, no matter how minimal, can be justified. He justifies a minimal state system, however, on the grounds that were people placed in a socially organized situation lacking a polity—John Locke's state of nature—then the inconveniences of their position, in particular the lack of protection for their rights, would drive them rationally to make arrangements with one another that approximate, without their necessarily foreseeing this, to a minimal state. Moreover, their individually rational choices would give rise to such a system without the infringement—or at least the uncompensated infringement—of anyone's rights. If the situation that the antistate libertarian would presumably have to hail as the ideal would lead under pressure of rationality, and without moral offence, to a minimal state system, then Nozick argues that this gives all libertarians reason to endorse such a system.

The difference between the quasicontractual procedure envisaged by Nozick and a contract proper, certainly a contract in Rawls's sense, is that although the parties in Nozick's procedure need have no idea where their individual bargains with others are collectively leading, the parties to a contract proper are concerned precisely with the choice between different collective and system-level arrangements. If they converge on some particular arrangement, they do so intentionally, not as the unforeseen and unintended result of more specific negotiations.

The second question to do with the nature of the contract envisaged is whether it is a political or economic contract. The terms in which the question is phrased are not self-explanatory, however, and we need to make clearer the matter at issue.

When two or more people seek to make an agreement that affects their interests differently, so that each would most prefer a different arrangement from the other, the agreement may be pursued in either of two ways: one I describe as economic and the other as political. The economic way is for each to calculate what best suits his own interests and then to try to get this: say, to bargain with the other or others, seeking to win the largest benefit possible at the least possible concession from themselves. The political way is for the parties to put aside their own particular interests and to debate about the arrangement that best answers to those considerations—usually considerations in some sense to do with the common good—that all can countenance as relevant. The economic approach is institutionalized in the process of market negotiation, the political—at least ideally—in the forum of

---

[13]*Anarchy, State and Utopia*, p. 132.

discussion in which the parties are blocked, if only by the sanction of social disapproval, from arguing by reference to special as distinct from common concerns.

Jürgen Habermas's theory is the clearest current example of a contractarian approach in which the contract envisaged is one of a political character.[14] He sees matters of justice as determined by what would be agreed to by the parties involved in an act of collective decision, under what he describes as conditions of ideal speech or communication: these conditions are meant to ensure that everyone has the same rights and opportunities of speech, that there are no distorting differences of power and influence, that the culture is one of radical questioning, and the like. A consequence of envisaging the relevant contract in this way is of course that Habermas leaves himself unable to tell how the parties would in fact decide. Thus this contractarian approach does not have the methodological attractions of alternatives.

Clearly Rawls's notion of the contract is economic rather than political. He sees the parties as each making up their minds by reference to how well the candidate arrangements discussed answer to their personal interests. There is no suggestion that they will step aside from those interests and try to judge arrangements by appeal to considerations of common concern, though of course their personal interests are assumed to incorporate the interests of their family lines.

The third and final question on the nature of contract is whether it is envisaged as a noninteractive or as an interactive exchange. The best example among contractarians of someone who thinks of the contract as an interactive procedure is David Gauthier.[15] In Gauthier's picture the parties are involved in a process of economic negotiation with one another, each seeking to drive the best bargain he can get. The distinguishing mark of Gauthier's work is that he tries to apply and indeed to develop bargaining theory in the attempt to show that there is a favored solution. In a sense he takes on a challenge put by Rawls, who would argue that if the original position generates a bargaining problem, then that problem will be "hopelessly complicated." "Even if theoretically a solution were to exist, we would not, at present anyway, be able to determine it."[16]

Rawls's own conception of the contract is noninteractive. He sees the parties as each deciding what to choose without the necessity of negotiating with one another. This conception is not motivated by a desire to avoid the bargaining problem, though he obviously welcomes it on those grounds. As he sees things, it falls out quite naturally once the

---

[14]See my "Habermas on Truth and Justice" and Jon Elster, "The Market and the Forum," both reprinted in this volume.

[15]See his *Morals by Agreement*.

[16]*A Theory of Justice*, p. 140.

original position is constrained so as to ensure that any agreements reached there are fair.

We can sum up the different positions on the nature of the contract in a tree diagram similar to that used for positions on the role of the contract. As before, Rawls's position lies on the right of each fork.

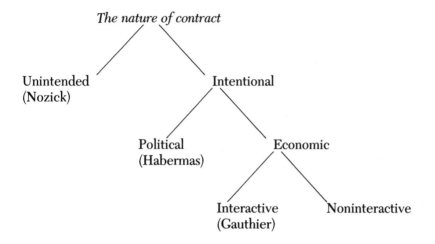

4. The Feasible

Contractarianism has been the most distinctive feature of recent political theory, but there is a second feature that may prove to be even of greater importance in the development of the discipline. In backing away from the study of the desirable, many political theorists have seen the best hope for the subject in the study, not of the eligible, but of the feasible.

When we ask which sort of political arrangement is most desirable, it has been common among political theorists to assume full compliance: to assume, for each arrangement considered, that it is possible to set it up and keep it going, with people being brought to behave as it requires. But clearly this is not always a reasonable assumption to make. We might argue that the best regime conceivable is one under which each maximizes overall utility. But it is not clear how interesting a result this is. After all, people are never going to be motivated to try to maximize overall utility and, even if they were, they would not have the capacity generally to get the sums right. The arrangement envisaged is not a feasible option.

The thought motivating the study of the feasible is that if we analyze alternative political arrangements on the score of feasibility, we may find that the feasible set of options is small: so small, ideally, that there is no trouble in determining which is the most desirable. As the study of the eligible is motivated by its promising an indirect route to the destination that is so elusive along the direct way of the desirable, so the study of the feasible is attractive for similar reasons.

The study of the feasible is possible only so far as we are able to make certain assumptions about human nature. If we think that human nature is utterly malleable, so that habitation can get people to act in just any old way, no matter how self-serving or how self-sacrificing, then we will think that no institutional arrangement can fail the feasibility test. The judgment that some arrangements are feasible, some not, presupposes the view that it is impossible for people to overcome certain natural or institutional restrictions; it is the arrangements that require such restrictions to be overcome that are then discounted as not being feasible.

A certain tradition of structural or functional thinking in social science, in particular a certain variety of Marxism, would suggest that there are important institutional restrictions on what people can be expected to be able to do. Thus a Marxist might hold that it is utopian to imagine any arrangement that, however abstractly attractive, requires the interests of the ruling class to be repressed. He will say that no such arrangement is going to be feasible, that it is an iron law that the interests of the ruling class are furthered by whatever political structure prevails in society.

Among contemporary social theorists there is less confidence than there once was that we can identify such universally valid institutional restrictions on how people can behave. Thus the study of the feasible, as that is pursued by political theorists, has tended to look to natural rather than institutional restrictions. In particular it has looked to the tradition of rational choice theory, rather than social theory in a structural or functional mold, for an account of restrictions that must be satisfied by any feasible political arrangement.

The rational choice tradition postulates, first, that people tend, at least in recurrent situations, to act in ways that advance their interests; and second, that the interests they have are in large part self-regarding. The first postulate is one of rationality and the second one of partiality. The partiality postulate is sometimes understood narrowly, so that people are said to be concerned only with the direct returns to themselves, in particular returns with more or less clear monetary values: their only interest is in economic gain. But under a more plausible reading, it postulates a concern both with economic gain and with social acceptance; this latter is an indirect return on action and it is difficult to put a monetary value on it. Thus John Harsanyi, a prominent rational choice theorist, writes: "People's behaviour can be largely explained in terms of two dominant interests: economic gain and social acceptance."[17]

Rational choice assumptions have been widely invoked in recent political theory to argue that various arrangements hitherto found attractive are in fact not feasible. Public choice theory, as it is called, has been particularly influential here.[18] Public choice theorists argue that the tradition of assuming that the state can step in to put right the failures of the market and of other such decentralized systems is uncritical and utopian. It fails to recognize that if we create political institutions that empower individuals to intervene in this way, we may be creating only further problems for ourselves; we may be opening the way to the abuse of power in the service of sectional interest, not to its benign employment.

The public choice school is closely linked with an economic approach to things political and sometimes the study of the feasible looks like an economistic takeover of political theory. But although the use of rational choice assumptions is distinctive of the economic method of thinking, it can in principle lead in directions far removed from traditional economic views of how things should be; it can even lead away from the faith in the free market that most economists display. There has been a growing literature in rational choice Marxism, for example, and this often harnesses the economic method to quite novel ends.[19]

It will be said by some that the rational choice assumptions are too pessimistic about human concerns, that people are more altruistic than they allow. But this criticism may be misplaced. If we are going to put our faith in a political arrangement, then we will want it to be resilient and feasible even under the pessimistic assumption that people are often partial in their concerns; we will want to err on the side of caution. The rational choice assumptions are well suited in this regard to the task of feasibility analysis: better suited, perhaps, than in the relative optimism that they display about people's rationality. In *A Theory of Justice* John Rawls spends nearly two hundred pages arguing, on the basis of certain psychological assumptions, that his two princi-

---

[17]"Rational Choice Models of Behaviour Versus Functionalist and Conformist Theories" (*World Politics*, Vol 22, 1969), quoted with approval by Michael Taylor in Michael Taylor, ed., *Rationality and Revolution* (Cambridge: Cambridge University Press, 1987, p. 66). See also my *"Virtus Normativa*: Rational Choice Perspectives," *Ethics*, Vol 100, 1990).

[18]See Iain McLean, *Public Choice* (Oxford: Blackwells, 1987).

[19]See, for example, G. A. Cohen, *Karl Marx's Theory of History* (Oxford: Oxford University Press, 1978); John Roemer, *A General Theory of Exploitation and Class* (Cambridge, Mass.: Harvard University Press, 1982); Jon Elster, *Making Sense of Marx* (Cambridge: Cambridge University Press, 1985).

ples of justice represent a stable and feasible basic structure for society. That part of his work has had little impact, however, on others and the reason may be that he allows himself to be too optimistic.

5. Conclusion

I hope that this overview suffices to give a sense of the lineaments of contemporary political theory. The division of concerns into my three categories is not standard, but I think it may be helpful. There are things to be said against it, no doubt, for as it gives prominence to some of the concerns of political theorists, so it downplays others. Thus it assumes that issues of political ethics, such as that of the political obligation of the citizen, belong with ethics rather than political theory. But it would scarcely be fruitful to go into such matters here.

In concluding this overview, however, there is one further matter that is worth discussing. Contemporary political theory, as it is represented here, is often accused of being uncritically individualistic, especially by communitarians.[20] Sometimes the charge is that such theory treats individual agents as if their relations with one another were not constitutive in any part of their identities: it is metaphysically atomistic. The charge in this form raises a question about the feasibility of any proposals that come of such theory but it is too wide-ranging to consider here.[21] The more usual form of the accusation, and the one we will address, is that the sort of theory represented in this book concentrates on the benefits that individuals can enjoy, to the neglect of more distinctively social returns: it is morally individualistic.

Moral individualists hold that if one political arrangement is better than another, that can be only because of how it affects individuals; this might be called the principle of individual relevance. Moral individualism in this sense is certainly assumed by the bulk of political theorists today and the question is whether it is a reasonable doctrine. In concluding this overview I would like to show that it is, drawing on work done elsewhere.[22]

The principle of individual relevance says that an arrangement is good so far and only so far as it constitutes or brings about something that affects individuals suitably: something that is good *for* individuals. I shall defend it by distinguishing it from three other doctrines. These

---

[20]See the authors represented, for example, in Michael Sandel, ed., *Liberalism and Its Critics* (Oxford: Blackwell, 1984).

[21]For the record, I endorse the rejection of atomism but derive a different sort of lesson. See my paper "The Freedom of the City: A Republican Ideal," in Alan Hamlin and Philip Pettit, eds., *The Good Polity*, op. cit. See also John Braithwaite and Philip Pettit, *Not Just Deserts: A Republican Theory of Criminal Justice* (Oxford: Oxford University Press, 1990).

[22]See Alan Hamlin and Philip Pettit, "Normative Analysis of the State: Some Preliminaries," op. cit.

say, respectively, that what makes any arrangement good is that it constitutes or brings about something that is a good *in* people, something that is a good *by* or according to people, or something that is a good *of* people. I believe that the only reason anyone could have for rejecting the principle of individual relevance — the *for*-individuals doctrine — is that he fails to distinguish it from these other theories.

The view that what makes a state or any other arrangement good is that it constitutes or brings about a good *in* people asserts an extreme moral individualism. It says that states are to be assessed by effects within people of a wholly atomistic kind: effects such that those people could logically have enjoyed them in isolation from one another. An example of such individualism is the utilitarian doctrine that what matters is just the pleasure, or the subjective preference-satisfaction, enjoyed by people taken separately. It says that all that matters in assessing a sociopolitical arrangement is the impact made by the arrangement on such private, subjective feelings.

It should be clear that moral individualism does not entail any such solipsistic view. Being a good *for* individuals does not entail being a good *in* individuals. For all that moral individualism says, the good brought about by a state may logically require social relations between individuals; it may not be something private that the individual can enjoy even in the absence of others. The good, for example, may be that of a person's actual equality in some regards with other people, or the good of his enjoying relations of friendship with them.

The second doctrine from which I distinguish moral individualism says that what makes the state good is that it constitutes or brings about something that is good *by* individuals: that is, something that individuals explicitly judge to be good. This doctrine will be found plausible by many, particularly those who insist that the state should respond to people's actual perceptions and preferences. Still, the appeal of the doctrine is not overwhelming. It rules out any political philosophy, for example, that praises the state for satisfying rights, needs, or other claims that individuals themselves do not recognize at the time of satisfaction.

Again, I hope it is clear that moral individualism does not entail this doctrine. Being a good *for* individuals does not entail being a good *by* individuals. It may be that something being a good *for* individuals entails that it would be a good *by* those people, that it would be something judged to be good among those people, if they were fully reflective concerning their preferences. But the proposition entailed falls far short of the approach embodied in the *by* doctrine.

The third doctrine from which I distinguish moral individualism says that what makes a state good is that it constitutes or brings about a good *of* individuals. This doctrine is less demanding, and less controversial, than either of the other two, but it is still more demanding than the moral individualism that contemporary political theorists endorse. The *of* doctrine decrees that the only goods in virtue of which a state can be praised are items that belong to individual people, such as their liberty, their happiness, their equality, or whatever. It rules out the approval of a sociopolitical arrangement for the production of goods that, though they affect people, belong in the first place to aggregate-level entities. Examples of such aggregate goods might be the solidarity of a community, the continuity of a culture, or the harmony of relations between racial groups. It is typical of such aggregate goods that although their realization affects individuals, there is no one way in which it affects them all. Thus there is a sense in which they are not goods of people and so the third doctrine would deny that a state ought to be approved for producing such benefits.

I think that moral individualism does not entail even this relatively mild doctrine. A good that is not a good *of* individuals can still be argued to be a good *for* individuals. Community solidarity may be judged good according to the extent that it furnishes good for the individuals involved, even though those individual goods may differ from person to person. When political theorists say that all that is relevant in the assessment of a sociopolitical arrangement is the good of those taking part in it, I think it is clear that they do not mean to rule out the possibility that an arrangement should be approved for producing aggregate goods that make a favorable impact on individuals.

I conclude that moral individualism, the *for*-individuals principle, is distinct from the three doctrines that we may describe as the *in*-individuals, the *by*-individuals, and the *of*-individuals principles. Once it is clear that moral individualism is indeed distinct from such approaches, I believe that it ought to be overwhelmingly attractive. Thus I do not think that the commitment to moral individualism entitles anyone to dismiss the sort of political theory represented in this book.

PART 1
THE DESIRABLE:
WHAT SHOULD WE VALUE?

THE ESSAYS IN this section represent some recent investigations, informed by contemporary perspectives, of old themes. The first five essays deal, respectively, with rights, with liberty, with democracy, with utility, and with an important element in discussions of equality, poverty. The last essay represents a critique of the evaluative concerns of most political theory, from a feminist standpoint. Both aspects to the study of the desirable are represented in the section: all the essays are focused to a degree on the analysis of values; and some are also concerned with the assessment of the values analyzed.

1

JOEL FEINBERG

The Nature and Value of Rights

1

I WOULD LIKE to begin by conducting a thought experiment. Try to imagine Nowheresville—a world very much like our own except that no one, or hardly any one (the qualification is not important), has *rights*. If this flaw makes Nowheresville too ugly to hold very long in contemplation, we can make it as pretty as we wish in other moral respects. We can, for example, make the human beings in it as attractive and virtuous as possible without taxing our conceptions of the limits of human nature. In particular, let the virtues of moral sensibility flourish. Fill this imagined world with as much benevolence, compassion, sympathy, and pity as it will conveniently hold without strain. Now we can imagine men helping one another from compassionate motives merely, quite as much or even more than they do in our actual world from a variety of more complicated motives.

This picture, pleasant as it is in some respects, would hardly have satisfied Immanuel Kant. Benevolently motivated actions do good, Kant admitted, and therefore are better, *ceteris paribus*, than malevolently motivated actions; but no action can have supreme kind of worth—what Kant called "moral worth"—unless its whole motivating power derives from the thought that it is *required by duty*. Accordingly, let us try to make Nowheresville more appealing to Kant by introducing the idea of duty into it, and letting the sense of duty be a sufficient motive for many beneficent and honorable actions. But doesn't this bring our original thought experiment to an abortive conclusion? If duties are permitted entry into Nowheresville, are not rights necessarily smuggled in along with them?

The question is well-asked, and requires here a brief digression so that we might consider the so-called "doctrine of the logical correlativity of rights and duties." This is the doctrine that (i) all duties entail other people's rights and (ii) all rights entail other people's duties. Only the first part of the doctrine, the alleged entailment from duties to rights, need concern us here. Is this part of the doctrine correct? It should not be surprising that my answer is: "In a sense yes and in a sense no." Etymologically, the word "duty" is associated with actions that are *due* someone else, the payments of debts *to* creditors, the keeping of agreements with promisees, the payment of club dues, or legal fees, or tariff levies to appropriate authorities or their representatives. In this original sense of "duty," all duties are correlated with the rights of those *to* whom the duty is owed. On the other hand, there seem to be numerous classes of duties, both of a legal and non-legal kind, that are *not* logically correlated with the rights of other persons. This seems to be a consequence of the fact that the word "duty" has come to be used for *any* action understood to be *required*, whether by the rights of others, or by law, or by higher authority, or by conscience, or whatever. When the notion of requirement is in clear focus it is likely to seem the only element in the idea of duty that is essential, and the other component notion — that a duty is something *due* someone else — drops off. Thus, in this widespread but derivative usage, "duty" tends to be used for any action we feel we *must* (for whatever reason) do. It comes, in short, to be a term of moral modality merely; and it is no wonder that the first thesis of the logical correlativity doctrine often fails.

Let us then introduce duties into Nowheresville, but only in the sense of actions that are, or are believed to be, morally mandatory, but not in the older sense of actions that are due others and can be claimed by others as their right. Nowheresville now can have duties of the sort imposed by positive law. A legal duty is not something we are implored or advised to do merely; it is something the law, or an authority under the law, *requires* us to do whether we want to or not, under pain of penalty. When traffic lights turn red, however, there is no determinate person who can plausibly be said to claim our stopping as his due, so that the motorist owes it to *him* to stop, in the way a debtor owes it to his creditor to pay. In our own actual world, of course, we sometimes owe it to our *fellow motorists* to stop; but that kind of right-correlated duty does not exist in Nowheresville. There, motorists "owe" obedience to the Law, but they owe nothing to one another. When they collide, no matter who is at fault, no one is morally accountable to anyone else, and no one has any sound grievance or "right to complain."

When we leave legal contexts to consider moral obligations and other extra-legal duties, a greater variety of duties-without-correlative-rights

present themselves. Duties of charity, for example, require us to contribute to one or another of a large number of eligible recipients, no
one of whom can claim our contribution from us as his due. Charitable
contributions are more like gratuitous services, favors, and gifts than
like repayments of debts or reparations; and yet we do have duties to
be charitable. Many persons, moreover, in our actual world believe that
they are required by their own consciences to do more than that
"duty" that *can* be demanded of them by their prospective beneficiaries. I have quoted elsewhere the citation from H. B. Acton of a character in a Malraux novel who "gave all his supply of poison to his fellow
prisoners to enable them by suicide to escape the burning alive which
was to be their fate and his." This man, Acton adds, "probably did not
think that [the others] had more of a right to the poison than he had,
though he thought it his duty to give it to them."[1] I am sure that there
are many actual examples, less dramatically heroic than this fictitious
one, of persons who believe, rightly or wrongly, that they *must do*
something (hence the word "duty") for another person in excess of
what that person can appropriately demand of him (hence the absence
of "right").

Now the digression is over and we can return to Nowheresville and
summarize what we have put in it thus far. We now find spontaneous
benevolence in somewhat larger degree than in our actual world, and
also the acknowledged existence of duties of obedience, duties of charity, and duties imposed by exacting private consciences, and also, let us
suppose, a degree of conscientiousness in respect to those duties somewhat in excess of what is to be found in our actual world. I doubt that
Kant would be fully satisfied with Nowheresville even now that duty
and respect for law and authority have been added to it; but I feel
certain that he would regard their addition at least as an improvement.
I will now introduce two further moral practices into Nowheresville
that will make that world very little more appealing to Kant, but will
make it appear more familiar to us. These are the practices connected
with the notions of *personal desert* and what I call a *sovereign monopoly
of rights*.

When a person is said to deserve something good from us what is
meant in part is that there would be a certain propriety in our giving
that good thing to him in virtue of the kind of person he is, perhaps, or
more likely, in virtue of some specific thing he has done. The propriety
involved here is a much weaker kind than that which derives from our
having promised him the good thing or from his having qualified for it
by satisfying the well-advertised conditions of some public rule. In the
latter case he could be said not merely to deserve the good thing but

[1]H. B. Acton, "Symposium on 'Rights'," *Proceedings of the Aristotelian Society*, Supplementary Volume 24 (1950), pp. 107–8.

also to have a *right* to it, that is to be in a position to demand it as his due; and of course we will not have that sort of thing in Nowheresville. That weaker kind of propriety which is mere desert is simply a kind of *fittingness* between one party's character or action and another party's favorable response, much like that between human and laughter, or good performance and applause.

The following seems to be the origin of the idea of deserving good or bad treatment from others: A master or lord was under no obligation to reward his servant for especially good service; still a master might naturally feel that there would be a special fittingness in giving a gratuitous reward as a grateful response to the good service (or conversely imposing a penalty for bad service). Such an act while surely fitting and proper was entirely supererogatory. The fitting response in turn from the rewarded servant should be gratitude. If the deserved reward had not been given him he should have had no complaint, since he only *deserved* the reward, as opposed to having a *right* to it, or a ground for claiming it as his due.

The idea of desert has evolved a good bit away from its beginnings by now, but nevertheless, it seems clearly to be one of those words J. L. Austin said "never entirely forget their pasts."[2] Today servants qualify for their wages by doing their agreed upon chores, no more and no less. If their wages are not forthcoming, their contractual rights have been violated and they can make legal claim to the money that is their due. If they do less than they agreed to do, however, their employers may "dock" them, by paying them proportionately less than the agreed upon fee. This is all a matter of right. But if the servant does a splendid job, above and beyond his minimal contractual duties, the employer is under no further obligation to reward him, for this was not agreed upon, even tacitly, in advance. The additional service was all the servant's idea and done entirely on his own. Nevertheless, the morally sensitive employer may feel that it would be exceptionally appropriate for him to respond, freely on *his* own, to the servant's meritorious service, with a reward. The employee cannot demand it as his due, but he will happily accept it, with gratitude, as a fitting response to his desert.

In our age of organized labor, even this picture is now archaic; for almost every kind of exchange of service is governed by hard bargained contracts so that even bonuses can sometimes be demanded as a matter of right, and nothing is given for nothing on either side of the bargaining table. And perhaps that is a good thing; for consider an anachronistic instance of the earlier kind of practice that survives, at least as a matter of form, in the quaint old practice of "tipping." The tip was

---

[2]J. L. Austin, "A Plea for Excuses," *Proceedings of the Aristotelian Society*, Vol. 57 (1956–57).

originally conceived as a reward that has to be earned by "zealous service." It is not something to be taken for granted as a standard response to *any* service. That is to say that its payment is a *"gratuity,"* not a discharge of obligation, but something given apart from, or in addition to, anything the recipient can expect as a matter of right. That is what tipping originally meant at any rate, and tips are still referred to as "gratuities" in the tax forms. But try to explain all that to a New York cab driver! If he has *earned* his gratuity, by God, he has it coming, and there had better be sufficient acknowledgment of his desert or he'll give you a piece of his mind! I'm not generally prone to defend New York cab drivers, but they do have a point here. There is the making of a paradox in the queerly unstable concept of an "earned gratuity." One can understand how "desert" in the weak sense of "propriety" or "mere fittingness" tends to generate a stronger sense in which desert is itself the ground for a claim of right.

In Nowheresville, nevertheless, we will have only the original weak kind of desert. Indeed, it will be impossible to keep this idea out if we allow such practices as teachers grading students, judges awarding prizes, and servants serving benevolent but class-conscious masters. Nowheresville is a reasonably good world in many ways, and its teachers, judges, and masters will generally try to give students, contestants, and servants the grades, prizes, and rewards they deserve. For this the recipients will be grateful; but they will never think to complain, or even feel aggrieved, when expected responses to desert fail. The masters, judges, and teachers don't *have* to do good things, after all, for *anyone.* One should be happy that they *ever* treat us well, and not grumble over their occasional lapses. Their hoped for responses, after all, are *gratuities*, and there is no wrong in the omission of what is merely gratuitous. Such is the response of persons who have no concept of *rights*, even persons who are proud of their own deserts.[3]

Surely, one might ask, rights have to come in somewhere, if we are to have even moderately complex forms of social organization. Without rules that confer rights and impose obligations, how can we have ownership of property, bargains and deals, promises and contracts, appointments and loans, marriages and partnerships? Very well, let us introduce all of these social and economic practices into Nowheresville, but *with one big twist*. With them I should like to introduce the curious notion of a "sovereign right-monopoly." You will recall that the subjects in Hobbes's *Leviathan* had no rights whatever against their sovereign. He could do as he liked with them, even gratuitously harm them, but this gave them no valid grievance against him. The sovereign, to be

---

[3]For a fuller discussion of the concept of personal desert see my "Justice and Personal Desert," *Nomos VI, Justice*, ed. by C. J. Friedrich and J. Chapman (New York: Atherton Press, 1963), pp. 69–97.

sure, had a certain duty to treat his subjects well, but this duty was owed not to the subjects directly, but to God, just as we might have a duty to a person to treat his property well, but of course no duty to the property itself but only to its owner. Thus, while the sovereign was quite capable of *harming* his subjects, he could commit no wrong against them that they could complain about, since they had no prior claims against his conduct. The only party *wronged* by the sovereign's mistreatment of his subjects was God, the supreme lawmaker. Thus, in repenting cruelty to his subjects, the sovereign might say to God, as David did after killing Uriah, "to Thee only have I sinned."[4]

Even in the *Leviathan*, however, ordinary people had ordinary rights *against one another*. They played roles, occupied offices, made agreements, and signed contracts. In a genuine "sovereign right-monopoly," as I shall be using that phrase, they will do all those things too, and thus incur genuine obligations toward one another; but the obligations (here is the twist) will not be owed directly *to* promisees, creditors, parents, and the like, but rather to God alone, or to the members of some elite, or to a single sovereign under God. Hence, the rights correlative to the obligations that derive from these transactions are all owned by some "outside" authority.

As far as I know, no philosopher has ever suggested that even our role and contract obligations (in this, our actual world) are all owed directly to a divine intermediary; but some theologians have approached such extreme moral occasionalism. I have in mind the familiar phrase in certain widely distributed religious tracts that "it takes three to marry," which suggests that marital vows are not made between bride and groom directly but between each spouse and God, so that if one breaks his vow, the other cannot rightly complain of being wronged, since only God could have claimed performance of the marital duties as his *own* due; and hence God alone had a claim-right violated by nonperformance. If John breaks his vow to God, he might then properly repent in the words of David: "To Thee only have I sinned."

In our actual world, very few spouses conceive of their mutual obligations in this way; but their small children, at a certain stage in their moral upbringing, are likely to feel precisely this way toward *their* mutual obligations. If Billy kicks Bobby and is punished by Daddy, he may come to feel contrition for his naughtiness induced by his painful estrangement from the loved parent. He may then be happy to make amends and sincere apology *to Daddy*; but when Daddy insists that he apologize to his wronged brother, that is another story. A direct apology to Billy would be a tacit recognition of Billy's status as a right-

---

[4]II Sam. 11. Cited with approval by Thomas Hobbes in *The Leviathan*, Part II, Chap. 21.

holder against him, some one he can wrong as well as harm, and someone to whom he is directly accountable for his wrongs. This is a status Bobby will happily accord Daddy; but it would imply a respect for Billy that he does not presently feel, so he bitterly resents according it to him. On the "three-to-marry" model, the relations between each spouse and God would be like those between Bobby and Daddy; respect for the other spouse as an independent claimant would not even be necessary; and where present, of course, never sufficient.

The advocates of the "three to marry" model who conceive it either as a description of our actual institution of marriage or a recommendation of what marriage ought to be, may wish to escape this embarrassment by granting rights to spouses in capacities other than as promisees. They may wish to say, for example, that when John promises God that he will be faithful to Mary, a right is thus conferred not only on God as promisee but also on Mary herself as third-party beneficiary, just as when John contracts with an insurance company and names Mary as his intended beneficiary, she has a right to the accumulated funds after John's death, even though the insurance company made no promise to her. But this seems to be an unnecessarily cumbersome complication contributing nothing to our understanding of the marriage bond. The life insurance transaction is necessarily a three party relation, involving occupants of three distinct offices, no two of whom alone could do the whole job. The transaction, after all, is defined as the purchase by the customer (first office) from the vendor (second office) of protection for a beneficiary (third office) against the customer's untimely death. Marriage, on the other hand, in this our actual world, appears to be a binary relation between a husband and wife, and even though third parties such as children, neighbors, psychiatrists, and priests may sometimes be helpful and even causally necessary for the survival of the relation, they are not logically necessary to our *conception* of the relation, and indeed many married couples do quite well without them. Still, I am not now purporting to describe our actual world, but rather trying to contrast it with a counterpart world of the imagination. In *that* world, it takes three to make almost *any* moral relation and all rights are owned by God or some sovereign under God.

There will, of course, be delegated authorities in the imaginary world, empowered to give commands to their underlings and to punish them for their disobedience. But the commands are all given in the name of the right-monopoly who in turn are the only persons to whom obligations are owed. Hence, even intermediate superiors do not have claim-rights against their subordinates but only legal *powers* to create obligations in the subordinates *to* the monopolistic right-holders, and also the legal *privilege* to impose penalties in the name of that monopoly.

2

So much for the imaginary "world without rights." If some of the moral concepts and practices I have allowed into that world do not sit well with one another, no matter. Imagine Nowheresville with all of these practices if you can, or with any harmonious subset of them, if you prefer. The important thing is not what I've let into it, but what I have kept out. The remainder of this paper will be devoted to an analysis of what precisely a world is missing when it does not contain rights and why that absence is morally important.

The most conspicuous difference, I think, between the Nowheresvillians and ourselves has something to do with the activity of *claiming*. Nowheresvillians, even when they are discriminated against invidiously, or left without the things they need, or otherwise badly treated, do not think to leap to their feet and make righteous demands against one another, though they may not hesitate to resort to force and trickery to get what they want. They have no notion of rights, so they do not have a notion of what is their due; hence they do not claim before they take. The conceptual linkage between personal rights and claiming has long been noticed by legal writers and is reflected in the standard usage in which "claim-rights" are distinguished from the mere liberties, immunities, and powers, also sometimes called "rights," with which they are easily confused. When a person has a legal claim-right to X, it must be the case (i) that he is at liberty in respect to X. i.e., that he has no duty to refrain from or relinquish X, and also (ii) that his liberty is the ground of other people's *duties* to grant him X or not to interfere with him in respect to X. Thus, in the sense of claim-rights, it is true by definition that rights logically entail other people's duties. The paradigmatic examples of such rights are the creditor's right to be paid a debt by his debtor, and the landowner's right not to be interfered with by anyone in the exclusive occupancy of his land. The creditor's right against his debtor, for example, and the debtor's duty to his creditor, are precisely the same relation seen from two different vantage points, as inextricably linked as the two sides of the same coin.

And yet, this is not quite an accurate account of the matter, for it fails to do justice to the way claim-rights are somehow prior to, or more basic than, the duties with which they are necessarily correlated. If Nip has a claim-right against Tuck, it is because of this fact that Tuck has a duty to Nip. It is only because something from Tuck is *due* Nip (directional element) that there is something Tuck *must do* (modal element). This is a relation, moreover, in which Tuck is bound and Nip is free. Nip not only *has* a right, but he can choose whether or not to exercise it, whether to claim it, whether to register complaints upon its infringement, even whether to release Tuck from his duty, and forget the whole thing. If the personal claim-right is also backed up by criminal sanctions, however, Tuck may yet have a duty of obedience to the law from which no one, not even Nip, may release him. He would even have such duties if he lived in Nowheresville; but duties subject to acts of claiming, duties derivative from and contingent upon the personal rights of others, are unknown and undreamed of in Nowheresville.

Many philosophical writers have simply identified rights with claims. The dictionaries tend to define "claims," in turn, as "assertions of right," a dizzying piece of circularity that led one philosopher to complain — "We go in search of rights and are directed to claims, and then back again to rights in bureaucratic futility."[5] What then is the relation between a claim and a right?

As we shall see, a right *is* a kind of claim, and a claim is "an assertion of right," so that a formal definition of either notion in terms of the other will not get us very far. Thus if a "formal definition" of the usual philosophical sort is what we are after, the game is over before it has begun, and we can say that the concept of a right is a "simple, undefinable, unanalysable primitive." Here as elsewhere in philosophy this will have the effect of making the commonplace seem unnecessarily mysterious. We would be better advised, I think, not to attempt a formal definition of either "right" or "claim," but rather to use the idea of a claim in informal elucidation of the idea of a right. This is made possible by the fact that *claiming* is an elaborate sort of rule-governed *activity*. A claim is that which is claimed, the object of the act of claiming. There is, after all, a verb "to claim," but no verb "to right." If we concentrate on the whole activity of claiming, which is public, familiar, and open to our observation, rather than on its upshot alone, we may learn more about the generic nature of rights than we could ever hope to learn from a formal definition, even if one were possible. Moreover, certain facts about rights more easily, if not solely, expressible in the language of claims and claiming are essential to a full understanding not only of what rights are, but also why they are so vitally important.

Let us begin then by distinguishing between: (i) making claim to . . . , (ii) claiming that . . . , and (iii) having a claim. One sort of thing we may be doing when we claim is to *make claim to something*. This is "to petition or seek by virtue of supposed right; to demand as due." Sometimes this is done by an acknowledged right-holder when he serves notice that he now wants turned over to him that which has already been acknowledged to be his, something borrowed, say, or improperly taken from him. This is often done by turning in a chit, a receipt, an I.O.U., a check, an insurance policy, or a deed, that is, a *title* to something currently in the possession of someone else. On other occasions, making claim is making application for titles or rights themselves, as when a mining prospector stakes a claim to mineral rights, or

<hr>

[5] H. B. Acton, *Op. cit.*

a householder to a tract of land in the public domain, or an inventor to his patent rights. In the one kind of case, to make claim is to exercize rights one already has by presenting title; in the other kind of case it is to apply for the title itself, by showing that one has satisfied the conditions specified by a rule for the ownership of title and therefore that one can demand it as one's due.

Generally speaking, only the person who has a title or who has qualified for it, or someone speaking in his name, can make claim to something as a matter of right. It is an important fact about rights (or claims), then, that they can be claimed only by those who have them. Anyone can claim, of course, *that* this umbrella is yours, but only you or your representative can actually claim the umbrella. If Smith owes Jones five dollars, only Jones can claim the five dollars as his own, though any bystander can *claim that* it belongs to Jones. One important difference then between *making legal claim to* and *claiming that* is that the former is a legal performance with direct legal consequences whereas the latter is often a mere piece of descriptive commentary with no legal force. Legally speaking, *making claim to* can itself make things happen. This sense of "claiming," then, might well be called "the performative sense." The legal power to claim (performatively) one's right or the things to which one has a right seems to be essential to the very notion of a right. A right to which one could not make claim (i.e. not even for recognition) would be a very "imperfect" right indeed!

Claiming that one has a right (what we can call "propositional claiming" as opposed to "performative claiming") is another sort of thing one can do with language, but it is not the sort of doing that characteristically has legal consequences. To claim that one has rights is to make an assertion that one has them, and to make it in such a manner as to demand or insist that they be recognized. In this sense of "claim" many things in addition to rights can be claimed, that is, many other kinds of proposition can be asserted in the claiming way. I can claim, for example, that you, he, or she has certain rights, or that Julius Caesar once had certain rights; or I can claim that certain statements are true, or that I have certain skills, or accomplishments, or virtually anything at all. I can claim that the earth is flat. What is essential to *claiming that* is the manner of assertion. One can assert without even caring very much whether any one is listening, but part of the point of propositional claiming is to *make sure* people listen. When I claim to others that I know something, for example, I am not merely asserting it, but rather "obtruding my putative knowledge upon their attention, demanding that it be recognized, that appropriate notice be taken of it by those

[6]G. J. Warnock, "Claims to Knowledge," *Proceedings of the Aristotelian Society*, Supplementary Volume 36 (1962), p. 21.

concerned . . . "[7] Not every truth is properly assertable, much less claimable, in every context. To claim that something is the case in circumstances that justify no more than calm assertion is to behave like a boor. (This kind of boorishness, I might add, is probably less common in Nowheresville.) But not to claim in the appropriate circumstances that one has a right is to be spiritless or foolish. A list of "appropriate circumstances" would include occasions when one is challenged, when one's possession is denied, or seems insufficiently acknowledged or appreciated; and of course even in these circumstances, the claiming should be done only with an appropriate degree of vehemence.

Even if there are conceivable circumstances in which one would admit rights diffidently, there is no doubt that their characteristic use and that for which they are distinctively well suited, is to be claimed, demanded, affirmed, insisted upon. They are especially sturdy objects to "stand upon," a most useful sort of moral furniture. Having rights, of course, makes claiming possible; but it is claiming that gives rights their special moral significance. This feature of rights is connected in a way with the customary rhetoric about what it is to be a human being. Having rights enables us to "stand up like men," to look others in the eye, and to feel in some fundamental way the equal of anyone. To think of oneself as the holder of rights is not to be unduly but properly proud, to have that minimal self-respect that is necessary to be worthy of the love and esteem of others. Indeed, respect for persons (this is an intriguing idea) may simply be respect for their rights, so that there cannot be the one without the other; and what is called "human dignity" may simply be the recognizable capacity to assert claims. To respect a person then, or to think of him as possessed of human dignity, simply *is* to think of him as a potential maker of claims. Not all of this can be packed into a definition of "rights;" but these are *facts* about the possession of rights that argue well their supreme moral importance. More than anything else I am going to say, these facts explain what is wrong with Nowheresville.

We come now to the third interesting employment of the claiming vocabulary, that involving not the verb "to claim" but the substantive "a claim." What is it to *have a claim* and how is this related to rights? I would like to suggest that *having a claim consists in being in a position to claim, that is, to make claim to or claim that.* If this suggestion is correct it shows the primacy of the verbal over the nominative forms. It links

---

[7]This is the important difference between rights and mere claims. It is analogous to the difference between *evidence* of guilt (subject to degrees of cogency) and conviction of guilt (which is all or nothing). One can "have evidence" that is not conclusive just as one can "have a claim" that is not valid. "Prima-facieness" is built into the sense of "claim," but the notion of a "prima-facie right" makes little sense. On the latter point see A. I. Melden, *Rights and Right Conduct* (Oxford: Basil Blackwell, 1959), pp. 18–20, and Herbert Morris, "Persons and Punishment," *The Monist*, Vol. 52 (1968), pp. 498–499.

claims to a kind of activity and obviates the temptation to think of claims as *things*, on the model of coins, pencils, and other material possessions which we can carry in our hip pockets. To be sure, we often make or establish our claims by presenting titles, and these typically have the form of receipts, tickets, certificates, and other pieces of paper or parchment. The title, however, is not the same thing as the claim; rather it is the evidence that establishes the claim as valid. On this analysis, one might have a claim without ever claiming that to which one is entitled, or without even knowing that one has the claim; for one might simply be ignorant of the fact that one is in a position to claim; or one might be unwilling to exploit that position for one reason or another, including fear that the legal machinery is broken down or corrupt and will not enforce one's claim despite its validity.

Nearly all writers maintain that there is some intimate connection between having a claim and having a right. Some identify right and claim without qualification; some define "right" as justified or justifiable claim, others as recognized claim, still others as valid claim. My own preference is for the latter definition. Some writers, however, reject the identification of rights with valid claims on the ground that all claims as such are valid, so that the expression "valid claim" is redundant. These writers, therefore, would identify rights with claims *simpliciter*. But this is a very simple confusion. All claims, to be sure, are *put forward* as justified, whether they are justified in fact or not. A claim conceded even by its maker to have no validity is not a claim at all, but a mere demand. The highwayman, for example, *demands* his victim's money; but he hardly makes claim to it as rightfully his own.

But it does not follow from this sound point that it is redundant to qualify claims as justified (or as I prefer, valid) in the definition of a right; for it remains true that not all claims put forward as valid really are valid; and only the valid ones can be acknowledged as rights.

If having a valid claim is not redundant, i.e., if it is not redundant to pronounce *another's* claim valid, there must be such a thing as having a claim that is not valid. What would this be like? One might accumulate just enough evidence to argue with relevance and cogency that one has a right (or ought to be granted a right), although one's case might not be overwhelmingly conclusive. In such a case, one might have strong enough argument to be entitled to a hearing and given fair consideration. When one is in this position, it might be said that one "has a claim" that deserves to be weighed carefully. Nevertheless, the balance of reasons may turn out to militate against recognition of the claim, so that the claim, which one admittedly had, and perhaps still does, is not a valid claim or right. "Having a claim" in this sense is an expression very much like the legal phrase "having a *prima facie* case." A plaintiff establishes a *prima facie* case for the defendant's liability when he establishes grounds that will be sufficient for liability unless outweighed by reasons of a different sort that may be offered by the defendant. Similarly, in the criminal law, a grand jury returns an indictment when it thinks that the prosecution has sufficient evidence to be taken seriously and given a fair hearing, whatever countervailing reasons may eventually be offered on the other side. That initial evidence, serious but not conclusive, is also sometimes called a *prima facie* case. In a parallel *"prima facie* sense" of "claim," having a claim to X is not (yet) the same as having a right to X, but is rather having a case of at least minimal plausibility that one has a right to X, a case that does establish a right, not to X, but to a fair hearing and consideration. Claims, so conceived, differ in degree: some are stronger than others. Rights, on the other hand, do not differ in degree: no one right is more of a right than another.[8]

Another reason for not identifying rights with claims *simply* is that there is a well-established usage in international law that makes a theoretically interesting distinction between claims and rights. Statesmen are sometimes led to speak of "claims" when they are concerned with the natural needs of deprived human beings in conditions of scarcity. Young orphans *need* good upbringings, balanced diets, education, and technical training everywhere in the world; but unfortunately there are many places where these goods are in such short supply that it is impossible to provision all who need them. If we persist, nevertheless, in speaking of these needs as constituting rights and not merely claims, we are committed to the conception of a right which is an entitlement *to* some good, but not a valid claim *against* any particular individual; for in conditions of scarcity there may be no determinate individuals who can plausibly be said to have a duty to provide the missing goods to those in need. J. E. S. Fawcett therefore prefers to keep the distinction between claims and rights firmly in mind. "Claims," he writes, "are needs and demands in movement, and there is a continuous transformation, as a society advances [toward greater abundance] of economic and social claims into civil and political rights . . . and not all countries or all claims are by any means at the same stage in the process."[8] The manifesto writers on the other side who seem to identify needs, or at least basic needs, with what they call "human rights," are more properly described, I think, as urging upon the world community the moral principle that *all* basic human needs ought to be recognized as *claims* (in the customary *prima facie* sense) worthy of sympathy and serious consideration right now, even though, in many cases, they cannot yet plausibly be treated as *valid* claims, that is, as grounds of any other people's duties. This way of talking avoids

---

[8]J. E. S. Fawcett, "The International Protection of Human Rights," in *Political Theory and the Rights of Man*, ed. by D. D. Raphael (Bloomington: Indiana University Press, 1967), pp. 125 and 128.

the anomaly of ascribing to all human beings now, even those in pre-industrial societies, such "economic and social rights" as "periodic holidays with pay."[9]

Still, for all of that, I have a certain sympathy with the manifesto writers, and I am even willing to speak of a special "manifesto sense" of "right," in which a right need not be correlated with another's duty. Natural needs are real claims if only upon hypothetical future beings not yet in existence. I accept the moral principle that to have an unfulfilled need is to have a kind of claim against the world, even if against no one in particular. A natural need for some good as such, like a natural desert, is always a reason in support of a claim to that good. A person in need, then, is always "in a position" to make a claim, even when there is no one in the corresponding position to do anything about it. Such claims, based on need alone, are "permanent possibilities of rights," the natural seed from which rights grow. When manifesto writers speak of them as if already actual rights, they are easily forgiven, for this is but a powerful way of expressing the conviction that they ought to be recognized by states here and now as potential rights and consequently as determinants of *present* aspirations and guides to *present* policies. That usage, I think, is a valid exercise of rhetorical licence.

I prefer to characterize rights as valid claims rather than justified ones, because I suspect that justification is rather too broad a qualification. "Validity," as I understand it, is justification of a peculiar and narrow kind, namely justification within a system of rules. A man has a legal right when the official recognition of his claim (as valid) is called for by the governing rules. This definition, of course, hardly applies to moral rights, but that is not because the genus of which moral rights are a species is something other than *claims*. A man has a moral right when he has a claim the recognition of which is called for — not (necessarily) by legal rules — but by moral principles, or the principles of an enlightened conscience.

There is one final kind of attack on the generic identification of rights with claims, and it has been launched with great spirit in a recent article by H. J. McCloskey, who holds that rights are not essentially claims at all, but rather entitlements. The springboard of his argument is his insistence that rights in their essential character are always *rights to*, not *rights against*:

> My right to life is not a right against anyone. It is my right and by virtue of it, it is normally permissible for me to sustain my life in the face of obstacles. It does give rise to rights against others *in the sense* that others have or may come to have duties to refrain from killing me,

[9]As declared in Article 24 of *The Universal Declaration of Human Rights* adopted on December 10, 1948, by the General Assembly of the United Nations.

but it is essentially a right of mine, not an infinite list of claims, hypothetical and actual, against an infinite number of actual, potential, and as yet nonexistent human beings . . . Similarly, the right of the tennis club member to play on the club courts is a right to play, not a right against some vague group of potential or possible obstructors.[10]

The argument seems to be that since rights are essentially rights *to*, whereas claims are essentially claims *against*, rights cannot be claims, though they can be grounds for claims. The argument is doubly defective though. First of all, contrary to McCloskey, rights (at least legal claim-rights) *are* held *against* others. McCloskey admits this in the case of *in personam* rights (what he calls "special rights") but denies it in the case of *in rem* rights (which he calls "general rights"):

Special rights are sometimes against specific individuals or institutions —e.g. rights created by promises, contracts, etc. . . . but these differ from . . . characteristic . . . general rights where the right is simply a right to . . . [11]

As far as I can tell, the only reason McCloskey gives for denying that *in rem* rights are against others is that those against whom they would have to hold make up an enormously multitudinous and "vague" group, including hypothetical people not yet even in existence. Many others have found this a paradoxical consequence of the notion of *in rem* rights, but I see nothing troublesome in it. If a general rule gives me a right of noninterference in a certain respect against everybody, then there are literally hundreds of millions of people who have a duty toward me in that respect; and if the same general rule gives the same right to everyone else, then it imposes on me literally hundreds of millions of duties — or duties towards hundreds of millions of people. I see nothing paradoxical about this, however. The duties, after all, are negative; and I can discharge all of them at a stroke simply by minding my own business. And if all human beings make up one moral community and there are hundreds of millions of human beings, we should expect there to be hundreds of millions of moral relations holding between them.

McCloskey's other premise is even more obviously defective. There is no good reason to think that all *claims* are "essentially" *against*, rather than *to*. Indeed most of the discussion of claims above has been of claims *to*, and as we have seen, the law finds it useful to recognize claims *to* (or "mere claims") that are not yet qualified to be claims *against*, or rights (except in a "manifesto sense" of "rights").

Whether we are speaking of claims or rights, however, we must notice that they seem to have two dimensions, as indicated by the

---

[10]H. J. McCloskey, "Rights," *Philosophical Quarterly*, Vol. 15 (1965), p. 118.
[11]*Loc. cit.*

prepositions "to" and "against," and it is quite natural to wonder whether either of these dimensions is somehow more fundamental or essential than the other. All rights seem to merge *entitlements to* do, have, omit, or be something with *claims against* others to act or refrain from acting in certain ways. In some statements of rights the entitlement is perfectly determinate (e.g., *to* play tennis) and the claim vague (e.g., *against* "some vague group of potential or possible obstructors"); but in other cases the object of the claim is clear and determinate (e.g., *against* one's parents), and the entitlement general and indeterminate (e.g., to be given a proper upbringing). If we mean by "entitlement" that *to* which one has a right and by "claim" something directed at those *against* whom the right holds (as McCloskey apparently does), then we can say that all claim-rights necessarily involve both, though in individual cases the one element or the other may be in sharper focus.

In brief conclusion: To have a right is to have a claim against someone whose recognition as valid is called for by some set of governing rules or moral principles. To have a *claim* in turn, is to have a case meriting consideration, that is, to have reasons or grounds that put one in a position to engage in performative and propositional claiming. The activity of claiming, finally, as much as any other thing, makes for self-respect and respect for others, gives a sense to the notion of personal dignity, and distinguishes this otherwise morally flawed world from the even worse world of Nowheresville.

2

QUENTIN SKINNER

Two Views on the Maintenance of Liberty

'Freedom always inclines to dialectical reversals.
She realises herself very soon in constraint, fulfils
herself in the subordination to law, rule, coercion,
system—but to fulfil herself therein does not
mean she therefore ceases to be freedom'[1]

JAMES HARRINGTON, MEDITATING on the idea of a free State in his *Oceana* in
1656,[2] began by suggesting that the theory and practice of government
may be divided into two distinct historical periods. The first, he declared, was initiated 'by God himself in the fabric of the commonwealth
of Israel', and was 'afterward picked out of his footsteps in nature and
unanimously followed by the Greeks and the Romans'. This gave rise to
the era of 'ancient prudence', an era in which the concept of political
authority was analysed in terms of civic liberty and equality. Later,
however, there followed a long and melancholy decline into the age of
'modern prudence', an age inaugurated by Julius Caesar when he
overthrew 'the liberty of Rome' and thereby 'opened up a pathway to
the barbarians', who eventually 'deformed the whole face of the world'
with their 'ill features of government'.

A determined effort has been made, Harrington goes on, to eradicate
the features of ancient prudence from modern political thought. The
leader of this destructive movement has been Hobbes, whose *Leviathan*
Harrington treats as the greatest monument to gothic barbarism in the
entire literature on the art of government. Fortunately, however, there
has been one modern commentator on politics who has shown himself a

[1]T. Mann, *Doctor Faustus*, H. Lowe-Porter (trans.) (Harmondsworth: Penguin, 1968),
p. 185.
[2]All my quotations from Harrington come from the opening paragraph of the 'Preliminaries' to his "Oceana", in J. Pocock (ed.), *The Political Works of James Harrington*
(Cambridge: Cambridge University Press, 1977).

'learned disciple' of the Roman theorists, and has managed to uphold the fabric of ancient prudence in the face of modern vandalism. This heroic figure is Machiavelli, 'the only politician of later ages', whose *Discourses on the first Decade of Titus Livy* constitute, according to Harrington, the one significant attempt by a modern political philosopher to retrieve and elaborate a classical theory of liberty.

These observations from the opening pages of *Oceana* seem well worth developing, and my principal aim in what follows will be to try to enlarge on them.[3] First of all, it is I think correct to suggest that there is a danger — far greater now than when Harrington was writing — that we may be losing touch with one fruitful way of thinking about the ideal of political liberty and how to maintain it. Secondly, it remains plausible to suggest that this may be due to the continuing influence of the major natural-law systems of the seventeenth century. These systems, first developed in the age of Grotius and Hobbes, quickly succeeded in obliterating the very different ways of thinking about law and the maintenance of liberty that had been characteristic of Renaissance thought. And their influence has remained hegemonal, even in contemporary political philosophy; in the writings of such leading contemporary theorists as John Rawls, Robert Nozick and their numerous disciples, we encounter a self-conscious attempt to revive and extend precisely the same 'gothic' vision of liberty as a natural right, of coercion as the antonym of liberty, and of the duty to maximise individual liberty as the chief (perhaps the sole) duty of enlightened governments.[4] Finally, it is I think valuable to suggest that, as a way of trying to re-establish some points of contact with earlier and contrasting ways of thinking about these same concepts, we can hardly do better than to focus on the political theory of the Renaissance, and in particular on Machiavelli's analysis of liberty in his *Discourses*,[5] the treatise on the

---

[3]For providing me with critical comment on earlier drafts of this article, I am extremely grateful to Thomas Baldwin, John Dunn, Richard Flathman, Susan James, J. G. A. Pocock, Russell Price and James Tully. To Russell Price I owe a special debt for discussing with me, in great detail, the many places where Machiavelli's *Discourses* pose special problems of translation, and for directing me, partly in consequence of this, to recast some of my arguments.

[4]For Rawls's characterisation of his own theory as one that 'generalises and carries to a higher level of abstraction the traditional conception of the social contract', see J. Rawls, *A Theory of Justice* (Cambridge, Harvard University Press, 1971: 3). For Nozick's invocations of the same tradition, especially as represented by Locke, see R. Nozick, *Anarchy, State and Utopia* (New York: Basic Books, 1974. 9, 10–12 and *passim*).

[5]For the fullest treatment of Machiavelli's views about liberty in the whole range of his political works, see M. Colish, 'The Idea of Liberty in Machiavelli', *Journal of the History of Ideas*, 1971, 32: 323–50. It is certainly true, as Colish demonstrates (and cf. Q. Skinner, *Machiavelli*, (Oxford: Oxford University Press, 1981: 78–86)), that Machiavelli's analysis of liberty in the *Discourses* is not merely reiterated but amplified in his later *History of Florence*. However, it seems to me that no significant general features of his views on political liberty are absent from the earlier work.

government of cities which he completed in 1519.[6] It is to this text, accordingly, and its possible implications for the somewhat blinkered analysis of liberty to be found in contemporary liberal thought, that the following discussion is addressed.

When we turn to the question of how we can hope to maintain our liberty within political society,[7] contemporary followers of the gothic way of thinking about this problem tend to begin by echoing and endorsing the classical assumption that the task is not merely one of paramount importance but also of exceptional difficulty. The deep gulf that separates the two traditions only begins to appear once they proceed to offer their very different accounts of what makes it so difficult to ensure that our freedom is safely preserved.

Contemporary exponents of the gothic approach are generally content to repeat the celebrated answer to this question provided by Hobbes in *Leviathan*. Consider the account given by John Rawls in *A Theory of Justice*. When Rawls considers what makes our liberty such a fragile commodity, he explicitly announces his agreement with what he calls 'Hobbes's thesis', the thesis that the ineliminable threat to our freedom arises out of our own natural selfishness. As rational egoists, Rawls begins by conceding, all of us have 'an inclination to self-interest', a disposition to follow a policy of seeking to increase our own freedom of action as far as possible, even at the expense of others (Rawls 1971:5; cf. 3–4, 239–40). But it is obvious that, if each of us seeks to act in this fashion, we shall soon find ourselves encroaching upon and interfering with the liberty of others. The fact of limited altruism is thus held to set the basic problem for the theory of justice.

For a classical theorist like Machiavelli, by contrast, the problem is more complicated. He agrees that the overwhelming majority of citizens in any polity can safely be assumed to have it as their fundamental desire to lead a life of personal liberty. A few men, it is true, will always want instead to dominate others, and will only be happy when their

---

[6]For the dating of the *Discourses*, see H. Baron, 'Machiavelli: the Republican Citizen and the Author of "The Prince"', *English Historical Review*, 1961, 76: 217–53. It is arguable that Baron overstates his case about the date at which Machiavelli began the work, but his account of the date of its completion is convincingly argued.

[7]Note that, in what follows, I shall adopt the contemporary practice of treating the terms 'freedom' and 'liberty' as exact synonyms. I also adopt the convenience of treating 'he', 'him' etc., as abbreviations, whenever appropriate, for 'he or she', 'him or her' etc. It is perhaps worth stressing at the outset the limited character of this investigation into Machiavelli's views about how to maintain liberty. My aim is simply to report what I take to be the structure of Machiavelli's beliefs about this topic as he presents them in his *Discourses*. I do not claim to be offering *an interpretation of his theory* of liberty, an undertaking which would in addition require, in my view, an account of what Machiavelli should be understood to be doing in asserting the beliefs about liberty which (I merely seek to show) are in fact asserted in the *Discourses*.

'thirst for power', their 'great longing to rule', is duly satisfied.[8] But most men 'simply want not to be ruled'; they want to be able 'to live as free men' (vivere liberi), pursuing their own ends as far as possible without insecurity or unnecessary interference.[9] They want, in particular, to be free (liber) to marry as they choose; to bring up their families without having to fear for their honour or their own welfare; and to be in a position 'freely (liberamente) to possess their own property'. This is what it means 'to enjoy personal liberty' (la libertà); and this is what enables people to recognise and rejoice in the fact 'that they have been born as free men (liberi) and not as slaves'.[10]

While these are the ends that most of us desire above all, however, there is no possibility of our being able to attain them, according to Machiavelli, unless we live in a community of which it can already be said that it enjoys uno vivere libero, a free way of life. Our community, that is, must be based on free institutions in which all of us as citizens participate. It must be kept free from subjection to the will of any particular individual or faction; free from any dependenza or servitù, whether imposed by a conqueror in the form of 'external servitude' or by a tyrant who arises from within the community's own political system.[11] And the only means, Machiavelli insists, of preventing our government from falling into the hands of such tyrannical individuals or groups is by organising it in such a way that it remains in the hands of the whole body of the citizens. It is only if everyone remains willing to place their talents at the disposal of the community that the bene comune, the common good or public interest, can be upheld and the rule of private or factional interests avoided; and it is only if this happens that the personal liberty of each individual citizen can in turn be secured.[12] In the classical oxymoron that Machiavelli is restating,

[8]For Machiavelli's view about the grandi, see N. Machiavelli's 'Discourses' — henceforth just Machiavelli—in A. Gilbert (trans.) The Chief Works and Others, 3 vols. (Durham, NC: Duke University Press, 1965), p. 204, 237, 432, 449–50. Note that, although I basically follow the translations given by A. Gilbert in Machiavelli, I have felt free—aided by the generous advice of Russell Price—to alter Gilbert's renderings in a considerable number of places, while continuing to give page-references to Gilbert's translations of the passages concerned.

[9]See Machiavelli, Discourses: 204–5, 237. It is true that Machiavelli occasionally speaks of all men as 'restless' and 'ambitious' in character. See Machiavelli 272, 478. But he generally insists that 'most people' have 'no desire for authority' and simply wish to be left in security to enjoy their liberty. See the refs. above and also 208, 222.

[10]Machiavelli, 236, 332—the two crucial passages in which the dependence of personal liberta upon the maintenance of uno vivere libero is stressed.

[11]For the claim that public liberty is automatically extinguished when there is subjection to a foreign conqueror, see Machiavelli, 296, 328, 461. For the claim that the same happens when a tyrant arises from within the community, see 219, 235, 269–70, 329–30.

[12]For this crucial contention, see especially Machiavelli 450–1, 461, 519 and for a fuller analysis, with further references, see G. Cadoni 'Liberta, repubblica e governo misto in Machiavelli', Rivista Internazionale di filosofia del diritto, 1962, 39: 479–80 and Q. Skinner Machiavelli (Oxford: Oxford University Press, 1981) p. 53–73.

freedom is thus a form of service, since devotion to public service is held to be a necessary condition of maintaining personal liberty. If we wish to maximise our freedom to control our private affairs without anxiety or interference, the moral is that we must first turn ourselves into wholehearted servants of the public good.[13]

Machiavelli's way of summarising these claims is to say that *libertà*, both personal and public, can only be maintained if the citizens as a whole display *virtù*, the quality of *virtù* being defined as a willingness to do anything that may be required (whether conventionally virtuous or not) in order 'to save the life and preserve the liberty of one's native land'.[14] But herein lies the rub. For the sad truth, as Machiavelli repeatedly insists, is that most men are not naturally *virtuoso* in character. On the contrary, most men are 'corrupt', by which Machiavelli means that their basic disposition, if left unchecked, will be to place their own private interests above those of the community.[15] There are two ways, he argues, in which this threat of *corruzione*, this negation of *virtù*, tends to arise. The ordinary run of citizens are prone to be lazy (*ozioso*), as a result of which they often fail to devote any energies to their civic obligations at all.[16] Even more dangerous to *libertà*, however, is the tendency for leading citizens to be moved by personal ambition (*ambizione*), and in consequence to pursue the corrupt course of trying to pervert the free institutions of their community in such a way as to favour their own family, faction or social group, whereas they ought of course, as *virtuosi* citizens, to be devoting themselves to upholding the interests of the community as a whole.[17]

For Machiavelli, accordingly, the fundamental threat to liberty is not simply posed by the fact of human selfishness; it is rather that, in pursuing their self-interested desires, men are at the same time self-deceived. They are prone, that is, to entertain the false belief that the best

---

[13]For a classic (in both senses) statement of the claim that the *libertas* of the *res publica*, and thus of its members, can only be maintained if the *virtus* of all the citizens is such that they are willing to devote all their *cura* and *labor* to serving the community in war and peace, see Sallust 'The War with Catiline', in J. Rolfe (ed.) *Sallust* (London: Heinemann, 1921) VI.5 and X–XI. For the constitutional implications, see Livy, Book II, I–II, and C. Wirszubski *Libertas as a Political Ideal at Rome* (Cambridge: Cambridge University Press, 1960) p. 5.

[14]Machiavelli, 519. Cf. also 218, 482, 496. For a full analysis of Machiavelli's uses of the term *virtù*, see R. Price 'The Senses of *Virtu* in Machiavelli', *European Studies Review*, 1973, 3:315–45.

[15]For this claim, see especially Machiavelli 242, 361, 385–6, 457–8 and 496; and for a fuller account of the notion of 'corruption' involved here, see Q. Skinner *The Foundations of Modern Political Thought*, Vol. I: *The Renaissance* (Cambridge: Cambridge University Press, 1978) pp. 163–7, 178–9.

[16]For the claim that to be *ozioso* is to be unfit for any deeds of *virtù*, see the general discussion in Machiavelli 194–5, and cf. 260, 330–2. On the need to avoid such laziness, see 202–4, 246–7.

[17]On the ambitions of the powerful, and especially the nobility, as both a manifestation and a cause of corruption, see especially Machiavelli, 216, 220, 242, 251, 257–60, 264–7, 272–5, 282–4.

way to attain their desired ends—including the maintenance of their personal liberty—will either be to evade their civic obligations altogether, or else to try to reshape the institutions of their community to serve their own ends. But this is to forget that, whenever we corruptly permit or pursue such policies hostile to the common good, we begin to subvert the free institutions of our community, and hence our own personal liberty at the same time. The paradox with which we have to reckon, as Machiavelli repeatedly reminds us, is thus that 'the people, deceived by a false image of good, many times desire their own ruin'.[18]

It follows that, for a classical theorist such as Machiavelli, the question of how to maintain our liberty in the face of our limited altruism appears as a more complicated problem than it does to the modern gothic theorists of liberty. For the latter, the dilemma is said to be resolved as we discover a fair means of regulating the tendency of self-interested individuals to threaten the freedom of others. They assume, that is, that the fundamental problem in theory of liberty—and indeed in the theory of the State—is simply that of devising the best method of adjudicating between competing rational egoists in such a way that each person is able to enjoy an equal right to the most extensive system of liberties compatible with a similar system of liberty for all.[19] For Machiavelli, by contrast, the further problem that remains to be solved is that of finding some means of transmuting our natural but self-destructive tendency to exhibit *corruzione* into a *virtuoso* concern for the common good. Or else, if this is rendered impossible by our incorrigible *ozio* or *ambizione*, the problem becomes that of devising some mechanism for preventing these inescapably corrupt motives from having their natural but self-destructive as well as politically destructive effects. For a classical theorist like Machiavelli, the deepest secret of psychology and statecraft is thus to understand how this act of alchemy can be performed.

Machiavelli's starting-point is of course to consider how these self-destructive tendencies arise. What causes us to behave corruptly? Why do we tend to pursue our own private advantage at the expense of the public interest? As we have seen, his answer (in general terms) is that although there are good reasons for all of us to pursue the common good, we are often prevented—and often prevent ourselves—from seeing that this is so, in consequence of which we tend not to be motivated to act as our interests dictate.[20] The point is conveyed in the

[18]Machiavelli, 302. For the idea of *corruzione* as the high road to *servitu*, see also 259, 295–6, 449–50.

[19]Here I allude to the 'final statement' of Rawls's 'first principle' of justice. See Rawls 302.

[20]This is of course merely to summarise—and in an idiom more familiar to us than to Machiavelli—what I take to be the general thrust of Machiavelli's argument. The closest Machiavelli comes himself to stating the issue in such abstract terms is in Machiavelli 303, in the course of glossing Dante's aphorism to the affect that 'the populace many times shouts "long live its own death" and "Down with its own life"'.

form of a recurrent visual metaphor: we are easily blinded, he asserts, to the nature of our own best interests. Such impairment of moral vision is even capable of afflicting men of the highest *virtù*, such as Quintus Fabius, who 'became blinded' to his duties as a result of his *ambizione* and eventually 'behaved like a tyrant' (285). So too with Manlius Capitolinus, who began 'by performing many excellent deeds for the advantage of his country', but later 'became so blinded' to his obligations that 'he set out to raise rebellion against the Senate and the laws of Rome' (449). The same danger is even more likely to be incurred by the rank-and-file of the citizenry, who are always liable to be 'blinded by a kind of false good' (493), and even to be 'so badly blinded' that they fail to recognise when 'they are putting a yoke around their own necks' [21] Machiavelli admiringly quotes a remark attributed to King Ferdinand of Spain, who once observed that the people are sometimes 'so completely blinded' that 'they often act like small birds of prey, who so strongly desire to catch their victims, as nature urges them to do, that they do not hear above them another and larger bird that will kill them' (284).

It is perhaps worth underlining that this is the general shape of Machiavelli's argument. For it is often supposed that, if we say of someone that there is a reason for them to act in a certain way, even though they are not motivated so to act, we must either be positing a 'higher self' with different and more rational motives,[22] or else implying that there are certain purposes it is objectively rational for all agents to pursue.[23] It is then held to follow that the only means of coming to see that there is indeed a reason for us to act which differs from any of our current motives is by finding some means of attuning ourselves to these objective reasons or to our higher self.

It is arguable that, if there are determinate human needs, there must be objective reasons of this character; and it is certainly true that, in a theory of liberty such as Kant's — which bears certain resemblances to Machiavelli's — we find their existence being powerfully defended.[24] As we shall see, however, Machiavelli's own view of the matter occupies a middle ground between the two poles of this long-standing dispute. In contrast with the assumption later made famous by Hume (1888:415) — the assumption that 'reason is and ought only to be the

[21]This exact phrase is used in Machiavelli 239; similar phraseology recurs at 270, 284, 303.

[22]This is, for example, Isaiah Berlin's supposition in Berlin *Four Essays on Liberty* (Oxford: Oxford University Press, 1969) pp. 132–4, 151 and note.

[23]For this assumption, see for example M. Hollis 'Rational Man and Social Science' in R. Harrison (ed.) *Rational Action* (Cambridge: Cambridge University Press, 1979) pp. 1–15.

[24]For a highly persuasive contemporary analysis of this character, partly indebted to Kant, see T. Nagel *The Possibility of Altruism* (Oxford: Oxford University Press, 1970) Chap. III, 13–17. Cf. also the discussion of 'real interests' in R. Geuss *The Idea of a Critical Theory* (Cambridge: Cambridge University Press, 1981) pp. 45–54.

slave of the passions' — Machiavelli shows that it is possible to argue coherently for the conclusion that there may be genuine reasons for action which are unconnected with — and perhaps unconnectable with — any of our present desires. But in contrast with Kant's attack on Hume, Machiavelli shows in turn how it is possible for this position to be defended without having recourse, even implicitly, to the idea of objective reasons or higher selves.

To understand how Machiavelli arrives at this conclusion, we need to focus on his explanation of the fact that all of us are so readily blinded to our own true interests. Turning to this question, he makes use in an informal way of the distinction he has already drawn between the conduct to be expected from the ambitious leaders of society on the one hand, and the conduct to be expected from ordinary citizens on the other. When our leaders become blind to the fact that it is in their interests to do their duty and promote the common good, this is generally because their *ambizione* has betrayed them into deceiving themselves. 'The nature of men', Machiavelli declares, 'is ambitious and suspicious, and does not know how to set a limit to its own *fortuna*'.[25] The most gifted of men are especially prone to over-reach and in consequence deceive themselves about what they can hope to achieve. This is what happened to Quintus Fabius, 'who was blinded by a little *ambizione*' (285), as well as to Manlius Capitolinus, whose early deeds of *virtù* were 'later cancelled out by a vicious longing to rule' which 'completely blinded his mind' (449). Machiavelli summarises these contentions in Book I, chapter 10, where he discusses — in a passage of unusual sententiousness — the characteristic failings of men who are given great opportunities. Almost all of them, he declares, 'in the end deceive themselves with a false idea of good and a false glory, and allow themselves to slide, either willingly or ignorantly, into the position of those who deserve more blame than praise. For while able, to their perpetual honour, to set up a republic or a kingdom, they turn to a tyranny, without recognizing how much fame, how much glory, how much honour, security, quiet, along with satisfaction of mind they give up by this decision, and into what great infamy, censure, blame, peril and disquiet they run' (220–1).

When he turns instead to consider how a body of citizens can fail or even refuse to recognise what is in their own best interests, Machiavelli argues in a rather different way. He stresses that they too may succeed in deceiving themselves, thereby falling into a condition which he describes at several points as one of 'collective self-deceit'.[26] But he

---

[25]Machiavelli, 257, 272. For the significance of *Fortuna* in this context, see Skinner *Machiavelli*, pp. 24–31, and for a full and very fine analysis see T. Flanagan 'The concept of *Fortuna* in Machiavelli', in A. Parel (ed.) *The Political Calculus* (Toronto: 1972).

[26]The phrase Machiavelli uses 386 is *uno comune inganno*. Cf. also the similar accounts at 271, 282–3, 292, 399.

lays his main emphasis on the fact that political leaders are 'often so corrupt and so ambitious' that they are willing to employ their positions of influence to blind, delude and deliberately mislead the people about the courses of action they need to adopt in order to gain their own desired ends.[27]

Machiavelli is especially preoccupied by two historical instances of this treasonous proclivity, both of which occurred in republican Rome. First he examines the case of the Decemvirs, a group of magistrates led and dominated by Appius Claudius. Assigned a special authority to make laws, they used this unlimited power 'to blind and deceive the people' so completely that 'without any scruple they were able to usurp the liberty of Rome'.[28] But the most shameless example is said to be that of Julius Caesar, against whom we are warned 'not to let ourselves be deceived by his glory' or by the flattery of later ages.[29] 'Those who praise him', Machiavelli insists, 'are unduly influenced by his success (*fortuna*) and by the long duration of his Empire' (221). The truth is that he offers us the best instance of an unscrupulous leader who 'so totally blinded the populace' that he eventually forced and deceived them 'into decreeing their own ruin' (239, 242).

These examples prompt Machiavelli to consider how it comes about that corrupt leaders usually find it so alarmingly simple to betray the populace. He first of all points to the capacity of great men to dazzle us with their greatness, thereby preventing us from seeing—until it is too late—that they may be misusing their outstanding gifts in order to seize power for themselves. The problem is outlined in general terms in Book I, chapter 33, where Machiavelli affirms that 'if in a state a young noble appears who possesses extraordinary *virtù*, all the citizens begin to turn to him and agree, without reservation, in honouring him. Hence, if he has any *ambizione*, through the union of the aid nature gives him with his situation, he soon gets to such a place that, if the citizens realise their mistake, they have few methods for putting a stop to the process, and if they try to make much use of all those they have, they do nothing else than hasten his rise to power' (265). Machiavelli cites several cases in which this happened in ancient Rome, including that of Horatius as well as Julius Caesar[30] but his chief example comes from much closer at hand, and concerns the insidious rise to power of the Medici in fifteenth-century Florence. 'Cosimo de Medici', he explains, 'through whom the Medici first grew great in our city, arrived at

[27]For the corrupting influence of the powerful, see Machiavelli, 309; for incidental references to the danger that the people may be blinded by their leaders, see 294, 295, 302–3.

[28]The point is first made at Machiavelli, 270 and repeated at 282–3.

[29]Caesar is frequently attacked in the *Discourses*. The quotation comes from Machiavelli 221; cf. also 239, 242, 266.

[30]For Horatius, see Machiavelli, 251; for Caesar, 266 and 267–8.

such a high reputation, by means of the credit derived from his own prudence and other citizens' ignorance, that he struck awe into the government, so that the citizens judged it dangerous to attack him, although it was even more dangerous to let him continue' (265).

But the most effective means available to the leaders of society for dazzling and misleading their followers is said to be through the corrupt use of their wealth. Sometimes the nobles may be so rich that they are able to employ their fortunes not merely to purchase men's loyalties, but even to build up private armies. 'They are able to command castles and procure subjects, a course of action altogether hostile to all free government' (308–9). Less spectacularly, but no less effectively, the rich are also in a position to prevent the people from seeing that their liberty is in jeopardy simply by bribing them to look the other way. Bribery, Machiavelli thinks, is in fact the most frequent cause of corruption in public life. He offers many instances of this depressing truth throughout the *Discourses*, as well as discussing the problem in general terms at several points.[31] Among the many cases he cites, one of the most instructive is said to be that of Spurius Cassius, a man who was *ambizioso* and 'was eager to seize unconstitutional power in Rome'. In an attempt to gain the plebeians' goodwill, he 'spoke to the people and offered to give them the money derived from the grain which the city imported from Sicily'. Being *virtuosi* citizens, they refused the bribe; but as Machiavelli points out, 'had they been corrupt, they would not have refused it', and would shortly have discovered 'that Spurius was trying to give them the price of their *libertà*' (449). But the most shocking example Machiavelli cites — shocking because it was successful, even in a period of great civic *virtù* — is again that of the Decemvirs under the early republic. Returning to their positions of absolute authority for a second year, they not only began 'to carry on the government with violence', but also 'created satellites for themselves among the young nobles by giving them the goods of persons who had been condemned'. Machiavelli refers us to Livy's solemn judgment on the results of such corruption: 'bribed with these gifts, the young men preferred license for themselves rather than liberty for all' (282).

The dilemma posed by this account of *corruzione* can now be summarised. On the one hand, there are good reasons for all of us to subordinate our private ambitions to the pursuit of the common good. Nor are these reasons 'external' to the boundaries of our present selves,[32] for we are certainly capable of seeing them, of reflecting and deliberating on the relationship between our current motives and our desired ends with enough clearsightedness to perceive that any tend-

[31]For general discussions of 'bribery and corruption' see Machiavelli, 270, 271, 290–1, 300, 493.
[32]For this way of putting the point, see Nagel 7 and note.

ency to behave corruptly will need to be eradicated if we are to avoid acting in self-destructive as well as anti-social ways. But on the other hand, the vices of ambition and avarice are so deeply rooted in human nature that it will always be difficult, perhaps impossible, to recollect our own patterns of motivation with sufficient tranquillity to prevent ourselves from falling into self-deception or being blinded by our leaders into acting against our own best interests. This being so, we are brought back to the questions that need above all to be answered if the value of liberty is to be upheld. How is such *corruzione* to be overcome? How can we hope, that is, to reform our naturally self-interested patterns of behaviour in such a way as to avoid undermining our own as well as other people's liberty? If such reform is impossible, what is to be done? Can we nevertheless hope to evolve some mechanism for preventing our incorrigible corruption from having its destructive — and self-destructive — effects?

Machiavelli begins by intimating that to some extent the answer to these questions lies beyond the boundaries of statecraft, since we can never hope to overcome the forces of corruption unless we happen to enjoy a large measure of good fortune. Just as he contends in *The Prince* that all great leaders are to some degree indebted for their ascendancy to the favourable attentions of the goddess Fortuna, so he affirms in the *Discourses* that no community has the least hope of avoiding *corruzione* — and hence of assuring its *libertà* — unless it happens to be blessed with two large and wholly gratuitous pieces of luck. He begins by arguing — in the opening chapters of Book I — that 'the first stroke of luck' any city needs to enjoy is that of starting life in the hands of a great founding father, a leader and lawgiver of outstanding *virtù* to whom 'as a daughter' the community may be said to owe its birth (223; cf. 196,200,244). Later he goes on to insist — this being the principal theme of Book III — that although this element of good fortune is necessary, it is by no means sufficient to enable a city to attain greatness. It is also necessary that the community should be lucky enough to acquire a succession of later leaders in whom the natural tendency of mankind towards *corruzione* is similarly and almost miraculously replaced by a willing and *virtuoso* commitment to the promotion of the public interest at all costs (481).

Machiavelli completely disagrees, however, with those writers who argue that the rise to greatness of any particular city is always and entirely a matter of luck (324–5). He assumes that the process is, at least to some degree, susceptible to *ragione* and thus to the formulation of rules. So his principal remaining task becomes that of furnishing an account of such guidelines as he believes can be formulated for the defence of liberty against its enemies.

One possibility, one that is canvassed at a number of different points throughout the *Discourses*, is that our natural tendency to behave corruptly, to pursue our private advantage at the expense of the public interest, can perhaps be successfully transcended.[33] Perhaps we can be persuaded to forswear our foolish ways; perhaps we can manage to reach out, if not to a higher self, at least to a heightened state of selfhood. Perhaps we can aspire to that condition which Machiavelli sometimes seems to attribute to the citizens of the Roman republic, who treated 'the love of their country as more powerful than any other consideration' (450), and came 'to love the glory and the common good of their native community' with apparent willingness and spontaneity (315; cf. 217).

One way in which this condition of naturally *virtuoso* citizenship can perhaps be attained, according to Machiavelli, is by means of education. It is hardly surprising to find him advancing this suggestion, since he lived in—and wrote for—an intellectual community in which it was widely believed that, in Erasmus's famous phrase, 'men are not born but made'.[34] It was commonplace for the political treatises of Machiavelli's contemporaries to take the form—as with the works of Erasmus himself—of pedagogic handbooks, indicating what forms of instruction might be expected to offer the best prospects of inculcating a *virtuoso* desire to serve the common good.[35] Nor does Machiavelli question the conventional wisdom at this point. On the contrary, he declares with great emphasis in Book I, chapter 4, that 'all instances of *virtù* have their origin in good education' (203), a judgment which he endorses at the start of Book II, declaring that 'if we ask why it is that people in ancient times were greater lovers of *libertà* than nowadays', we are bound to conclude that the answer lies in 'the difference between our education and that of ancient times'.[36] Finally, he reiterates the same conclusion at the end of Book III, blaming 'men's feebleness in our day' upon 'their feeble education', and reminding us that the impressions of our tender years 'serve to govern our conduct in all the subsequent periods of our life'.[37]

[33]This element in Machiavelli's argument seems to me underestimated in most recent discussions of Machiavelli's views about liberty, my own included. Cf. Skinner *Machiavelli* and M. Colish 'The Idea of Liberty in Machiavelli', *Journal of History of Ideas*, 1971, 32: 347, who confines her attention exclusively to the coercive effects of the law in discussing 'the means of instituting *libertà*', thereby overlooking this more voluntarist aspect of Machiavelli's theory altogether.

[34]For this phrase, and its place in Erasmus's views about education, see Skinner *The Foundations of Modern Political Thought* pp. 241–3.

[35]Erasmus's own main contribution of this nature was his Latin treatise on *The Education of a Christian Prince* (1516). For the genre as a whole, see Skinner *The Foundations of Modern Political Thought* Chaps. 5 and 8.

[36]This passage is omitted in Gilbert's translation in Machiavelli. It ought to occur at 331.

[37]Machiavelli, 490 and 525. But for a fuller and partly contrasting analysis of Machiavelli's argument at this point, cf. J. Pocock *The Machiavellian Movement* (Princeton: Princeton University Press, 1975) pp. 195–6.

Despite his endorsement of these familiar humanist premises, however, Machiavelli appears uncertain about the value of this particular argument. He tells us very little about the precise relationship he discerns between the right system of education, the promotion of *virtù* and the upholding of *libertà*. And he tells us nothing at all about the types of training — the actual contents of the curriculum — that might be expected to provide us with the best preparation for a life of effective citizenship. Instead he devotes far more of his attention to a second possibility, the possibility that a body of citizens may perhaps be capable of transcending their natural selfishness if they are inspired by the example of truly *virtuoso* leadership. The working out of this line of thought occupies much of the third Book of the *Discourses*, the chief aim of which, as Machiavelli explains at the outset, is to indicate 'how the deeds of individuals increased Roman greatness' (423).

Great leaders are capable of inspiring deeds of *virtù* among their followers, Machiavelli suggests, simply by the force of their own example. This general claim is put forward at the beginning of Book III, and is subsequently illustrated at considerable length. The reformation of a republic, we are told, 'can always be brought about by the sheer *virtù* of a single man', since truly *virtuosi* leaders 'are of such reputation, and their example is so powerful, that good men wish to imitate them, while the wicked are ashamed to live a life contrary to theirs' (421). The *locus classicus* of this general truth is said to be provided by Manlius Torquatus, who invariably acted 'wholly for the benefit of the republic, without the least consideration for his personal ambitions', thereby demonstrating that it is possible to reanimate 'the ancient *virtù* of a republic' by means of exemplary deeds (481–2).

As before, however, Machiavelli seems unwilling to place much weight on this argument. As he makes clear, the arrival on the political scene of a truly *virtuoso* leader is always in part a matter of fortune, and accordingly constitutes an unreliable, unstatesmanlike means of promoting *virtù* in the citizen body as a whole. He concedes that 'if a republic were fortunate enough to manage on many occasions' to nurture leaders of Manlius's quality, the effect 'would not merely be to stop it from running to ruin' but 'would actually be to make it everlasting' (481). But he also points out that, even under the Roman republic, the supply of such *virtuosi* leaders eventually dried up, 'there being no further examples after Marcus Regulus' in the middle of the third century, 'after which corruption began to increase' (421). His final word on the subject accordingly takes the form of a warning against treating the idea of an everlasting republic with any seriousness. We must never forget — and fortune's caprice is there to remind us — that 'the ruin of republics always comes in a thousand unexpected ways' (471).

There is one further consideration Machiavelli explores in discussing whether it is possible to inspire large bodies of people to rise above their ingrained selfishness: that it may be possible to do so by manipulating their religious beliefs. One of the first general claims he makes about Roman religion in the sequence of chapters devoted to this topic in Book I of the *Discourses* is that king Numa, Romulus's immediate successor, understood perfectly how religion can be 'well used' in this way. In particular, he appreciated the value of exploiting popular superstitions about portents and auguries, as a result of which 'the religion Numa introduced was among the chief reasons for the prosperity of Rome' (225).

A portent or augury, Machiavelli goes on to explain, is an alleged sign that the gods desire you to perform a certain action and will reward you with success if you duly perform it. The aim must therefore be to exploit this belief. It is not important that the people's leaders should believe in these signs themselves. Indeed, Machiavelli implies, they will obviously be in a stronger position to manipulate such superstitions if they remain sceptical themselves (227). All that matters is that the body of the people—especially if called upon to fight a battle—should go into action believing that the gods are on their side. This will inspire them to fight with a preternatural degree of *virtù*, a *virtù* which in turn will be very likely to win the day, simply because 'confidence is the first cause of every victory' (503).

Once again, however, Machiavelli seems uncertain about the strength of this argument, or at least about its relevance in Christian societies. Although he mentions a number of cases in which the Romans were dramatically successful in the manipulation of auguries,[38] he concedes at the same time that Christianity is much less susceptible to being 'well used' in this way (227–8). Striking a somewhat wryer note, he adds that in any case Numa had an easier time of it, 'since those ages were very religious, and the people with whom he had to deal were rough and ignorant', as a result of which 'he was able to mould them in any shape he desired' (225).

As Machiavelli's tone throughout the above discussion suggests, he is pessimistic about the prospects of changing human nature, of transforming our natural selfishness into a willing and *virtuoso* concern for the common good. He prefers to take men as they are, and to recognise that in general they exhibit a strong tendency to be corrupt. As he puts it in a vehement passage near the beginning of Book I, it is not merely prudent but essential 'for anyone who lays out a republic and establishes its laws to presuppose that all men are evil, and that they are always going to act according to the wickedness of their spirits when they are given free scope' (201). But if this is the most realistic axiom

[38]Three different examples are cited in *Discourses* Bk I, Chap. 13. See Machiavelli, 229–31.

from which to work, it follows that the problem of how to uphold our liberty in the face of our own egoism still remains to be solved. If we cannot hope to transcend our selfish desires, it becomes a matter of even greater urgency to discover how to curb and bridle them, so that our self-interested behaviour can somehow be prevented from having its self-destructive consequences.

The general solution Machiavelli proposes to this dilemma is a very familiar one: he puts all his trust in the coercive powers of the law. It is obvious, he assumes, that 'men will never do anything good except by necessity' (201); but it is no less obvious that 'they can be kept better and less ambitious by fear of punishment' (259). It is this consideration which enables the law to act as a guardian of our liberty. For it is always open to our legislators 'to bridle human appetites' and 'regulate the multitude' by means of 'taking from us any hope of erring without punishment' (285,314). The indispensable role of the law is thus to deter us from *corruzione* and impose on us the 'artifical necessity' of behaving as *virtuosi* citizens by making it 'less eligible' (as Bentham would say) to follow our natural tendency to pursue our own interests at the expense of the common good.[39] 'For this reason', Machiavelli concludes, 'it is said that hunger and poverty make men industrious, while the laws make them good' (201). In a strikingly Rousseauvian phrase, he adds that all citizens ought ideally to be 'chained by the laws' as a means to coerce them into respecting the ideal of liberty and behaving 'in a well-ordered way' (317).

The best illustration of the law's capacity to maximise public (and hence personal) liberty is said to be provided by the constitution of republican Rome. When Machiavelli asks himself at the beginning of Book I how Rome managed 'to avoid corruption for so many centuries', his basic answer is that what made this possible was 'the many necessities imposed upon her by the laws of Romulus, Numa and the rest' (195). From the outset the Romans recognised that 'a republic can never hope to be perfect unless she provides for everything by means of her laws and furnishes a legal method for dealing with every unexpected event' (268–9). Perceiving the significance of this fact, the Romans continually 'devised new laws whenever new necessities appeared' (295) and thereby managed 'to establish the city's liberty upon an increasingly firm base' (280). This eventually brought them their unique success: by maintaining 'law and order' they were able to preserve the city's liberty; and by preserving their free way of life, they were able to reach their peak of *grandezza* as 'rulers of a great and mighty empire' (268, 271).

---

[39]The idea of the law as an 'artificial' as opposed to a natural form of coercion, and thus as an artificial necessity, is a leading theme of *Discourses* Bk.I, Chap. I. See Machiavelli 192–5.

The most obvious way in which the law can be used to protect liberty is by stopping us from unfairly interfering with other people's freedom to pursue their own ends. To understand Machiavelli's specific programme for using a system of 'laws and ordinances' to bring this about, we first of all need to recall what he takes to be the most dangerous methods a citizen can use to threaten or undermine the freedom of others. One method—employed by the Decemvirs and later perfected by Julius Caesar—is to engineer for oneself a position of supreme authority, either civil or (even better) military, and then use it to promote one's corrupt ambitions at the expense of the common good. Machiavelli's suggested response is a very simple one: there must be laws to prevent such positions of command from ever being instituted, unless they are set up 'for a limited term' and with the sole purpose 'of dealing with the emergency that caused them to be set up' (268). Otherwise there is no surer method of placing everyone's liberty at risk than to assign supreme power to one particular citizen. Rome, as always, is offered as the most instructive example: it was the habit 'first of prolonging the magistracies, and later the supreme commands' that 'eventually ruined the republic' and 'rendered Rome unfree' (485–6).

The other means by which a leading citizen can always hope to undermine *libertà* is, as we have seen, by the corrupt use of his wealth. If he is very rich, he may be able to equip enough military retainers to threaten the liberty of an entire city; even if he is only somewhat richer than average, he can always hope to buy himself unfair advantages by the judicious payment of bribes. Machiavelli's solution to the first of these problems is typically dramatic: 'anyone who wishes to set up a republic in a place where there are many such gentlemen has no hope of doing so unless he first of all wipes them all out' (309). He is unspecific about how this is to be done, and about the nature of the legislation needed to prevent any later recrudescence of such feudal arrangements. But he is emphatic in pointing out that 'those republics where government is kept uncorrupt must never allow any citizen of theirs to live in the fashion of such gentlemen', and he even adds with obvious approval that truly *virtuosi* republics 'put such people to death, if ever they fall into their hands, as the beginners of corruption and the cause of all discord', since they recognise that 'men of that type are altogether hostile to all forms of free government' (212, 308–9).

This still leaves the problem of bribery and corruption, to which Machiavelli responds with the same devastating simplicity. To maintain a well-ordered republic, he declares, the laws must ensure 'that the treasury remains rich while the citizens remain poor' (272). Again, he does not specify the nature of the *ordini* required to preserve such a condition of virtuous austerity. But he insists throughout the *Discourses* that, because 'corruption and slight aptitude for a free way of life spring from inequality in cities' (240), it follows that 'the most useful thing *uno vivere libero* can bring about is to keep its citizens poor'.[40] 'I could show' he concludes, 'with a long speech that poverty produces much better fruit than riches, and that one has honoured cities, provinces and religions while the other has ruined them, if the subject had not been well-treated on many occasions by other men' (488).

As well as these specific suggestions, Machiavelli has a more all-embracing proposal to make about the best means of preventing our freedom from being undermined by the selfish ambitions of our fellow-citizens. What is required, he argues, is a special magistracy charged with the duty of acting as 'the guardian of our liberty' against any who seek to undermine it (204). This is the first and most general idea put forward — in Book I, chapter 5 — about the best means of ensuring equity among essentially self-interested men. A special court or assembly must be established 'with the power to bring charges before the people' in the case of 'any citizen who in any way sins against free government' (211). Machiavelli considers it a matter of nice judgment to decide how such courts are to be set up, and in particular whether their membership should be drawn from the nobility or from the rank-and-file of the citizens.[41] He merely insists that some such arrangement is indispensable as a means of preventing encroachments upon our liberty. He not only points out that 'those who have prudently founded republics have regarded the establishment of a guardian for liberty as one of the most important matters they have to arrange'; he concludes that 'according to whether this arrangement has been well or badly made, the *vivere libero* thus set up has lasted a longer or a shorter time' (204).

Up to this point, Machiavelli's analysis of the relationship between law and liberty has been founded on familiar premises. But as we have seen, he is not merely concerned with the obvious fact that, if we behave in a consistently self-interested fashion, this will inevitably violate the liberty of others. He is also moved by the further consideration that, if we are blinded by the stratagems of corrupt leaders, or corrupted by 'collective self-deceit', this will have the effect of making us behave not merely in anti-social but in self-destructive ways. When he contends, therefore, that the indispensable means of preventing corruption is to invoke the coercive powers of the law, he is not merely endorsing the familiar observation that the law can be used to make us respect each other's liberty. He is also suggesting that the law can act to free us from our natural but self-destructive tendency to pursue our

---

[40]This moral is several times repeated. See Machiavelli, 486; and cf. also 378 and 469.
[41]This is the chief issue debated in *Discourses* Bk. I, Chap. 5 and 6. See Machiavelli 204–11.

selfish interests, forcing us instead to promote the public interest in a genuinely *virtuoso* style, and thereby enabling us to preserve our own individual liberty instead of undermining it. He is claiming, in effect, that the law can — and must — be used to force us to be free.

Any consideration of this further possibility tends to be stigmatised by contemporary gothic theorists of liberty as an obvious — even a sinister — misunderstanding. Liberty, they point out, entails absence of constraint; so to speak of rendering people free by means of constraining them is simply to propagate a blatant confusion of terms.[42] It follows, as Isaiah Berlin has maintained with particular eloquence, that there must be 'something amiss in the premises of the argument' if we find ourselves endorsing the conclusion that 'to be at once wholly law-abiding and wholly free' represents a coherent possibility.[43]

Given the prevalence and prestige of these arguments, it is worth examining in some detail how Machiavelli nevertheless develops the case for saying that it is possible, and indeed essential, for the law to protect and enhance our liberty by means of coercing us. The general structure of the argument he presents is based on two assumptions we have already discussed. The first is his generally pessimistic view of human nature, his view that it is wisest to regard our tendency to act corruptly as ineliminable. The second concerns the nature of the problem this generates: that, since corruption is the antithesis of *virtù*, while *virtù* is indispensable for the maintenance of personal as well as public *libertà*, it follows that our corrupt behaviour must somehow be neutralised if a *vivere libero* (and hence our own *libertà*) are both to be preserved. What the law can hope to achieve in the face of these difficulties, Machiavelli suggests, is to coerce and direct us in just such a way that, even if we continue to act solely out of a corrupt desire to further our own individual or factional advantage, our motivations may nonetheless be capable of being harnessed to serve the public interest, although the outcome of precisely the same motivations, in the absence of any such coercion, would have been destructive not merely of the public interest, but also — and in consequence — of our own individual liberty at the same time.

This process is not envisaged as one in which the agent is made to

---

[42]For a representative example of this argument, see J. Gribble *Introduction to the Philosophy of Education* (Boston: 1969) pp. 158–60. Gribble's claims are discussed and endorsed in L. Allison 'Liberty: A Correct and Authoritarian Account', *Political Studies*, 1981, 29: 390–1. For a similar commitment, see W. Parent 'Some Recent Work on the Concept of Liberty', *American Philosophical Quarterly*, 1974, 11: 149–67. But for a classic corrective see G. MacCallum 'Negative and Positive Freedom', in P. Laslett *et al.* (ed.) *Philosophy, Politics and Society* Fourth Series (Oxford: Oxford University Press, 1972) and cf. C. Taylor 'What's Wrong with Negative Liberty?', in A. Ryan (ed.) *The Idea of Freedom* (Oxford: Oxford University Press, 1979).

[43]Berlin 154. Cf. also 155, 171 for the contention that it is 'illiberal' to argue otherwise.

bring his desires in line with those of a 'higher self'. On the contrary, he retains his selfish patterns of motivation and in consequence his self-destructive proclivities. All that happens is that the law operates to channel his behaviour in such a way that, although his reasons for action remain self-interested, his actions have consequences which, although not intended, are such as to promote the public interest, and hence his own individual liberty. The agent is thus enabled, by means of the coercive powers of the law, to attain the freedom he actually desires, and to avoid the servitude his unconstrained behaviour would otherwise have produced.

There are two important passages in Book I where Machiavelli relies on this exact structure of argument. The first occurs in the course of the elaborate discussion of constitutional law in the opening chapters, an account which contrasts very instructively with the handling of the same theme by current gothic theorists of liberty. It seems obvious to Machiavelli, no less than to contemporary theorists that there must be one distinctive set of constitutional arrangements which offers those living under it the best prospects of maintaining their liberty. It is true that Machiavelli differs sharply from current theorists in his views about how to uncover the nature of these arrangements. He assumes that the surest method must be to investigate the common elements of the most successful constitutional codes of antiquity, hoping that, if the causes of their durability can be uncovered, it may be possible to repeat their political success.[44] For a contemporary gothic theorist like John Rawls, by contrast, the aim is to stand at an Archimedean point outside history, with the results that Rawls prefers to reflect on his intuitions about justice at an imagined 'constitutional convention' in order to elucidate the legal foundations of a free society (Rawls 196–9). Despite these divergent approaches, however, the fruits of Rawls's hypothetical convention and of Machiavelli's historical reflections prove to be exactly the same — a fact so extraordinary as to cast some doubt, perhaps, on whether Rawls has really succeeded in freeing himself from the imaginative constraints imposed by history in the way his thought-experiment claims. The conclusion at which both theorists arrive is that the optimum legal basis for a free polity consists of a republican constitution founded on a bicameral legislature,[45] a system to which Machiavelli adds the need for a strong consular or presidential element, while Rawls stresses in addition the need for an independent judiciary.[46]

[44]For this assumption see especially the Preface to *Discourses* Bk. I in Machiavelli 190–2, and for the assumption deployed cf. 195–200.

[45]For Machiavelli's preference for such a republican constitution, see Machiavelli, 199–200 and 202–4. For Rawls's preference, see Rawls 222–4.

[46]Machiavelli, 200; Rawls 224. Machiavelli, 202 and 211–14 also has remarks germane to the question of independent judicial processes.

When we turn, however, to their reasons for supposing that this particular structure best serves to maximise our freedom, we encounter a deep disparity between the individualistic premises governing Rawls's theory and the more classical understanding of the relationship between law and liberty embodied in Machiavelli's account. For Rawls, the special value of the constitution he outlines is that it provides everyone, at least potentially, with equal access to power, equal means to prevent any encroachments upon their personal rights and an equal capacity in consequence to defend their liberties.[47] For Machiavelli, by contrast, the reason for preferring the same type of constitution lies in its unique potentiality for converting private vices into public benefits, thereby coercing us into respecting our own as well as other people's liberties.

This is achieved, according to Machiavelli, essentially by exploiting the fact — which he again repeats — that 'in every republic there are two opposed factions, that of the people and that of the nobility' (203 – 4). By instituting a bicameral system, he suggests, this rivalry can be exploited to the public advantage, as happened in republican Rome. The nobles held control of the Senate,[48] the people 'enjoyed a measure of popular control' through various magistracies,[49] and each group 'kept guard over the other' to prevent its rival from acting purely in its own interests.[50] The effect was that 'all the laws made in favour of liberty' resulted 'from this discord between the populace and the ruling group' (203). Even when both sides were motivated solely by the desire to advance their own ends, the constitution served to coerce them into acting in such a way that all purely sectarian proposals were blocked, and the interests of the whole community were in consequence upheld. By the force of law, the people were thereby liberated from the natural consequences of their own *corruzione* and transformed in effect into *virtuosi* citizens; and by these means they were in turn channelled into acting in such a way that their individual as well as their civic liberties were preserved.

The other point at which Machiavelli considers how to force people to respect their own freedom is in his sequence of chapters on Roman religion, a sequence that occurs immediately after his analysis of the Roman republican constitution. The issue of religion arises in this context because of Machiavelli's belief — one that he again shares with

[47]This is the argument of section 36 of Rawls.

[48]Machiavelli, 200; cf. also 202 – 4.

[49]This was originally achieved by the establishment of the Tribunate, which was not only designed 'for the protection of Roman liberty' (Machiavelli, 204) but also to provide 'a measure of popular control' over the government (202). For the resulting system in outline see 200 and 298. This element of balance was later strengthened by further magistracies, notably the Censorship. For this point see 295 – 6.

[50]Machiavelli, 204. There are several later references to the same idea of a tensely-balanced equilibrium. See for example the discussions at 270 and 282 – 4.

most contemporary theorists of liberty — that religious susceptibilities are capable of posing a threat to well-ordered societies, so that a series of 'laws and ordinances' will be needed to prevent this danger from materialising. Again, however, there is an instructive contrast to be drawn between Machiavelli's discussion of this issue and that of modern gothic theorists of liberty such as Rawls. Rawls assumes (212) that the only way in which the adherents of a particular sect can jeopardise our freedom is by undermining what he calls 'the common interest in public order and security'. He starts out (208) from the observation that deeply religious people are prone to insist that 'others ought to recognise the same beliefs and first principles' as they themselves do, and 'are grievously in error' if they fail to do so. This tends to breed intolerance, which in turn carries with it a danger of 'interference with the essentials of public order' and a consequential threat to the liberties of anyone who fails to endorse the outlook of the intolerant group (Rawls 213, 215, 218). Machiavelli, by contrast, has a broader sense of the power of religion — and especially of Christianity — to threaten our liberty. To be deeply religious, he assumes, is to be motivated in all one's actions by the hope of going to heaven and the corresponding fear of incurring God's wrath and failing to be saved (224, 231–3, 331). But this means that the most fervent Christians care nothing for 'worldly glory' or the welfare of their community in this present life; they care only for heavenly glory and their own welfare in the life to come. They despise the pagan ideals of 'greatness of spirit and bodily strength'; instead 'they glorify humble and contemplative men' and 'set up as the greatest good humility, abjectness and contempt for worldly affairs' (331). Machiavelli's daring suggestion is thus that Christianity, as habitually practised, has served to encourage *ozio*, and has thereby acted as a corrupting influence on civic life. 'It has made the world weak and turned it over as prey to wicked men, who can easily control it, since the generality of men, in the hope of going to heaven, think more about enduring their injuries than avenging them' (331).

The threat to liberty posed by any religion which, like Christianity, is based on our hopes and fears about the world to come is thus the threat of corruption, not intolerance. To preserve our liberty, we need above all to possess *virtù*; but to possess *virtù* is to be willing to place our city's salvation above all personal considerations, whereas Christianity instructs us to treat our personal salvation as more important than anything else. 'Pondering, then, why it can be that in ancient times people were greater lovers of freedom than in these', Machiavelli arrives at the conclusion that Christianity must carry a considerable burden of the blame, having taught us 'not to esteem worldly honour', whereas the pagans always held the quintessentially *virtuoso* belief 'that such honour constitutes the greatest good' (330–1).

As a result of these divergent views about the relationship between religion and civic freedom, Machiavelli presents an analysis completely at variance with that of most contemporary theorists of liberty when he goes on to consider what 'laws and ordinances' will be needed to prevent our religious susceptibilities from undermining our freedom. To a modern gothic theorist such as Rawls, the problem is simply that of adjudicating between the values of liberty of conscience and public tranquillity. Liberty of conscience must never be limited unless 'there is reasonable expectation that not doing so will damage the public order which the government should maintain' (Rawls 1971:213). But as soon as it becomes clear that a given religion poses 'considerable risks to our own legitimate interests', the law can and ought to intervene in such a way as to 'force the intolerant to respect the liberty of others' (Rawls 1971:219, cf. 212). For Machiavelli, by contrast, the laws required to regulate religion in the name of liberty will be such as are capable of harnessing the self-interested motivations of the religious in such a way as to enable the fear of God to be turned to public account and used 'to bring about the greatness of States' (224–5). The question, in short, is how to interpret religion 'according to *virtù*' instead of (as at present) 'according to *ozio*': how to prevent it from corrupting us and thereby threatening our liberty, how to enable it instead to contribute 'to our country's exaltation and defence' (331).

The most basic requirement, according to Machiavelli, is to enact a series of *ordini* designed, if possible, to encourage religious belief, or at least to compel the observance of religious practices (231,234). Unless the people are genuinely religious in their outlook, there will obviously be no hope of manipulating their beliefs in such a way as to serve the common good. It follows that, just as 'the right use' of religion 'is capable of bringing about the greatness of states', so 'contempt for it brings about their ruin' (225, 234). The moral is thus that 'those princes or republics that wish to keep themselves uncorrupted must above all else keep the ceremonies of their religion uncorrupted and hold them always in respect, because one can have no better indication of the ruin of a country than to see divine worship little valued' (226,419).

Even if the people are deeply pious, however, there remains the question of how to channel their fears of God and hopes of salvation in such a way as to promote instead of undermining the public interest. Machiavelli presents his fundamental suggestion at the start of his first chapter on Roman religion: it is essential, he claims, that the *ordini* concerning religion should insist with deep seriousness on the absolute sanctity of oaths. It was due above all to the fact that the Romans 'feared much more to break an oath than to break the laws' that their leaders were able to make use of religion 'to facilitate whatever undertaking the Senate or the great men of the city planned to carry out' (224).

An oath is a promise in which the name of God is invoked as a guarantee that the promise will be kept. We can readily see the political significance of such oaths if we consider the case, as Machiavelli does, of a body of citizens acting, or planning to act, in a corrupt and self-interested fashion in relation to some important public enterprise. It will be essential for their leaders to find some means of coercing them into upholding the public interest and hence their own liberty. Machiavelli's suggestion is that, as long as the prevailing religion emphasises the sanctity of oaths, it will always be open to the leaders of such a people to force them to overcome their natural selfishness by imposing an oath binding them to behave in the manner of genuinely *virtuosi* citizens. This will not of course have the effect of changing the people's disposition; but it will certainly have the effect of making them more frightened of evading their public duties than of performing them, since their greatest desire, if they are truly religious, will now be to keep their promise and avoid the wrath of God. By means of the *ordini* governing their religion, they will thus be coerced into acting, against their natural disposition, in such a way as to promote the freedom of their community and in consequence their own freedom at the same time. By means of coercion, in short, they will be assured of their liberty.

Machiavelli offers numerous instances of political leaders playing upon the religious susceptibilities of their followers in such a way as to force them to be free.[51] Of all his examples, perhaps the most striking is that of Scipio Africanus and his conduct at the time of the second Punic war. 'After Hannibal defeated the Romans at Cannae', Machiavelli relates, 'many citizens met together who, despairing of their native land, agreed to abandon Italy and go to live in Sicily. Hearing of this, Scipio went to them with a naked sword in his hand and forced them to swear an oath not to abandon their native land'. The result was that 'although the love of their country and its laws had not been enough to keep them in Italy, they were kept there by the oath they were forced to take'. Being forced, in short, to become *virtuosi*, they stood their ground, eventually defeated Hannibal and thereby secured, by means of their enforced *virtù*, the liberty they had been ready to give up (224).

Machiavelli's account of how to maintain public (and hence personal) liberty may thus be said to reverse the usual relationship between liberty and the law, the relationship expressed in most contemporary theories of liberty. Among contemporary theorists, the coercive apparatus of the law is generally pictured as an obvious affront to individual freedom. The power of the law to constrain us is only held to be

---

[51]See for example the discussion of Lucius Manlius in Machiavelli, 224; of Titus Quintus, 231, and of the Samnite leaders, 233–4.

justified if, in diminishing the extent of our natural liberty, it serves at the same time to assure more effectively our capacity to exercise the freedom that remains to us.[52] The proper relationship between the law and liberty is thus held to be expressed by saying that — as Isaiah Berlin puts it — the law should create a framework within which as many individuals as possible can realise as many of their ends as possible, without assessment of the value of those ends, save in so far as they may frustrate the purposes of others'.[53]

For a classical theorist like Machiavelli, by contrast, the law is in part justified because it ensures a degree of personal freedom which, in its absence, would altogether collapse. If the coercive apparatus of the law were withdrawn, there would not be a greater degree of personal liberty with a diminished capacity to enjoy it without risk. Due to our self-destructive natures, there would rather be a diminution of personal liberty, a rapid slide towards a condition of complete servitude. The proper relationship between liberty and the law is not to be expressed, therefore, by treating the law as a neutral framework within which we then pursue our own purposes. The law is rather to be seen as a liberating agency, one that serves to constrain us — if our legislators have been wise — in just such a way that we are released from the bondage which our natural selfishness would otherwise impose on us, and are granted our freedom by means of being coerced.

---

[52]As J. Gray 'On Negative and Positive Liberty', *Political Studies* 1980, 28: 523, emphasises, this account of how coercion is to be justified constitutes a central feature of classical liberalism. Rawls 302 expresses it in the form of the axiom — which he calls the 'First Priority Rule' — that 'liberty can be restricted only for the sake of liberty'. For a valuable account of the inconsistencies to which this commitment gives rise, see H. Hart 'Rawls on Liberty and its Priority', in N. Daniels (ed.) *Reading Rawls* (New York: Basic Books, n.d.).

[53]Berlin 153, note. Cf. also Berlin 161 for Mill's and Constant's formulations of the point. The same commitment underlies Rawls. See especially 236 and, more generally, section 38 on 'The rule of law', 235–43.

3

RICHARD WOLLHEIM

A Paradox in the Theory of Democracy

THE INVENTION OF Democracy is traditionally attributed to Cleisthenes. Many will object to this attribution, not so much on factual grounds, as because it savours too much of a heroic or Promethean view of history. But in this case at least such a view might seem justified. We know little enough of the motives or sentiments of the great reformer, but of the enduring significance of what he achieved there can be no reasonable doubt. The institutions that he devised survived with only minor modifications as the political structure of Athens: around them there developed a creed or theory of popular government, of which only fragments have come down to us: and, finally, it was to those institutions that the word Δημοκρατια was initially applied. By the middle of the fifth century B.C. Democracy existed as a set of institutions, as a theory of government, and as a word. Since the institutions came first and prompted the rest, he who devised them may with good reason be celebrated as the inventor of Democracy.

From the days of Cleisthenes onwards Democracy has enjoyed a continuous, if often exiguous, history in Western culture. The political experience of Athens has never been forgotten and never totally dismissed, if only because it is recorded in texts that for quite extraneous reasons have made a sustained claim upon the attention or reverence of the educated.

However, although there has been continuity, there has also been change. In several important respects the Democracy of Antiquity differs, and should be distinguished, from the Democracy of the modern world: and this not just in practice, but also in theory. To take an obvious case: to the classical mind Democracy was linked *in an essential way* with certain specific political institutions. These links no longer exist. For the institutions with which the Ancients so intimately connected Democracy either are no longer held to be connected, or even consistent, with Democracy, as in the case of public scrutiny or the lot, or else *are* still held to be connected with Democracy but not in a way which can be directly derived from the nature of Democracy, as, for instance, with the Rule of Law.

But the most important respect in which modern Democracy differs from classical Democracy is that whereas classical Democracy was a form of sectional government, to the modern mind Democracy is opposed to all forms of sectional government. The etymology of the word Democracy gives a clue to what the Ancients meant by it. For Democracy was regarded as a form of government parallel to, though different from, other forms of government designated by names having a parallel structure: Aristocracy, Oligarchy, Plutocracy, Ochlocracy. In each case power lay with a certain section of the population: the forms differed from one another according to the section with which power lay: and in each case the section was indicated by the prefix. In Aristocracy, it was the *aristoi* or the best: in Oligarchy, it was the *oligoi* or the few: in Plutocracy it was the *plutoi* or the rich: in Ochlocracy it was the *ochlos* or mob: in Democracy it was the *demos*. And the *demos* in the Greek city-state was a specific or determinate section of the population: the populace or the poor.

By contrast the modern conception of Democracy is of a form of government in which no restriction is placed upon the governing body: the governing body is identical with the citizen body. We might put the difference between the ancient and modern conceptions of Democracy like this: in both cases Democracy is the rule of the people; but in the classical theory the people is identified with a section or part of the population, whereas in modern theory the people is identified with the population as a whole.

Immediately a problem arises: if Democracy means the rule of the people *as a whole*, how can it be realized? For in any modern state the people is bound to be both *numerous* and *diverse*, and either of these characteristics by itself—let alone the conjunction of the two—surely must make a group of individuals incapable of effective rule. In antiquity, or at any rate in the political theory of antiquity, the problem does not arise. For the *demos* of the Greek city-state was, in the first place, relatively small: and, secondly, it was, or was supposed to be, united in interest, and therefore uniform in desire or want.

One solution to this problem is to suggest a return to the Greek conditions: or the suggestion is, rather, that the conditions which hold for the Greek *demos* should be made to hold for the population of a modern democracy. This population should, in the first place, be considerably reduced in size. And when it is no longer numerous, it will automatically cease to be diverse. Or if any diversity remains, this diversity will be purely phenomenal or apparent. This solution — which can roughly be equated with Rousseau's ideal of 'legitimate rule' — is obviously unacceptable. The restriction upon population is Utopian: and the 'true' or 'real' uniformity that it advocates, which is consistent with any degree of conscious diversity, is worthless.

Another solution consists in weakening the criteria attached to the notion of effective rule. For if we mean by 'ruling' 'devising and composing laws' — as the Greeks did — then it is clearly impossible for a numerous and diverse population to exercise collective rule. One answer, as we have seen, is that we should bring it about that the population in a Democracy is neither numerous nor diverse. Another answer is that we should mean something different by 'ruling': or that in elucidating Democracy we should employ a different concept of 'rule'. And it is this second answer that is, explicitly or implicitly, incorporated in most modern democratic theories. If modern theory insists that in a democracy the people in the sense of the whole population, not just a section of the population, should rule, it also insists that the people should rule in the sense not of devising or initiating legislation but of choosing or controlling it. And the significance of this is that it permits a people to rule despite its size and its diversity.

That size is no obstacle to the people ruling in what might be called this weakened sense should be evident. Since the control or choice of legislation does not require that the people should meet in general assembly, numbers do not impair its effectiveness. That diversity is equally no obstacle may be less apparent. That it is not derived directly from the fact that whereas to say that the people rule in the strong sense entails that everyone assents to the legislation enacted, to say that the people rule in the weak sense has no such entailment: popular rule, where rule means control, can be said to hold, even if a sizeable proportion of the population dissents from what is enacted.

However, even if popular rule is consistent with some degree of dissent, there must also be a degree of dissent with which it is inconsistent. Or to put it another way: for legislation to be said to be by the people, it must stand in some positive relation to what the individual citizens would like legislation to be like. How is this relation to be characterized?

In practice, of course, we say that legislation is democratic if (1) it concurs with what the majority of the population would like and (2) it is enacted because of this concurrence. It has however been argued that though the majority principle may be all right in practice, it certainly is inadequate to any ideal construction of Democracy: and since any justification of Democracy is most likely to relate to an ideal construction, this is important.

Before the inadequacies of the majority-principle can be brought out, an ambiguity in its formulation needs to be resolved. For the principle may be insisting on a concurrence of the legislation with an absolute majority, or merely with a plurality, of citizens' choices. If an absolute majority is intended, then the majority principle is acceptable in that it never selects legislation that is intuitively unacceptable, given the choices of the individual citizens: the trouble is, however, that over too large a range not just of possible but of likely cases the majority principle selects no absolute majority legislation at all. Accordingly if government is to be continuous, the absolute-majority principle needs to be supplemented by another principle, and for this role the obvious candidate is the plurality principle. This principle in all likely cases at any rate *does* select specific legislation, but the trouble is that the legislation it selects is in some cases counter intuitive — given, that is, the choice of the citizens.[1] An example will illustrate this.

Let us suppose that there are three policies from which the population must choose: A, B, C. Forty per cent choose A, 35 per cent choose B, and 25 per cent choose C. On the simple majority principle A is selected. However, those who choose B prefer C to A, and those who choose C prefer B to A. In the light of this information, it is far from clear that A is the right selection if democratic rule is to be observed. For 60 per cent prefer both B and C to A.

What this example brings out is that it is not always clear which policy or legislation should be enacted in a democracy, given the choices of the individual citizens — if all we take into account are the first choices of the citizens. We need to go below this and consider the whole preference-schedule of the individual citizens.

Following up this kind of criticism of the majority-principle, political scientists have envisaged the problem of Democracy as that of devising a function which would allow us to derive what might be called the 'democratic choice' from the ordered choices or preference-schedules of the individual citizens. It is only if we can construct such a function —the argument runs—that we can claim to have explicated the weak sense of 'rule' in which, according to *modern* theory, the people rule in a Democracy.

Recently, however, this approach has met with a reverse. For in his *Social Choice and Individual Values*, Arrow[2] has proved that it is impossible to construct a function that satisfies certain intuitive criteria. Arrow's specific concern was with what he called a 'social welfare function' whose task was to determine a complete 'social' preference schedule given the individual preference-schedules. However, it has more recently been shown[3] that Arrow's Impossibility Theorem also

[1]Duncan Black, *Theory of Committees and Elections* (London, 1958), pp. 67–68.
[2]Kenneth J. Arrow, *Social Choice and Individual Values* (New York, 1951), Ch. V.
[3]R. D. Luce and H. Raiffa, *Games and Decisions* (New York, 1957), Ch. 14.

applies to the less ambitious project, which is more directly relevant to democracy, of constructing a function which would merely give us a 'social' first-choice on the basis of the individual preference-schedules.

I mention this problem, however, solely *en passant*: not because I intend to tackle it, but because I intend to ignore it. For the purpose of this paper, I intend to assume that the so-called problem of aggregation has been solved: that there exists a method or rule[4] for going from individual choices to some specific legislation such that we can justifiably call the enactment of that legislation an instance of democratic rule.

Having made this assumption, I now want to go on and envisage Democracy in terms of a certain machine which operates according to this method or rule. The machine — which we may for convenience call the democratic machine — operates in a discontinuous fashion. Into it are fed at fixed intervals the choices of the individual citizens. The machine then aggregates them according to the pre-established rule or method, and so comes up with what may be called a 'choice' of its own. Democratic rule is said to be achieved if throughout the period when the machine is not working, the most recent choice of the machine is acted upon. The question now arises: What is the authority of the choice expressed by the machine? More specifically, why should someone who has fed his choice into the machine and then is confronted by the machine with a choice non-identical with his own, feel any obligation to accept it?

In order however to advance the inquiry we must now note a distinction. For the choices that the individual citizen feeds into the democratic machine and on the basis of which the democratic 'choice' is made, are susceptible of two very different interpretations.

On the one hand, we may regard the choices as expressions of *want*. To say that a certain citizen chooses policy A or that he prefers policy A to policy B, is to say that he wants policy A more than any other policy or that he wants it more than policy B. The wants which the citizens' choices express need not, of course, be selfish or egotistical wants. When a man decides that he wants policy A more than policy B, he may well be moved not just by his own narrow interests but by a concern for the welfare of others. But all the same, in choosing A he is not asserting that the others want A, nor that A ought to be realized; he would be asserting *tout court* that he wants A.

If we conceive the democratic machine as operating on choices in the sense of expressed wants, then our questions resolves into something approximating to the old Utilitarian problem: Why should a man who

[4]'Rule' or 'method' here is to be understood in some very general sense that will satisfy even those who hold that 'the essence of democracy is something which must escape definition in terms of any functional relation between decisions and individual preferences'. I. M. D. Little, 'Social Choice and Individual Values', *Journal of Political Economy*, Vol. LX, no. 5, October 1952, p. 432.

wants A think that B ought to be the case, when B is not consistent with A but is arrived at by considering the wants of all the other citizens of the society? And I think that in this connexion it is only necessary to make two quite brief observations.

In the first place, there is no inconsistency whatsoever in wanting A and thinking that B ought to be the case, even when A and B are themselves inconsistent. We may well have a desire and a moral belief that runs counter to that desire. Indeed there are moral philosophers who have held that morality would be inconceivable unless *some* of our moral beliefs ran counter to our desires.

However, though there is no inconsistency between wanting A and thinking that B ought to be the case, it should be equally obvious that the former could not serve as a reason for the latter nor the latter be derived from the former. Yet there seems a presumption in the question that just this is what is to be shown. Paradoxically though, Utilitarians (and I use the expression in a rather general way) seem to have held both that there was a *prima facie* inconsistency between wanting A and thinking that B ought to be the case, and also that this inconsistency was to be removed by showing that the belief that B ought to be the case was grounded in the want for A. But of course this last demand is an absurdity. It springs either from an absurdly exaggerated conception of what it is to prove consistency, i.e. that to prove two propositions are consistent one must show that one can be derived from the other, or else from a fundamentally egotistic conception of the basis of morality, i.e. that all one's moral beliefs are grounded in wants.

In fact the citizen who expresses a want for A and then, in deference to the operation of the democratic machine, thinks that B ought to be the case, thinks that B ought to be the case as the result of applying some higher-order principle to the effect that what the democratic machine chooses ought to be the case. He consults, in other words, his principles, he does not go back and consult again his wants. All he needs to be certain of is that his principles and his wants, though they may lead in different directions, are not actually inconsistent: and it seems very difficult to attach any sense even to the *possibility* that they could be.

However, it is now time to turn to another interpretation that can be put on the material which is characteristically fed into the democratic machine. On this view when the citizen chooses a certain policy or prefers one policy to another, he is expressing not a want but an *evaluation*. He chooses A or prefers A to B, because he thinks that A is the best policy, is the policy that ought to be enacted, or, alternatively, that A is a better policy than B or ought to be enacted in preference to B—not because he wants A more or needs it more than B. If it is objected at this stage that evaluations are based upon wants and therefore not to be contrasted with them, I can only reply that this may well be true if what is meant is that a man will often enough take his wants into account in arriving at his evaluations. But it does not follow from this that his evaluations are not different from his wants, nor that they cannot be placed in contrast to them. Indeed, the fact that evaluations may be based on wants is no more germane to our present discussion than it was to our earlier discussion that wants can be affected by evaluations.

Let us then regard the democratic machine as being fed with choices in the sense of evaluations. The evaluations are then aggregated by the machine in accordance with its established rule, and the machine comes up with a choice of its own. Anyone who accepts democracy is then obliged to think that the policy that the machine selects is the policy that ought to be enacted.

But immediately a difficulty arises. Let us imagine a citizen who feeds his choice for, say, A, or for A over B into the democratic machine. On the present interpretation, he is to be regarded as thereby expressing his opinion that A ought to be enacted. And now let us further suppose that the machine into which this and other choices have been fed comes up with its own choice, and its choice is for B. How can the citizen accept the machine's choice, which involves his thinking that B ought to be enacted when, as we already know, he is of the opinion, of the declared opinion, that A ought to be enacted?

Observe that we are confronted with a far more serious problem now when we interpret choices as evaluations than we were when we interpreted them as expressions of wants. For on the original interpretation the problem was (it will be remembered) that the acceptance of the machine's choice did not follow from one's own choice, which one had fed into the machine: the problem on this new interpretation is that the acceptance of the machine's choice seems to be incompatible with — not just not to follow from, but to be incompatible with — one's own original choice. For if a man expresses a choice for A and the machine expresses a choice for B, then the man, if he is to be a sound democratic, seems to be committed to the belief that A ought to be the case *and* to the belief that B ought to be the case.

Now, this is a serious matter. For I think it is fairly self-evident that, even if the dichotomy of 'expressed want' 'evaluation' is somewhat harsh, the choices that the citizens of a democracy make when they are called upon to make a choice are far closer to evaluations than to expressions of want. And I hold this not because of any particularly elevated view I have of political behaviour but because I think that the ordinary citizen, confronted by a political choice, is far more likely to know which of the two policies he thinks *ought to be* enacted than which of them he *wants* enacted. Accordingly he is more likely to vote in a way that reflects his evaluations than in a way that reflects his wants. If this is so, then the difficulty that I have described would seem to constitute a paradox in the very heart of democratic theory.

There are two obvious ways in which the paradox might be broken. One is by denying that in the circumstances the man is committed to the belief that A (i.e. the policy of his choice) ought to be enacted: the other is by denying that the man is committed to the belief that B (i.e. the policy of the machine's choice) ought to be enacted. Either of these two ways would be effective in resolving the paradox: both have considerable plausibility: but neither, I submit, is ultimately acceptable. Let me review the arguments:

1. It might be claimed that the man who feeds his choice for A into the democratic machine is not in fact committed to believing that A ought to be the case in the face of the machine's verdict, since, though the choice that he feeds into the machine is certainly an evaluation, it is an *interim*, not a final or definitive, evaluation. When he expresses his preference for A or for A over B, his preference (properly understood) is hypothetical. Written out it would be formulated in some such way as 'I think that A ought to be enacted, provided that other people, or enough other people, are of the same opinion'. The preference, the argument runs, is necessarily hypothetical, because when it is expressed, the man cannot know the preferences that will be expressed by his fellow-citizens. It is only when all these preferences have been fed into the machine, and the machine has operated on them and has come up with a preference of its own, that he has the requisite information on which to base a final as opposed to a provisional or interim choice. And then when he is in this position what he does is to reiterate the preference of the machine: he chooses as it has chosen — that is to say, in the present case he chooses B.

Once we understand this — the argument runs — the paradox disappears. No longer is there any temptation to think of the unfortunate citizen as committed both to the belief that A ought to be enacted and to the belief that B ought to be enacted — for it should now be clear that he continues to hold that A ought to be enacted only up to the moment when he has reason to think that B ought to be enacted: as soon as he has reason to commit himself to B, i.e., as soon as the machine has expressed *its* choices on the basis of all the choices in the community, his commitment to A dissolves. The man, in other words, withdraws his support from A and gives it to B.

The argument has some plausibility; but not, I think, enough. For, to begin with, it cannot be correct to interpret the choices fed into the democratic machine as interim or hypothetical, i.e. as of the form 'I think that A ought to be enacted if other people or enough other people are of the same opinion'. And this for two reasons. First, a hypothetical choice, or a choice hypothetically expressed, generally implies some doubt whether the condition upon which the choice is dependent is or is not fulfilled. It would be inappropriate to express a choice hypothetically if one knew that the protasis was fulfilled: and it would be pointless to express it so if one knew that the protasis was unfulfilled. And yet in politics people sometimes vote knowing how the vote as a whole will go: sometimes, indeed, knowing full well that it will go in the opposite direction to that in which they cast their own vote. And we don't think that the behaviour of such people is irrational. Suppose that a man votes Liberal, knowing full well that only a rather small minority of the population is of his opinion. We may disagree with his behaviour, but surely we don't think it irrational. Yet surely we ought to do so, if in casting his vote for the Liberals he was in effect saying 'I want a Liberal policy to be enacted if other people or enough other people are of my opinion', though he was quite certain that there was no chance whatsoever of there being enough people who were of his opinion.

Secondly, to interpret the citizens' choices as hypothetical is to imply that there is a dependence between what policy the citizen prefers and some other condition — in this case, how he thinks that others will vote: so that the citizen allows this consideration effectively to enter into his calculations when he decides which policy he supports. But this implication is surely, in many cases at least, unfounded. The citizen who votes for A cannot, without further qualification, be understood as expressing a view that A ought to be enacted if enough other people think so: because he may well be of the opinion that whether A ought to be enacted or not is *in some sense or other* independent of what other people think. Or even if he thinks that there is some dependence between what ought to be enacted and what others think, he may not think that there is a *total* dependence: so that if a policy is out-voted, then it automatically follows that it ought not to be enacted. Indeed, it would seem that democracy not merely allows but positively demands that our political preferences have a certain constancy to them and that they do not fluctuate with the preferences of others. In other words, when the machine's choice has been declared and we have given our adherence to it, there is a sense in which we still do and should stand by our original choice. What this sense is is still unclear, but that such a sense exists is surely indubitable.

However, suppose we allow that the citizen's choices are really hypothetical. Once we make this admission it is far from clear why a choice which is reached by aggregating them on the assumption that they are categorical or unconditional should have any particular appeal or authority. It is not very difficult to see why a choice which is based upon what are genuinely the unconditional choices of individual citizens should have authority: for such a choice would have been arrived at by considering what the citizens of the society actually think ought to be done. But if the democratic choice is the result of aggregating hypothetical choices, then it is arrived at merely by considering what the citizens of the society think ought to be done *under a certain set of conditions*, i.e. when other people agree with them. But why is this of such paramount significance? For is it not possible — indeed, is it not suggested by the form of words employed — that under a different set of conditions the citizens might well want something different done? Why then should we attach special prestige to what they think ought to be done if other people agree with them? Why is this a privileged condition? And, as far as I can see, the only reason for regarding any condition as privileged — in the sense that we are justified in detaching the remaining part of the preference and aggregating it — is that we are of the opinion that the condition is actually fulfilled. But it is quite clear that not in all cases of hypothetical choices will the condition be fulfilled. In some cases it will be, in others it will not be.

Moreover, if we take this suggestion for resolving the paradox of democracy *as a whole* we shall find a far stronger reason for thinking that a choice reached by aggregating hypothetical choices, where these hypothetical choices are choices conditional upon general agreement with the voter, has no natural authority. For it will be remembered that the voter who votes 'A if enough others agree with this', switches to B when the democratic machine comes up with B. Now if this is so, surely he might equally well have in the first place have voted B — for in voting B he would on this view merely have been expressing the view (which *is* surely his) that B ought to be enacted if enough people are of that opinion. Indeed it now seems as if the voter could quite legitimately have voted for *any* of the policies placed before him — provided only, of course, that he neither knows that enough other people would prefer that policy nor knows that not enough other people will prefer that policy, i.e. if the uncertainty proviso, which, as we have seen, is necessary for the making of a hypothetical choice, is fulfilled. In other words, if the vote for A is interpreted as 'A ought to be enacted if enough people are of the same opinion', and the voter is prepared to switch to support B if enough people are of that opinion, it is obvious that 'A' as it appeared in his original vote was a variable, not a constant: a variable ranging over all the policies that are not obviously either winners or losers, not a constant designating one particular policy. If this is so, then it would be quite improper to take his vote literally, as meaning what it says — as one surely would do if one accepted a choice arrived at by aggregating it and similar votes. Accordingly the first attempt to solve our paradox must be rejected.

2. The other obvious way of breaking the paradox of Democracy would be by denying the other limb of the offending conjunction. Democracy — the argument would run — is government by compromise, and the role of the democratic machine is to function as a kind of impersonal arbitrator. In so far as the machine chooses a policy, it

chooses a policy that it would be wise or prudent to follow, not a policy that the citizen ought to follow. And in so far as to believe in Democracy is to be prepared or disposed to accept the machine's choice, it is to accept it as the most sensible thing to do. The functioning of the democratic machine influences one's behaviour, actual and potential: what it does not do is increase one's obligations. On this view what one feeds into the machine are one's evaluations to the effect that this or that policy ought to be enacted: and these evaluations one continues to adhere to even after the machine has operated upon them. What the machine comes up with is the choice of a policy that it would be prudential for all to support, and there is no reason to postulate any incompatibility between the acceptance of such a policy, on the one hand, and, on the other, the continued adherence to one's own political beliefs. So once again the paradox disappears.

Once again the argument is plausible, but I do not think that ultimately it carries conviction. For, in the first place, it seems to me unrealistic to say that our commitment to the machine's choice, when the machine's choice does not concur with ours, is purely tactical or prudential. For if it were, then some argument analogous to that of Gyges's ring would apply. Suppose, once again, that our choice is for A and that of the machine is for B. Then if our support for B were purely tactical or prudential, we should surely be content if the B government were somehow outwitted and they found themselves, contrary to their own inclinations but with the continued support of their electors, putting through policy A. Yet I think it is fairly clear that if this happened in reality, we should be displeased and would think that something undesirable had occurred. If the machine chooses B, there is a sense in which we think that B ought to be enacted whether or not A could be. And this is more than tactical or prudential support.

Secondly it does not seem correct to equate — as the present argument does — belief in Democracy with a disposition to accept the successive choices of the democratic machine. For surely a man could be so disposed without believing in Democracy. He might, for instance, be prepared to go along with Democracy, because he thought that he could achieve power by no other means: although once he had achieved power he would probably try to end the democratic process. The problem, then, arises how we are to distinguish such a man from the genuine believer in Democracy. Surely the disposition to accept democratic results is common, and what must distinguish one from the other is the reason that each has for his acceptance. The genuine believer in Democracy is disposed to accept the successive choices of the democratic machine *because he believes that what the democratic machine chooses ought to be enacted.*

But once we make this concession the present solution to the paradox stands condemned. For if the believer in Democracy believes that what the democratic machine chooses ought to be enacted, then, whenever the machine actually chooses a policy, he must believe that that policy ought to be enacted: not just that it would be wise or tactical to support its enactment, but that it ought to be enacted. In other words, the believer in Democracy is in our example committed to the belief that B ought to be enacted.

So we must abandon this solution to the paradox: which, it might be said, requires the same sort of systematic reinterpretation of our ordinary behaviour that Hobbes (on the traditional interpretation, at any rate) found himself committed to when he asserted an analogous theory about the obligation or commitment we have not just simply to Democracy but to government as such.

The paradox of Democracy cannot, it seems, be resolved by denying either of the limbs of the offending conjunction that gives rise to it. The only remaining way of resolving it is to show that the two limbs are, contrary to appearances, not inconsistent, and therefore their conjunction is not offensive. In other words, what is now required is to show that in our example it is perfectly in order for one and the same citizen to assert that A ought to be enacted, where A is the policy of his choice, and B ought to be enacted, where B is the policy chosen by the democratic machine, even when A and B are not identical.

Now, if my arguments have been sound so far, it is evident that either the two assertions *are* compatible, or else Democracy is inconsistent. I doubt that any of us are prepared to regard Democracy as inconsistent: in consequence we are committed to the view that, in the circumstances of my example, A ought to be enacted and B ought to be enacted are compatible. What we need to see, though, is *how* they are compatible, and the rest of this paper I shall devote to expounding, I fear rather sketchily, one explanation.

The explanation I proffer presupposes a distinction between direct and oblique moral principles. Direct principles refer to the morality of actions, policies, motives, etc., where these are picked out or designated by means of some general descriptive expressions, e.g. *murder, envy, benevolence, birth-control, telling lies,* etc. Oblique principles, by contrast, refer to the morality of actions, policies, motives, etc., where these actions, policies, motives, etc., are not picked out by reference to some common quality or characteristic that they possess, but are identified by means of an artificial property bestowed upon them either as the result of an act of will of some individual or in consequence of the corporate action of some institution. This is a far from satisfactory formulation of the distinction, neither very clear nor very precise, but I think that it will do for my present purposes. Examples of direct principles would be *Murder is wrong, Birth-control is permissible.* Examples of oblique principles would be *What is commanded by the sovereign ought to be done,* or *What is willed by the people is right.*

Now, my suggestion is that two judgements of the form 'A ought to be the case' and 'B ought to be the case' are not incompatible even though A and B cannot be simultaneously realized *if* one of these judgements is asserted as a direct principle whereas the other is asserted as a derivation from an oblique principle — provided that the direct and the oblique principle are not themselves incompatible. Now, I am aware that the proviso might give rise to some difficulty, for it might be natural to think that A ought to be enacted was incompatible with any oblique principle from which B ought to be enacted could be derived, *ipso facto*. For my principle to have any area of operation, it is of course important to exclude incompatibility of a more immediate kind. And I hope that this restriction will be seen to be less artificial when it is realized that a judgement of the kind B ought to be enacted is derived from an oblique principle only by the introduction of certain further factual premises, e.g. B has been commanded by the Sovereign, B is the will of the people, etc.

Now I think it should be clear that my suggestion, if accepted, would resolve our paradox by the only means still available to us, i.e. by showing that the two limbs of the conjunction are not inconsistent. For — to return to the example — 'A ought to be enacted' is asserted by the citizen who has been outvoted as a direct principle, whereas 'B ought to be enacted' is asserted by him as a derivation from an oblique principle, i.e. the principle of Democracy.

But the question now arises, What reason have I for putting forward my suggestion? How is its truth to be established? And the only answer I can give is, I am afraid, disappointing. The most I can do is to try to dispose of two reasons, two reasons which I am sure are misguided, for rejecting it.

1. Someone might maintain that 'A ought to be the case' and 'B ought to be the case' are clearly incompatible, and being incompatible they are incompatible in all circumstances: *a fortiori*, they are incompatible no matter what reasons may be adduced in favour of either of them. Against this forthright position I would like to urge a more sceptical attitude. It seems to me fairly evident that any judgement of the form 'X ought to be the case' acquires a different meaning when it is asserted as a derivation from an oblique principle from that which it has when it is asserted directly, cf., e.g. Jews ought to be given privileged treatment asserted in the 1930s as a derivation from some principle to the effect that victims of persecution should be given exceptional treatment, and the same proposition asserted simply as an expression of Jewish chauvinism. Now if this is so, if the meaning of a principle can vary with the reasons for which it is asserted, and if — as is usually admitted — incompatibility is intimately associated with meaning, there seems, at the very least, good reason not to be dogmatic that of the two principles it is true that, once incompatible, always incompatible.

2. Again, it might be argued against my suggestion, that 'A ought to

be the case' and 'B ought to be the case' can never be consistently conjoined by anyone because the assertion of the first commits one to the implementation of A and the assertion of the second commits one to the implementation of B, and *ex hypothesi* this is impossible: for one cannot simultaneously commit oneself to the implementation of two policies that cannot be simultaneously realized.

Now this objection rests upon the identification of asserting (honestly asserting) that A ought to be the case with committing oneself to the implementation of A. And the identification is by no means self-evident. *Perhaps* honestly asserting 'I ought to do A' does commit one to the implementation of A—but it is surely megalomania further to identify 'A ought to be the case' with 'I ought to do A' or to think that belief in the one commits one to belief in the other.

However, even if we do allow that there *is* an element of commitment in any evaluation to the effect that, e.g. A ought to be the case, it is by no means clear in the present case that the degree of commitment is such as to preclude any commitment to the other. For it is surely evident that the commitment cannot be total. The democrat who believes in his political heart that A ought to be enacted cannot be totally committed to A. And if the commitment is short of totality, then there is in principle room for some commitment to B, even when B diverges from A. Indeed, when we think of the actual situation, it seems that our degree of commitment to the political policy we directly support never goes beyond arguing on its behalf, persuading others of its truth, etc. —whereas the degree of commitment we can plausibly be said to have to the choice of the democratic machine extends only to not resisting its implementation or perhaps to resisting any attempt to resist its implementation—and it seems perfectly possible to be simultaneously committed in these two different directions. Hence I conclude that the second objection to my suggestion fails.

4

JAMES GRIFFIN

Modern Utilitarianism

I WANT TO discuss how utilitarianism is formulated today, concentrating especially on the issues of the last ten years.[1] I shall have to be extremely selective but shall hope that much of what I miss in the text I register in the references. And I shall not try to be neutral but shall, in compensation, say where and why there is dispute.

1. Definitions of 'Utility'

Utilitarianism, in common with other moral theories, starts with an everyday, vague, and depressingly elusive notion: that of a person's welfare or well-being, of the quality of his life, of his life's being happy or successful in the broadest sense. But all of those terms, because so vague and elusive, need content put into them by intelligent stipulation. That is a need which Bentham and Mill never sufficiently recognized,[2] but which now is more felt. But there is a problem. We want the best explanation of welfare. Yet 'best' cannot mean 'most accurate', as if our job were to describe a concept already existing independent of our search. 'Welfare', in the context of utilitarianism, is a theoretical

---

[1] For a survey of work on utilitarianism from 1961 through 1971, see D. Brock, 'Recent Work in Utilitarianism', *American Philosophical Quarterly*, 1973, 10.

[2] Bentham, for example, thought that 'pleasure' and 'pain' offered some specification but immediately turned around and undid whatever specificity the ordinary uses of those terms lent in adding, 'By utility is meant that property in any object, whereby it tends to produce benefit, advantage, pleasure, good, or happiness", *An Introduction to the Principles of Morals and Legislation*, ch. 1, sect. 3.

term, figuring in value theory (What makes a person's life valuable?)
and in moral theory (What behaviour is morally wrong?). So we cannot
properly define it without knowing its role in, and the special demands
of, the theories. After all, while a parent may be concerned with the
'happiness' of his children and the donor of a gift with the 'pleasure' of
the recipient, and a prudent person with the overall 'quality' of his life,
a moral agent may think relevant only certain limited, especially fundamental 'interests' of people affected by his actions. Why think that one
concept of welfare will do service in all of these very different contexts? On the other hand, we can scarcely develop a theory until we
know what its central notions mean, what contribution they can make
to the theory. And how can we tell how much mileage we can get out of
'welfare' until we have judiciously stipulated a sense for it? This may
look like an impasse: no definition without theory; no theory without
definition. But it means only that we must define and build the theory
together, and that as each job progresses it will alter how we do the
other.

One main choice in defining 'welfare' or 'utility' lies between making
it a state of mind or a state of the world.[3] Does 'utility' have to do with
conscious states (e.g. pleasure, pain) or with the state of the world
which satisfies a desire (e.g. economists' 'preference')? If with conscious states, is there only one sort that counts, or many? If many, what
links them? If with fulfilment of desire, desires as they happen to be, or
in some way improved? If improved, how?

2. Mental State Accounts

Of course, when some utilitarians have spoken of conscious states
such as pleasure and pain, they have meant these terms to be taken so
widely as to approach desire accounts of 'utility'. But the two accounts
do not quite meet. The trouble with thinking of utility as *one* kind of
conscious state is that there is no one discernible mental state common
to all that we regard as having utility — eating, reading, working, creating, helping. What one mental state runs through them all in virtue of
which we rank them as we do? The truth seems, rather, that often we
just rank them, *period*; often they are basic preferences, not resting
upon further judgements about quantities of some homogeneous mental state present in or produced by each.

[3]For an account of contributions from economic theory see A. Sen *Collective Choice
and Social Welfare* (San Francisco: Holden-Day 1970), and for recent philosophical
discussions see R. Brandt *A Theory of the Good and the Right* (Oxford: Clarendon Press,
1979) chap. 7 and 13, R. Hare 'Ethical Theory and Utilitarianism', in H. Lewis (ed.)
Contemporary British Philosophy, Fourth Series (London: Allen & Unwin, 1976), A. Sen
'Plural Utility', *Proceedings of the Aristotelian Society*, 1980–1, 81, R. Dworkin 'What Is
Equality? Part I: Equality of Welfare', *Philosophy and Public Affairs*, 1981, 10, J. Glover
Causing Death and Saving Lives (Harmondsworth: Penguin Books, 1977) Chap 4, sect. 1.

Suppose, then, we said that utility consisted of several different conscious states. But what then makes them into a set? The obvious candidate would be desire; we could say, following Sidgwick in borrowing something from each of the competing accounts, that utility combines a mental element and a preference element. 'Utility', we could say, is 'desirable consciousness'.[4] But the trouble with this eclectic account is that we do seem to desire things other than states of mind, and independently of the states of mind that they produce. This is a point that Robert Nozick has forcefully made with some science fiction.[5] Imagine an experience machine programmed to give you any experience you want; it will stimulate your brain so that you think that you are living the most ideal life, while all the while you float in a tank with electrodes in your brain. Would you plug in? 'What else can matter to us', Nozick asks, 'other than how our lives feel from the inside?' And he replies, surely rightly, that we also want to *do* certain things, to *be* certain things, and to be receptive to what there is in life beyond what humans make. This fact presents a serious challenge to the eclectic account of utility. If not all desirable things are mental states, the eclectic account is fissile. Which part of it will one retain: desire or mental states? Of course, 'mental state' is vague enough to be very stretchable. But it is hard to stretch it enough to fit all objects of desire, so it seems better to abandon it in favour of a more purely desire account.

3. Desire Accounts

'Utility', one could then say, consists in the fulfilment of the desires that people actually have. Economists have been drawn to this account because one's actual desires are often revealed in one's choices, and 'revealed preferences' are observable and hence a respectable subject for empirical science.[6] The trouble here is that, notoriously, people mistake their own interests, and if, as we want, 'utility' is to be close to well-being, then what must matter for 'utility' will be, not people's actual desires, but their desires in some way sanitised. But how sanitised? One way would be to say that desires count towards utility only if 'rational' on some definition—for instance, that they 'survive maximal criticism by facts and logic'. This is an account of 'rational' worked out

[4]H. Sidgwick *The Methods of Ethics* (London: Macmillan, 1970) esp. pp. 111–2, 127, 396–398. For a good discussion of Sidgwick's account see J. Schneewind *Sidgwick's Ethics and Victorian Moral Philosophy* (Oxford: Clarendon Press, 1977) pt. II esp. chap 11–12.
[5]R. Nozick *Anarchy, State, and Utopia* (Oxford: Blackwell, 1974) pp. 42–45.
[6]But for acute criticism from economists, see J. Vickers 'Utility and Its Ambiguities', *Erkenntnis*, 1975, 9, A. Sen 'Plural Utility', sects. 3 and 6, F. Hahn and M. Hollis (eds.) *Philosophy and Economic Theory* (Oxford: Oxford University Press, 1979), intro.

with exemplary rigour by Richard Brandt.[7] But it is hard to get the balance between actual and sanitised desires quite right. Although 'utility' cannot simply be equated with 'actual desires', it cannot simply be equated with 'rational desires' either. It is doubtless true that if I were acquainted with all facts now obtainable, I should change some of my desires. But if that daunting education were not given to me, yet the objects of my potentially thus sanitised desires were, I might well not be glad to have them; the education, after all, may be necessary for my getting anything out of them. If I knew all the discriminations of flavours *premier cru* clarets allow, I might then prefer them to the soda pop I now love. But you do me no favour by giving me grand clarets now, unless it is part of some well conceived education. Utility must, it seems, be tied at least to desires that are actual when satisfied or are part of the education that will change desires. One might say that 'utility' should be explained in terms of 'informed desires', which is meant to cover the sort of complex combination of actual and sanitised desires sketchily indicated here.[8]

This seems to me the best direction for accounts of utility to take. But much remains to be done. Brandt's criteria for a sanitised desire perhaps put too much stress on information, as if all that criticism of desires needs, besides logic, is facts, the more the better. Yet sometimes desires are defective because we have not got enough, or the right, concepts. Theories need developing which will supply new or better concepts, including value concepts. And with information, more is not always better. It might cripple me to know what someone thinks of me, and I might sensibly prefer to remain in ignorance.[9] What seems most important to the desire account is that our desires have a structure; they are not all on one level. We have local desires (say, for a drink) but also higher order desires (say, to distance oneself from consumer's material desires) and global desires (say, to live autonomously). The structure of desires may provide the criterion for 'informed' or 'sanitised' desire: *information* is what advances plans of life; information is *full* when more, even when there is more, will not advance it further. This structure also provides part of the explanation of *strength* of desire. One does not most satisfy someone's desires simply by satisfying as many as possible, or as large a proportion. One must assess their strength, not in the sense of felt intensity (because my most intense

[7]See Brandt *A Theory of the Good and the Right* esp. chs. 2–7; for that definition of 'rational' see p. 10. Brandt, however, does not himself adopt the 'rational desire' account of 'utility', but thinks a happiness (mental state) account superior, as presently we shall see.

[8]For further discussion of 'informed desire', but still too brief, see J. Griffin 'On Life's Being Valuable', *Dialectics and Humanism*, 1981, 8, where topics in the following paragraph are also pursued more fully.

[9]I owe the example to Derek Parfit.

desires, in that sense, could be satisfied by your constantly imperilling my life and saving me only at the last moment, whereas I should clearly prefer peace to peril) but in a sense supplied by the natural structure of desires. That I prefer peace to peril suggests that global desires provide, in large part, the relevant notion of strength of desire: I desire the one form of life more than the other. They do not supply the whole notion of strength, because sometimes we form global desires only on the basis of having summed local desires (for example, a global desire for a way of life based on a belief that day to day pleasures will be maximized that way). Perhaps the situation is this: some global desires (for instance, to live autonomously) are basic, not based on any other judgements about the value of things; and some (say, for a life that will, in total, be more productive of day to day pleasures) are not. This means that the relevant notion of aggregation is not simply that of summing up small utilities from local satisfactions; the structure of desires already incorporates, constitutes, aggregation. It means also that the relevant sense of 'strength' is not simply the desire that wins out in motivation. If my doctor tells me that I shall die if I do not lay off drink, I shall want to lay off. But I may later crack and go on a binge, and at that point my desire to drink will, in a perfectly clear sense, be strongest. If 'strength' were interpreted as motivational force, then 'utility' would lose its links with a person's good; what would be good for him would then be satisfaction not of his 'informed desires' but of what he 'ought to desire' or 'has reason to desire'. But to retain the links with a person's good, the relevant sense of 'strength' should be, not motivational force, but rank in a cool preference ordering, an ordering that reflects some appreciation of the nature of the objects of desire. All of this is too sketchy to be left as it stands and raises problems as well as settles them, but it can serve to make an important point about procedure. Our essentialist tradition in philosophy makes it hard for us to shake the idea that definitions expound the nature of preexistent concepts. Yet our job with concepts like 'utility' is to give them an existence that they have never before had. And this may well require tinkering, patching, and re-working to meet well-founded objections.

4. Problems with Desire Accounts

There are strong objections to all such accounts. Brandt, indeed, finds them unintelligible, for the following reason.[10] If our desires never changed with time, then each person would have a single preference order, by reference to which what most satisfied his desires over

[10]Brandt A Theory of the Good and the Right, chap. 7 sect. 3 esp. pp. 146–148 and chap. 13 sect. 1; for a discussion of Brandt's charge see Sen 'Plural Utility'.

the course of his life could be calculated. However, they do change, and not simply in a way that allows us totally to discount the earlier ones. Suppose that for much of his life a person wanted his friends to keep him from vegetating when he retired but, now that he is retired, wants to be left to vegetate. There is, Brandt thinks, no plausible, intelligible programme for weighing desires that change with time and hence for maximizing satisfaction. We are, he concludes, driven back to a happiness or mental state account, to some such Benthamic notion as intensity of happiness or distress, multiplied by duration. 'This conception', Brandt says, 'is at least clear'.

Yet all the problems that we have just seen with mental state accounts remain; defects in one account do not disappear with the appearance of defects in another. How do we determine how happy a person is? Is happiness a single mental state? If many, how are they linked? 'Clear', I should think, is the last description mental state accounts deserve. Moreover, there may well be an acceptable programme for handling the cases that Brandt finds difficult. It is some complex notion of *informed* desire, I believe, that is the best candidate for defining 'utility'. Perhaps the notion of informed desire can be got to supply the weighting of desires that we need in these troublesome cases. Has our retired friend simply forgotten the satisfactions of a busy life? If so, his later desire has much less weight. Is it just a change in taste, on the model of no longer liking ice cream? If so, his earlier desire has much less weight. The notion of *informed* desire has yet to be worked out, and from it may emerge the programme that Brandt despairs of finding. The prospects of making a desire account work are certainly not less rosy than those of making a happiness account work.

Even if the desire account survives the charge of unintelligibility, problems remain. I shall mention only a particularly serious one.[11] We desire things other than states of mind; someone might prefer, say, bitter truth to comforting delusion. The desire account, as we have seen, has the advantage of being able to accommodate such desires. But the desire account does this by severing the link between 'satisfaction of desire' and the requirement that a person in some way experience its satisfaction, dropping what we might call the Experience Requirement. If the delusion is complete, one believes that one has the truth; the mental states involved in believing something that really is true and

---

[11]See Glover *Causing Death and Saving Lives* pp. 63–64; for further objections to desire accounts see L. Sumner *Abortion and Moral Theory* (Princeton: Princeton University Press, 1981) sect. 21. On obligations to the dead see J. Feinberg 'Harm and Self Interest', in P. Hacker and J. Raz (eds.) *Law, Morality and Society* (Oxford: Clarendon Press, 1977), A. Gombay 'What You Don't Know Doesn't Hurt You', *Proceedings of the Aristotelian Society*, 1978–9, 79, and E. Partridge 'Posthumous Interests and Posthumous Respect', *Ethics*, 1981, 91.

believing a successful deception are the same. Or if a parent wants his children to be happy, what he wants, what is valuable to him, is a state of the world, not a state of his mind; merely to delude him into thinking that his children flourish, therefore, does not give him what he values. That is the important point; the desire account does not require that satisfaction of desire translates itself in every case into experience, and that is what gives the account its breadth and attraction as a theory of value. But if we drop the Experience Requirement, why then would utility not include even the desires of the dead? And would that not mean that the account had gone badly awry? And if we exclude the desires of the dead, would we not, in order to avoid arbitrariness, have to re-introduce the Experience Requirement, thus losing the breadth that makes the desire account attractive? The difficulty goes deep in the theory.

Excluding the desires of the dead raises the general question of whether the best account of 'utility' will not exclude desires of several different sorts, a question which has received useful attention recently. Should not other-regarding desires be excluded?[12] Those who not only want their own welfare but also, luckily for them, have others wanting it too count more heavily than those who do not; for instance, orphans count less than children with loving parents. But that seems to yield Bentham out of Orwell: each to count for at least one but some for more than one. Should not irrational desires be excluded?[13] The principle of utility is a normative principle and ought perhaps, therefore, to grant weight only to what are, by its own standards, good reasons, such as benefit and freedom from harm, and to grant weight only to desires justifiable in terms of these reasons. Should not, for obvious reasons, immoral desires be excluded?[14] Indeed, should not desires of any sort of moral character be excluded? If the concern of the principle of utility is with what ought to be done, then the desire for something because it is what ought to be done appears when the principle delivers its result and seems improper as a ground for the result. Do we not, in general, need a Theory of Types in utility theory to exclude certain desires from the argument place in utility functions?

The various cases for exclusion are arresting, but to my mind none in the end succeeds. The best account still seems to me the old one, on which, as F. P. Ramsey puts it, what count for utility are desires for

[12]See R. Dworkin *Taking Rights Seriously* (London: Duckworth, 1977) chap. 9, for an argument that they should; for further discussion of some of the issues see B. Williams 'A Critique of Utilitarianism', in J. Smart and B. Williams (eds.) *Utilitarianism: For and Against* (Cambridge: Cambridge University Press, 1973).

[13]See Williams 'A Critique of Utilitarianism', pp. 105–106, for an argument that they should.

[14]J. Harsanyi *Rational Behavior and Bargaining Equilibrium in Games and Social Situations* (Cambridge: Cambridge University Press, 1977) p. 62, says they should.

pleasure or 'anything else whatever'.[15] One consideration to keep in mind, although it will not meet all the cases, is that the question 'What is the best account of "utility"?' should be kept distinct from the question 'What is the account of "utility" — perhaps highly artificial and *ad hoc* — that yields a one principle, utility maximizing, moral theory that is closest to adequacy?'. One should not always build into the notion of 'utility' restrictions that one thinks morality requires, when they are more naturally expressed in a separate moral principle.

5. Sen's Suggestion

Amartya Sen has recently asked whether we really need regard these various formulations of 'utility' as exclusive alternatives.[16] What instead we should do, he suggests, is to regard 'utility' as a plural notion, a vector of many different considerations. Suppose some person prefers bitter truth to comforting delusion, but is palmed off with the latter. We feel sorry for him. Then later he learns that it was all a deception. We feel sorrier for him. Why not take our sympathy as an indicator of the person's utilities? Bare desire fulfilment and experienced desire fulfilment are both relevant, and to insist on a choice between them, Sen says, seems 'arbitrary and uncalled for'. Similarly for the other choices we have been considering, for example the choice between actual and informed desires.

But the doubt about Sen's proposal is that, if one accepted it, one would have to supply some weighting for these various vectors when they merge in decision, and the weighting would have to be neither arbitrary nor left to haphazard intuitions. In this respect, the informed desire approach seems superior. It encompasses Sen's various 'vectors' and attaches weights to them in a manner motivated by the spirit of the notion of welfare. When the person we alluded to learns that it was all deception, his experienced hurt counts too, Sens says. But so it does on a desire account, because few want to be hurt. Similarly for the choice between actual and sanitised desires; as we have just seen, a plausible desire account gives weight to them both. If the lacuna in Sen's notion of 'plural utility' is properly filled, it is likely to lead in the end to something like the informed desire account. It may not be that all elements that he has in mind for his 'plural utility' will be accommodated, but perhaps all that the notion of 'welfare' should be made to carry will be.

---

[15]F. Ramsey 'Truth and Probability', in his *The Foundations of Mathematics* (London: Routledge and Kegan Paul, 1931) p. 173.

[16]Sen 'Plural Utility' esp. pp. 203–204. Sen is also concerned here to expound his very useful taxonomy of moralities which vary the role of welfare; see also Sen 'Utilitarianism and Welfarism', *Journal of Philosophy*, 1979, 76.

6. Non-utilitarian Accounts of Welfare

A particularly radical attack on definitions of 'utility' has been made recently. Utilitarians, it argues, are up the wrong definitional tree. The notion of 'welfare' that morality needs is not the broad one from the utilitarian tradition, whether in terms of happiness or of desire, but an altogether narrower one in terms of 'basic needs'—which are to be understood as what we need in order to function even minimally, what if denied will make us fall from some norm and ail.[17] These attacks, while requiring the context of moral theory or a theory of justice for their final assessment, are often launched outside that context, and we can briefly consider them now.

At first glance, the attack has force. It is easy to find a link between needs and obligation—namely, the urgency of ailment. In contrast to ailment, what claim do my mere desires, let alone my whims, make on others?[18] Moreover, basic needs, connecting as they do with objective matters of ailment and malfunction, are more easily identified, measured, and agreed upon; so they have the great practical advantage of providing an interpersonal measure for social decisions that can command society's assent.[19] What is more, to take all desires as relevant to 'welfare' would seem to distort moral calculation. For one thing, it would give scope to blackmail; a person could develop expensive tastes to skew allocations in his favour, and others might follow suit if only in self-defence. If someone develops a burning desire to study quasars with powerful radio telescopes, then so long as other members of society had more modest aims, equality of welfare would require that he be given more.[20] Then there is a related objection.[21] Even if the student of quasars does not manipulate his desires in order to blackmail society, the mere fact of defining his welfare as the satisfaction of his desires will lead to patently unjust distributions. Certain abilities—for instance, great intelligence—are the result of the genetic lottery. Perhaps the desire of the student of quasars is the natural product of his great intelligence, but if it is allowed to get him more of the social pie,

---

[17]On 'basic' needs see e.g. J. Feinberg *Social Philosophy* (Englewood Cliffs: Prentice-Hall, 1973) p. 111, D. Miller *Social Justice* (Oxford: Clarendon Press, 1976) chap. 4 sect 2, D. Richards *A Theory of Reasons for Action* (Oxford: Clarendon Press, 1971) pp. 37–38, R. Wollheim 'Needs, Desires and Moral Turpitude', in R. Peters (ed.) *Royal Institute of Philosophy Lecturers*, vol. 8 (London: Macmillan, 1975) pp. 163, 171–172.

[18]See Feinberg *Social Philosophy* p. 10, Wollheim, pp. 176–177.

[19]See J. Rawls *A Theory of Justice* (Oxford: Clarendon Press, 1972) sect. 15 and, for connection with needs, 'Fairness to Goodness', *Philosophical Review*, 1975, 84; T. Scanlon 'Preference and Urgency', *Journal of Philosophy*, 1975, 72: 658.

[20]This is John Rawls' example; see his discussion in 'Fairness to Goodness' p. 552.

[21]See its statement in Rawls p. 552. Neither of these objections, as stated, does justice to the discussions from which they are abstracted. An important further consideration is the fact that our basic needs are unavoidable, what human flesh is heir to; our mere desires, on the other hand, although sometimes not consciously adopted, or easily changed, fall more into the realm of our life for which we can be held responsible.

then he gets it for reasons that have nothing to do with merit, or with anything else that would seem to justify it. We might then succeed in making people's utilities (on the desire account) equal, but we should, it would seem, be making the wrong thing equal.

But these attacks are less strong than they seem. First the distinction between 'basic needs' and 'mere desires' lacks the power that the attack requires, 'Basic needs' are defined as those whose satisfaction is necessary for health or proper function, but the key notions of 'health' and 'proper function' are too indeterminate to work. It is no good repeating the much used example of food: certainly without food we shall ail. But it is not enough that a few needs fall clearly this side or that of the boundary of 'basic needs' if most sit right on the boundary. Is interesting work a basic need? Well, without it, alienation, a kind of social pathology, results. Is education a basic need? Without it, one's intellect will atrophy. And how much education? Of course, many supporters of a need account readily admit this indeterminacy; they admit what is sometimes called the 'conventional' nature of many needs.[22] But they say that, although the line between basic and nonbasic needs may change as society changes, there is still a rationale for locating the division where we do in each era. But even after all these points are taken into account, the line is still too broad. As a society becomes progressively richer, does the amount of education that is a 'basic need' increase in pace? Does the notion of a 'basic need' ever provide a cut-off point, except by fairly arbitrary stipulation? If not, it is playing very little role.

This indeterminacy loosens the link between need and obligation. If, over a wide area, what is ailment and malfunction is a matter for stipulation, then over that area what constitutes an obligation is also a matter for stipulation, which would be odd. A second consideration that weakens the link is this. Whatever in the end goes on the list of basic needs, there are likely to be people who want things off the list more than they want things on it. A group of scholars may, with full understanding, prefer an extension to their library to exercise equipment for their health. And part of what makes us think that basic needs, such as health, are more closely linked to obligation than desires are is that basic needs seem the 'bread' of life and desires mere 'jam'. But an extension to the scholars' library may not seem like 'jam' to them. On the contrary, if the scholars' preference is clear-sighted, then the library is of greater value to them. But then to maintain that needs create obligations where mere desires do not, or that they create stronger obligations, is to say that we have an obligation, or a stronger obligation, to the scholars to give them what they themselves value less, which would be odd.

[22]See, e.g., the discussion in Miller *Social Justice* pp. 136–138.

Nor do the various objections that the desire account distorts moral calculation succeed, at least as they now stand. The Blackmail Objection is simply a mistake. Anyone who develops expensive desires to skew allocation in his favour will have his strategy backfire. True, if his society is welfare egalitarian, he will get more *goods* than his mates to bring him up to their level of welfare. But he will not get more welfare that way, either than they get or than he would otherwise have got; in fact — this is why his strategy backfires — he will be worse off for his stratagems than he would otherwise have been, because everyone's welfare level will go down, his included, as a result of his expensive tastes. The Patent Unfairness Objection is weak, because it is not true that expensive tastes are largely a matter of chance. Some people have expensive tastes because of ways of life that they have chosen after reflection — say, the life of the mind that requires expensive libraries and laboratories. It is no good informing them that they could develop less expensive tastes, although it is true that they could, because these tastes are central to what they see as making life valuable. I shall stop here, although my replies to these objections are far too quick. The objections themselves have, I think, been far too quickly stated too, and what we now need in the immediate future is less speed over this terrain.[23]

7. *Scanlon's Objective Account*

Most need accounts blunder by being too rigid: they rank needs above mere desires, regardless of the levels of satisfaction of each, which is implausible. That was the moral of the story of the scholars' choice between a library extension or exercise equipment. But T. M. Scanlon has made an important contribution to the debate by proposing an account of welfare retaining the objectivity of the need accounts while avoiding their rigidity.[24] It goes like this. We have many concerns, health and learning being two of them. These concerns will be met to varying degrees. Various combinations of these degrees of satisfaction of our concerns constitute different overall levels of welfare. One concern can be morally more urgent than another, the notion of 'urgency' here being a relation holding between various increments and decrements in degrees to which concerns are met. That is, it is a relation between the importance to Mr Black of a certain drop in the degree to which a concern of his is met, given the rest of his circum-

---

[23]See Dworkin 'What Is Equality?' Part 1, *Philosophy and Public Affairs*, 1981, for a long and interesting discussion; I owe him the point about blackmail's back-firing, but he goes on to raise other problems connected with expensive tastes, although none, to my mind, damaging either to the desire account or (which is his primary concern) to the attractiveness of the aim of equalizing utility, so defined.

[24]Scanlon 'Preference and Urgency'.

stances (i.e. the degrees to which his other concerns are met) with the importance of Mr White of a certain increase in the degree a concern of his is met, given his circumstances.[25] In morality we should be interested in urgency of concern, not strength of desire; that is, we should focus on the reasons for which a benefit is desired, the concern behind it, where the reasons change in strength as the amounts of benefits already assured change.[26] Some concerns are relatively peripheral (i.e. what a person might or might not be moved by, depending upon his choices or chance factors in his life) and others are central (i.e. what virtually anyone must have as concerns). These considerations lead us to a definition of 'welfare', that core use of 'welfare' where it is the interpersonally measurable notion employed in determining distributions of social goods: *welfare is the satisfaction of these central concerns, so long as they retain urgency*. It is an 'objective' account of welfare, because which concerns are central is a fact about humans in general, whereas desire accounts employ each individual's varying subjective preferences. It is not a rigid account, unlike ordinary need accounts, because central concerns diminish in urgency as they are satisfied.

But why restrict welfare to central concerns? One ground might be a putative link between responsibility and obligation. Peripheral concerns are, in a sense, in our control; they are not always immediately alterable by choice, not always the result of choice, but they are constitutive of the individual we have become and, in a sense, need not have become and so may be held responsible for looking after the consequences of having become. Central concerns, in contrast, are not of our choosing; they are what human flesh is heir to. But the point here is obscure. The special needs of an intelligent person are not his needs qua human, because other humans do not have them, but neither are they what he chooses, even at an early stage. The desire of an intelligent child in school for more stimulation, or his thirst for more understanding later in life, is not in any obvious sense his responsibility.

But the main problem for Scanlon's account seems to me to be this. It rests on the assumption that we can determine which concerns are central and when they are urgent without appeal to people's subjective desires, that the urgency of what is invariant in our concerns is independent of the content of what is variant. That is the force of saying that urgency is an objective matter. But if, as I suspect, determining urgency necessarily involves appealing to people's actual, differing preferences, then the desire account will seem to be less easy to escape. There must be a point, we all agree, at which the moral demands of health are fully met and beyond which we are not obliged to go. But there is little consensus at present on where that point is. Moreover, it

---

[25]*Op. cit.*, p. 660.
[26]*Op. cit.*, pp. 660–661.

is hard to see how consensus could arise. If two people differ widely in the value they attach to self-reliance, they are likely to disagree about where society's obligation to protect life and limb ceases. Furthermore, if one greatly values learning, or any other expensive social activity, then if some further protection of health can be made only at cost to this highly valued goal, it may, for that reason, be unacceptable. In general, whether one finds a reduction in risk unacceptable must depend upon what else one values and how much one values it. It is unlikely that urgency can be, as Scanlon needs it to be, independent of one's individual conception of the good.

8. Common Misunderstandings of 'Utility'

There is a crude copy-book account of 'utility' still in circulation. It crops up, for instance, in Nozick's thinking that his experience machine makes a point against utilitarianism, when at most it is a pointer towards one particular definition of 'utility'. It crops up even in authors who are aware of the variety of possible accounts of 'utility': for instance, in David Wiggins' complaint that philosophy, especially utilitarianism, puts *happiness* in the place which should be occupied by *meaning*, the meaning of life.[27] But he overlooks the role that global desires and plans of life play in 'utility'; they shift the concept far closer to what he means by 'meaning' than to what he means by 'happiness'. Moreover, utilitarianism need not be tied to a Humean account of action. It need not root obligation in desire. It is not committed to monism in values; it can be (and on what seems to me the best account of 'utility' is) compatible with pluralism in values, because 'utility' can be seen not as the single overarching substantive value, in fact, not as a substantive value at all, but instead as a formal analysis of what it is for something to be of value to someone. All of this needs explanation and development, but in general philosophers have not yet come to terms with the far-reaching consequences of contemporary definitions of 'utility'.[28]

9. Method in Normative Ethics

There is another contribution of Brandt[29] and Hare[30] that should at least be briefly recorded, because, while it is not strictly part of utilitar-

---

[27]D. Wiggins 'Truth, Invention, and the Meaning of Life', *Proceedings of British Academy*, 1976, 62: 332.

[28]For recent discussions of one person's well-being, see Richards pt. I, P. Bricker 'Prudence', *Journal of Philosophy*, 1980, 77.

[29]Brandt *A Theory of the Good and the Right* chap. 1 esp. sect. 3, but also sects. 1–2.

[30]R. Hare 'Ethical Theory and Utilitarianism', in H. Lewis (ed.) *Contemporary British Philosophy*, Fourth Series, (London: Allen & Unwin, 1976), 'Rawls' Theory of Justice', Parts I and II, *Philosophical Quarterly*, 1973, 23, 'The Argument from Received Opinion', in his *Essays on Philosophical Method* (London: Macmillan, 1971), and esp. *Moral Thinking* (Oxford: Clarendon Press, 1981) chap. 8.

ian theory, it matters immensely to its assessment. By far the most common objection to utilitarianism is that it does not square with moral intuitions. Both Brandt and Hare argue, with deadly effect, that this method is not allowable, that intuitions, on their own, have no probative force. They each draw a heroic conclusion from this: we must totally renounce appeal to intuitions, and each offers his own very different proposal of an alternative procedure. The danger in the heroic position is that many will find it untenable and will therefore slip back into the old ways of piecemeal appeal to intuitions, on the grounds that there is nothing else to do. But there is; there is, for example, Rawls' method of 'reflective equilibrium', although Rawls has not applied his method in anything like a demanding enough form.[31] And whatever one thinks of Brandt's and Hare's positive proposals, their negative case cannot, I think, be gainsaid. It ought to change the face of moral argument.

10. Justice and Rights

Utilitarianism's greatest problem has been, is now, but need not always be sounding plausible on these topics. The deepest criticism of utilitarianism in the last ten years has been Rawls' charge that it ignores 'the separateness of persons'.[32] Utilitarianism proceeds by the simple device of trading off goods and bads by their magnitudes, not distinguishing intrapersonal and interpersonal trade-offs. This means that in awkward circumstances utilitarianism might send someone to the wall. It is clearly this lack of distinction that invites Rawls' charge of ignoring the separateness of persons and such similarly inspired ones as: 'One person may not be sacrificed, without limit, for the good of others'; 'The well-being of one person cannot simply be replaced by that of another'. But what is the restriction on utilitarian trade-offs that these various vague remarks seek to impose? At the base of them all there is some conception or other of what might be called 'treating people as equals': not meting out equal portions but that deeper matter of showing people equal regard. But which conception? There is an *embarras de choix*: does 'equal regard' require (i) granting equal weight ('everybody to count for one, nobody for more than one'); or (ii) a minimum level of welfare, above which obligations cease; or (iii) an equal start with equal prospects, after which inequalities resulting from just transactions are themselves to be regarded as just; or (iv) maximin; or (v)

---

[31]See Rawls *A Theory of Justice* sect. 4, 9, 87, Schneewind chap. 9, P. Singer, 'Sidgwick and Reflective Equilibrium', *Monist*, 1974, 58, J. Rawls 'The Independence of Moral Theory', *Proceedings of the American Philosophical Association*, 1974–1975, 48.

[32]Rawls *A Theory of Justice* p. 27, Nozick pp. 32–33; for an excellent discussion see H. Hart 'Between Utility and Rights', in A. Ryan (ed.) *The Idea of Freedom* (Oxford: Oxford University Press, 1979).

equal goods with equal prospects; or (vi) equal welfare? Our intuitions are not going to help us here; we will not find an answer by plumbing further the depths of our intuitions about equality or separateness or respect for persons, because intuitions are superficial things, without depths themselves and needing moral theory to supply them.

Suppose that, for some reason, one chose maximin as the interpretation of equal regard. That would still not be enough, if intuitions are what we are to go by. Maximin, intuition tells us, has exceptions; rich societies where the worst off are well off do, on the face of it quite reasonably, allocate resources — to art, for instance — in a way that further benefits the well off. Suppose then, to accommodate this, one said that what are not allowed are *sacrifices* of one person for another already better off, disastrous drops in welfare or, at least, drops to dismally low levels. But the French government knows that some people, through no fault of their own, die each year in automobile accidents because of the beautiful roadside avenues of trees, but it does not cut them down. So we do allow trade-offs between the common good and disastrous drops, even when the drop is as disastrous as death and the good is merely more aesthetic pleasure. Suppose, therefore, that one concluded that both of these principles were too strong and that one looked for something weaker. Sen once formulated what he meant to be close to an absolutely minimum requirement, what he called the Weak Equity Axiom, which goes: if one person is a less good utility producer than another, say because he is handicapped, so that at any level of goods he is less well off, then he must be given *something* more than the other.[33] One might even make the requirement weaker still: the unfortunate one must not be given less, if he is below and the more fortunate one already above a minimum acceptable level of welfare. But these 'weak' requirements are still too strong. Surgeons, in choosing between patients for a kidney transplant, are often guided by a patient's prospects. If Jones has been chronically ill, below the minimum acceptable level for most of his life, with poor prospects of surviving long after an operation, and Smith, never as ill, has good prospects, Smith may be operated on.[34]

It is not at all easy to find a cut-off for utilitarian trade-offs. It is easy enough, altogether too easy, to say things like 'No one may be sacrificed, without limit, for another', as if that had wrapped up in it somewhere the key to where the limit is. But what is not at all easy is to

[33]A. Sen *On Economic Inequality* (Oxford: Clarendon Press, 1973) p. 18; for a still weaker version see Sen 'Rawls versus Bentham: an Axiomatic Examination of the Pure Distribution Problem', *Theory and Decision* 1974, 4; reprinted with some revisions in N. Daniels (ed.) *Reading Rawls* (Oxford: Blackwell, 1975) p. 285.

[34]For further argument see J. Harsanyi *Essays on Ethics, Social Behavior, and Scientific Explanation* (Dordrecht: D. Reidel, 1976) chap. 5 sect. 3, J. Griffin 'Equality: On Sen's Weak Equity Axiom', *Mind*, 1981, 90.

supply the key. It may look, at this point, as if the best bet is not to search for an absolute cut-off for trade-offs but to fall back on the familiar structure of equipollent principles: a principle of utility maximization, a principle of equality independent of it, with sometimes the one and sometimes the other dominating in conflict. On this approach, moral thinking would not contain a line beyond which a person may not be sacrificed, but a moral counterforce on the maximizing trade-offs which may otherwise lead to his sacrifice. In the earlier case, Smith, who is better off, could be helped a lot and Jones, the worse off, only negligibly, and it is obviously this great disparity that points towards helping the better off. But suppose that the disparity is less great. Smith, we shall say, is an otherwise healthy man of sixty who with a transplant will live about another ten years; Jones is a chronically ill man of thirty who with a transplant will live about another five years. Smith, we are strongly inclined to think, has had a fairly good go at life, and although his prognosis is better than Jones', the pull towards equaling the balance is obvious. The benefit to Jones is less but not negligible, and he has had, and will at the end of his life still have had, so much less than Smith has already had.

This mode of argument seems to me a perfect example of the inadequacy of piecemeal appeal to intuition. One might invoke such an example and conclude from it that equality has moral weight independent of utility maximization. But suppose that one went on appealing to intuitions: if the method is worth anything, the more appeals the better. Well, suppose we take more cases with the features which in the last case seemed decisive against a purely utilitarian trade-off. Suppose Jones were a six year old child with a prospect of five more years, and Smith twelve years old with prospect of ten. Fickle intuition now favours Smith. What if Jones were fifteen with five more years, and Smith thirty with ten? Perhaps, ever inconsistent, intuition is now just silent. So if we appeal to enough intuitions, it is by no means clear that they supply grounds for concluding that there are two independent forces at work in our moral thought, utility and equality. One of the glaring faults of appeals to intuition is their selectivity; if one took the method seriously enough to appeal to more than just one or two intuitions, the method would often start yielding contrary results. This is not surprising. Intuitions are not just superficial; they are vague. At best, they are glimpses of fragments of outlines of principles. When principles get worked out fully enough, they may well look very different from what a first fleeting glimpse suggested. In fact, if one collected the trade-offs that fairly widespread intuitions support, and if one took the task seriously enough to collect a very large number of them over a wide range of cases, this 'undisputed set of trade-offs', so to speak, would undermine every proposal that moral philosophy has yet produced of a principle checking utilitarian trade-offs. This is true not just of principles of distribution of the sort that we have been considering, such as maximin and minimum acceptable level of welfare and sets of equipollent principles, but also of the various systems of rights also meant to check utilitarian trade-offs. None of these proposals squares with the 'undisputed set of trade-offs', if that is a wide enough sample. This is not fatal to them, but it shows how difficult it is to see what principle or principles to use in thinking about trade-offs, and how very far we are from having any satisfactory arguments on the subject.

It is possible, in all this, to see the point at which we all start diverging. We all begin at the same place, with the same rough idea of 'equal regard'. The moral point of view is constituted, we agree, by granting some sort of equal status to everyone. Hare, by drawing on the semantics of key moral terms, derives first the universal prescriptivity of moral judgements and then, from that, his formal notion of 'equal regard', namely the utilitarian 'everybody to count for one, nobody for more than one'. Rawls sees Hare's sort of 'equal regard' as an undesirable impersonality rather than impartiality, which he sees as captured by the fiction of people in the original position and the principles they would select. Nozick sees Rawls' interpretation of 'equal regard' as unacceptably ahistorical, and he finds the central notion of 'equal regard' in a small set of rights that all persons possess equally, requiring an equal start but allowing inequalities that result from just actions. But although we can see just where we diverge, we can hardly see what steps are being taken to carry us off on our different courses, and we certainly cannot see at all clearly why they are taken. This, I think, is the most important lesson of the last ten years: we should all be focusing our attention on those first few steps. How should we move? What reasons can we give for our moves? Is our method adequate? It has to be admitted that for the most part, the moves that have been made have been prompted by the briefest and least rigorous appeals to intuition, and I think that we can bring almost everyone to agree that such a method is far from adequate.

11. Other Recent Criticisms

I shall mention three other criticisms that have been important in the last ten years.

(A) WILLIAMS ON INTEGRITY

Utilitarianism, Williams says, 'essentially involves the notion of *negative responsibility*': that I am as responsible for what I allow as for what I myself do.[35] It does, he says, by being consequentialist, by regarding

---

[35]Williams 'A Critique of Utilitarianism', p. 95; in general use see sects. 3 and 5, Williams 'Persons, Character and Morality', in A. Rorty (ed.) *The Identities of Persons* (Berkeley: University of California Press, 1976) and 'Utilitarianism and Self-Indulgence' in H. Lewis (ed.) *Contemporary British Philosophy* (London: Allen & Unwin, 1976).

only the states of affairs that actions produce and not who produces them, or why, as relevant to moral right and wrong.[36] But this is to attack 'the value of integrity'.[37] Any fully developed person has 'commitments' or 'ground projects' that he 'takes seriously at the deepest level, as what his life is about',[38] projects which are 'closely related to his existence and which to a significant degree give meaning to his life'.[39] He cannot abandon such projects just because the reports from the utility network indicate that, as chance or the actions of others have stacked things, utility would be maximized by his doing so. That would be to ask him to commit a kind of suicide, to abandon himself.

This point about 'negative responsibility' is familiar; Williams' fresh contribution is to justify it by linking it with the survival of 'integrity'. Yet that is just where his remarks are most obscure.[40] Is his point that a normative theory must pass the test of psychological realism, that it must accept into the theory and employ as part of the ground on which it builds the deep, inescapable sources of human action? If it is, then he is surely right, but it is no longer clear how this would upset those forms of utilitarianism that do this. Or is his point, rather, that judgements about right and wrong should not be as much determined by what others do, or even by what happens naturally, as the outlook of 'negative responsibility' makes them. Well, certainly he means that, but does his rhetorical invocation of 'integrity' go any way to supporting the claim? What does the term mean here? Whereas 'integrity' as ordinarily used, to mean something like 'honesty' or 'general uprightness', does name something valuable, 'integrity' as Williams uses it, in its more literal etymological sense of 'wholeness', does not. People often actually have as their 'ground project', as what their life is about, morally hideous, or merely shabby or shallow, ambitions. To ask a person whose life is centred on resentment or revenge or vanity or one-upmanship to 'abandon' himself may be exactly what he needs. Some people most need, and all of us to no small degree would benefit from, some well chosen 'disintegration' and 'reintegration'.

Even if everyone's values were perfectly respectable, there would be a more general difficulty. Williams needs to explain 'integrity' in a way that makes it, at once, valuable in some non-question-begging way and yet incompatible with acting, utilitarian fashion, as reports from the

[36]Williams 'Critique of Utilitarianism', p. 96.
[37]Williams 'Critique of Utilitarianism', p. 96–99.
[38]Williams 'Critique' p. 116.
[39]Williams 'Persons, Character and Morality' p. 209.
[40]For powerful criticism of Williams see N. Davis 'Utilitarianism and Responsibility', *Ratio*, 1980, 22, S. Carr 'The Integrity of a Utilitarian', *Ethics*, 1975–6, 86; J. Harris 'Williams on Negative Responsibility and Integrity', *Philosophical Quarterly*, 1974, 24; for a further discussion of 'integrity' see G. Taylor 'Integrity' *Proceedings of the Aristotelian Society*, Suppl. 1981; and R. Gaita 'Integrity', *Proceedings of the Aristotelian Society*, Suppl. 1981.

utility network demand. That is no easy task. There are, it is true, other interpretations of 'wholeness' for us to appeal to. We might, for instance, take it to mean a person's being all of a piece — not hypocritical, nor insincere, nor self-deceived, nor inconsistent in the beliefs that importantly influence his behaviour. 'Integrity', so interpreted, would clearly be something worth protecting, but the trouble is that it would not be, at least in any obvious way, incompatible with utilitarianism. Or we might take 'wholeness' to require commitment that involves the whole of one's person; 'wholeness' could then be seen as a kind of 'wholeheartedness' such that a person who takes, say, truthfulness as one of his central values must see certain features of particular situations as morally dominant and certain others — especially calculations of utility gains — as morally minor. Here we have an interpretation of 'integrity' incompatible with utilitarianism, but now the trouble is that integrity, so construed, is no longer valuable in a non-question-begging way. Integrity, on this interpretation, would simply be the rejection of the utilitarian approach to values, and so could not be a ground for rejecting that approach. The argument, on this interpretation, would simply degenerate into a *petitio principii*.

(B) Hampshire on Incommensurable Values

This too is an old criticism, but Hampshire finds that recent workings of cost-benefit analysis have given it new force. He writes of the 'coarse, quantitative, calculative Benthamism' of 'Mr. McNamara and his defense advisors' and contends that what in utilitarianism led the United States to war in Vietnam was nothing peripheral to it, but rather something at its heart: its treating all values as commensurable.[41] Others make much the same point.[42]

One trouble with their claim is the vagueness of the word 'value'; it is usually, but by no means always, used of 'good' rather than of 'right', of activities or states of affairs that people value rather than of obligations that, perhaps quite independently of what makes life good, people find that they must accept. Now, when 'value' is used broadly to include both 'good' and 'right', then what people might have in mind, at least in part, when they say that values are incommensurable, is the old deontological claim that there are some obligations that simply fall outside the ken of utility maximization, or of any other considerations of what makes life good. They might mean, for instance, that the structure of moral thought has more features than even sophisticated utilitarianisms supply, that a consideration such as liberty plays a role in moral deci-

[41]S. Hampshire *Morality and Pessimism* (Cambridge: Cambridge University Press, 1972) for remark quoted see *New York Review of Books* 8 Oct. 1970.
[42]See e.g. I. Berlin *Fathers and Children* (Oxford: Clarendon Press, 1972) p. 55, Williams *Morality* last section.

sion that falls off the end of any utility scale.[43] But anyone who says this must be able to supply, what no one has yet come near supplying, an adequate substantive theory of rights which settles the question, among others, whether or not rights are instrumental and, if they are, of what ends they are the instruments. Until he supplies it, he has no ground to stand on. If he finds it obvious that the desiderated theory, whatever in the end its details, will have certain general features such as rights that are non-instrumental, then he has missed the difficulties, both of subject matter and of method in normative theory building.

However, even if 'value' is taken narrowly and confined to 'good', the claim that there are incommensurable values can still mean many very different things, few of them plausible. Consider, for instance, Bernard Williams' complaint that nowadays in social decisions of all kinds 'values . . . quantified in terms of resources, are confronted by values which are not quantifiable in terms of resources: such as the value of preserving an ancient part of a town, or of contriving dignity as well as comfort for patients in a geriatric unit'. It is not, he concedes, that utilitarians have to think that these other values do not matter but, rather, that they are committed to what 'in practice has these implications: that there are no ultimately incommensurable values'.[44] Yet how should we decide between, say, on the one hand, enhancing the dignity of some geriatric patients by giving them greater privacy or, on the other, enhancing their comfort by giving them more heat? The utilitarian answer is that we are to be guided by how the patients themselves value the options, provided that they understand them. It is unclear whether Williams' point is that these two considerations, dignity and comfort, cannot both be put on a single scale of informed desires or that, although they can, their value is not determined by their place there. If the first, he is pretty clearly wrong. If the second, then would he say that, even if the patients clearsightedly prefer the heating, we decision-makers might have grounds to value their privacy more and give them that instead? But that is an implausible claim. This example is not untypical; a good deal of work has still to be done simply to state a clear and plausible thesis of the incommensurability of values.[45]

(c) DWORKIN ON EQUALITY

Although they occur in the course of an attack on utility as a candidate for what an egalitarian should equalize, Dworkin's arguments are worth considering here too, because they hold an important moral about 'utility'.

---

[43]T. Nagel means this; see T. Nagel 'The Fragmentation of Value', in his *Mortal Questions* (Cambridge: Cambridge University Press, 1979) Chap. 9.

[44]Williams *Morality* pp. 102–103.

[45]This point is more fully argued in J. Griffin 'Are There Incommensurable Values?', *Philosophy and Public Affairs*, 1977, 7.

Dworkin provides several ingenious arguments, but his strongest is this.[46] Suppose that 'utility' is best defined as 'satisfaction of desire', and that the proper desires to consult are our broadest ones, ones that embody the overall value that we attach to our lives. But then how should one compare Jack's level of overall desire satisfaction with Jill's? We might try different ways. One technique would be to ask each of them, 'How would you compare your present life with the best life you can imagine, with whatever physical and mental powers and material resources and opportunities you could ask for?'. Now suppose Jack, who thinks that with all that he could ask for he could then go on to solve the riddle of the origin of the universe, replies that his present life is *much* less valuable than his ideal life would be. But Jill, who, let us suppose, is much more down to earth, thinks the riddle insoluble and has no comparably grand dream at hand, and so she replies that her present life is not much below what her ideal life would be. We could then proceed to take what each considers ideal as marking the same level of utility. This would allow us to treat their answers as indicating their present actual level: Jack would be at a much lower level than Jill. But we would not, for a minute, want to see transfers of goods from Jill to Jack, in order to raise Jack somewhat closer to the ideal. Equality of welfare, on that account of utility, provides no attractive goal at all.[47]

Suppose, therefore, that we try another technique. We ask Jack and Jill, as perhaps a better way to get at their utility levels, 'How would you compare your present life with a life that seemed to you to have no value at all?'. Now suppose that Jack is the sort who believes that an everyday life fully immersed in projects is immensely valuable, and that he is leading such a life, and that he replies that his present life is *much* better than a valueless one. And suppose that Jill, who is much more demanding and regards such life as of little value, replies that her present life is only *slightly* better than a valueless one. We could now take what they mean by a valueless life as representing the same level of utility and so regard their answers as establishing that Jack is at a far higher level of utility than Jill. But, again, to transfer resources from Jack to Jill in the name of equality would be a thoroughly unattractive move. Equality of utility, once again, has no plausibility as a goal.[48]

Of course, one could try other techniques, but Dworkin thinks that they will all turn out to have some fault or other. What we need to get at, he correctly observes, are differences in Jack's and Jill's lives, not differences in their grand fantasies or beliefs or theories of values. We need, he concludes, a new standard: we would consider people actually to have lives of less utility if they have more 'reasonably to regret' that they do not have or have not done, where the notion of 'reasonably'

---

[46]Dworkin *Taking Rights Seriously* pp. 209–220, but also pp. 224–226.
[47]p. 215.
[48]p. 215.

carries a lot of weight.[49] 'Reasonably' has to rule out false belief, speculative fantasies, and unsound views about values. No one can *reasonably* regret not having the life span of Methuselah, or supernatural mental or physical powers, or more than his fair share of resources.[50] From these considerations Dworkin immediately draws a series of conclusions, of increasing disturbance to dogmatic slumberers. Equality of utility must make the idea of reasonable regret pivotal. Hence it must include, in its statement of what it aims at, an account of what a fair distribution would be. Hence equality of utility cannot be used to constitute or justify a theory of fair distribution; indeed the account of fair distribution that it must incorporate as one of its parts would 'contradict' it.[51]

But the argument is not persuasive. Dworkin canvasses several ways of identifying 'utility', all of them pretty inadequate, so it is unsurprising that in the end he finds them all inadequate for his purposes. Then for their genuine inadequacy he proposes a remedy, from which he draws his startling conclusions, but his remedy is neither the only, nor the best, available.

Look again at Dworkin's examples. In the first Jack and Jill compare their present lives to the best lives that they can imagine. Jack, because of his 'speculative fantasy' about solving the riddle of the origin of the universe, sees a huge gap; Jill, without that or any comparable 'dream', sees a small gap. If we take their ideals as marking the same level of utility, there is, of course, no resisting the conclusion that Jack is at a lower level of utility than Jill. Dworkin concludes that the aim of equalizing utility, on such a scheme, is unattractive. No doubt. But the fault goes deeper than Dworkin acknowledges: not that utility is not what we should be equalizing, but that it could not be, in any case, the right way to locate utilities. Why on earth think that Jack's and Jill's ideal lives mark the same level of utility? They clearly do not: Jack sees the best life as something high in the clouds; Jill sees it close to the ground. That technique for introducing comparability is about as subtle and plausible as some of the collosally arbitrary and rather similar devices from the economic literature, such as the zero-one rule.[52] The most obvious and sensible response to the familiar inadequacy Dworkin points out is to look for better techniques for identifying utility levels and for introducing comparability. And one can come up with more plausible techniques if one starts with a fairly adequate account of 'utility'. 'Utility' is 'the satisfaction of informed desire', where a lot is built into 'informed'. Jack's speculative fantasy about solving an impor-

[49]p. 216.
[50]pp. 216–217.
[51]p. 217.
[52]For good discussions see Sen *Collective Choice and Social Welfare* chap. 7 sect. 3, Rawls *A Theory of Justice* pp. 322–325.

tant problem marks a real utility level only if it is true that, with more brains and leisure, he would actually solve it. His regret at not solving it has certainly in that sense to be 'reasonable' — to use Dworkin's term. What is not 'reasonable' must, as Dworkin says, be eliminated. But so it will be with an account of 'utility' of any subtlety. If the riddle is soluble and Jack could solve it, that would be a life of enormous value. If Jill is wrong to think the riddle insoluble, then she is wrong about how valuable her life could really be. But no account of utility is any good if it treats Jack's delusions, if such they be, as marking a real utility level, or Jill's lack of imagination, if that is what it is, as marking a real utility ceiling for her. And no theory is improved by introducing comparability through the arbitrary assumption that these two possibly delusive and disparate utility levels are the same real level. There is no even remotely adequate account of 'utility' in use here.

In Dworkin's second example, Jack and Jill compare their present lives to lives they see as having no value. Jack, absorbed in everyday projects, finds a huge gap; Jill, equally absorbed but valuing the absorption less, finds a small gap. Dworkin is entirely right that if we assume, first, that they mean the same by a life of no value and, second, that their answers of 'huge' and 'small' can be taken to be employing the same rough cardinal scale, then they are at different utility levels. But why the example has the rhetorical effect Dworkin wants it to have is that we think of them as being at more or less the same utility level. They are, Dworkin says, equal in resources, in enjoyment of life, in relative success with their projects — indeed, the difference between them, Dworkin says, seems only to be 'differences in their beliefs, not differences in their lives'.[53] In other words, their lives are, for all real purposes, at the same level but this mode of identifying utility places them at different levels. But, then, this mode must be pretty bad. Why think that Jack's and Jill's answers employ the same cardinal scale? That would be an extremely simple-minded assumption. Jack says that his everyday life is worth 'a lot'; Jill says that her exactly similar life, equally enjoyed, is worth 'not much'. Clearly their scheme of values may be influencing their language. Perhaps the difference between their answers is only one of expression and can be resolved by some sensible translation. Does Jill actually regard her everyday life as less valuable than Jack's? Since there is only a difference in their beliefs and not in their lives, it is doubtful that she, or we, would. But perhaps the difference in their answers comes from a more serious cause. Perhaps one or other of them is using a scheme of values that is, as Dworkin puts it, 'confused or inaccurate or just wrong'.[54] If Jill's scorn for everyday life comes from her thinking that Nietzschean supermen live lives of far

[53]p. 216.
[54]p. 209.

greater value, her beliefs may well be, if not demonstrably false, at least ones that no wise and experienced person holds, or holds in such an extreme form. But a plausible account of 'utility' also subjects desires to whatever criticism, or whatever reform in categories, that value theory is subject to.

So Dworkin is, I think, right that to get a good indication of real differences in people's lives we need to eliminate false belief, unreal fantasies, unsound philosophical convictions and the like. But at the last minute, in drawing up this list, Dworkin slips in something not at all like these others.[55] He says that one cannot reasonably regret not having the life span of Methuselah, or not having supernatural mental or physical powers; they are denied us by reality and so such wishes, if we should suffer from them, cannot make the sort of real difference to life that we are interested in. Quite so. But then he adds to the list that one cannot reasonably regret not having more than one's fair share of resources. But here the sense of 'reasonable' radically changes. It is no longer that a lion's share of resources could not come one's way or would not actually make any difference to one's life if it did; in many cases it could and most patently would. Dworkin slips the anomalous item in without, so far as I can see, justification. He seems to confuse 'rational' in the sense in which his argument does successfully show rationality to be an essential part of any notion of well-being—viz. 'purged of false belief and the like'—and 'rational' in the inflated sense that he provides no ground for—viz. 'also purged of unfairness'. A good account of 'utility' must rule out desires irrational in the first sense. No doubt greedy desires for more than one's fair share also need ruling out, only not out of the notion of 'utility' (where they belong), but out of morality (where they do not). But then principles of distribution that come anywhere near adequacy rule them out there.

There is an important moral here. The literature does not yet contain a really adequate account of 'utility'. To proceed to use an inadequate one, either with the aim of theory building or theory busting, leaves one with the problem of locating the cause of any inadequacy that may result. Often it is nothing more revealing than the inadequacy of the account of 'utility' chosen at the outset. One of the things that moral philosophy most badly needs is a serviceable definition of 'utility'.

15. Applications

The greatest change of the last ten or fifteen years has not been in theory, but in interest in its application. This new concern is entirely beneficial, first of all because applying relatively well, instead of ill, considered principles to our problems must be an improvement but, second, because applications constitute the best possible test for nor-

---

[55]pp. 216–217.

mative theory. There is no quicker way to show up a normative principle as jejune or cant or muddled than to confront it with real life. In fact, the pay-off so far has been mostly for theory: if we have not yet got many good practical answers, we have got some very good theoretical questions, many important to utilitarianism.

The pivot for many practical concerns is the value of life. How do we assess it? The cost-benefit approach goes a long way towards measuring simple things like the value of saving twenty minutes travel time, but its deliverances on the value of life have been profoundly unsatisfactory. Some cost-benefit analysts see potential Pareto optimality as the rationale of their whole practice,[56] but whenever life is at stake, the purely ordinal Pareto approach runs into trouble: one cannot just ask a person about to die what he would take in compensation, because one risks getting the answer 'Nothing', and it takes only one person implacably going to his death for the Pareto test not to apply. Economists have suggested ways around this difficulty, usually by asking us to make the false assumption that we never know which particular persons will die but only which ones will have their actuarial risks changed. Still, it is not clear that anything short of getting the value of life onto some sort of cardinal scale will do,[57] and it is scarcely easy to do that. Nor is it even easy to settle which desires, on the 'informed desire' account, are the relevant ones to consult.[58]

However, supposing that utilitarianism can come up with a plausible account of the value of life and a way to determine it in the real situations where it is needed, can it explain why deliberately killing an innocent person is wrong? Of course, it can bring in side-effects: the sadness and insecurity for others, say, that killing causes. But that misses the point; it is wrong apart from side-effects and that needs adequate explanation. Can we get anything approaching one from utility maximization alone?[59]

[56]See e.g. E. Mishan *Elements of Cost-Benefit Analysis* (London: Allen & Unwin, 1972) p. 14.

[57]E.g. T. Schelling 'The Life You Save May Be Your Own', in S. Chase (ed.) *Problems in Public Expenditure Analysis* (The Brookings Institute, 1968), E. Mishan 'Evaluation of Life and Limb: A Theoretical Approach', *Journal of Political Economy*, 1971, 79; J. Broome 'Choice and Value in Economics', *Oxford Economic Papers*, 1978, 30, and Broome 'Trying to Value Life', *Journal of Public Economy*, 1979, 12; for a case for cardinality see Griffin 'Are There Incommensurable Values', pp. 53–54.

[58]See Dworkin 'What is Equality', pp. 209–220, also Glover 'Assessing the Value of Saving Lives', in G. Vesey (ed.) *Human Values* Royal Institute of Philosophy Lectures, vol. 11 (Sussex: Harvester Press, 1978).

[59]For fuller discussion see Glover *Causing Death and Saving Lives* chap. 3–5; also R. Henson 'Utilitarianism and the Wrongness of Killing', *Philosophical Review*, 1971, 80; R. Talmadge 'Utilitarianism and the Morality of Killing', *Philosophy*, 1972, 47; L. Sumner 'A Matter of Life and Death', *Nous*, 1976, 10; T. Roupas 'The Value of Life', *Philosophy and Public Affairs*, 1978, 7; M. Kaplan 'What Is Life Worth?', *Ethics*, 1978, 89; M. Lockwood 'Singer on Killing and the Preference for Life', *Inquiry*, 1979, 22; P. Singer *Practical Ethics* (Cambridge: Cambridge University Press, 1979), chap. 4. R. Young 'What Is Wrong with Killing People', *Philosophy*, 1979, 54.

Abortion is a special case, with special difficulties. Its problems fall right outside the domain that moral language has been designed for. Utilitarianism explains the wrongness of killing, apart from side-effects, in terms of the victim's loss of future valuable life. A foetus, too, loses future valuable life; there are doubts about whether a foetus is a 'person' but no comparable doubts about the fact of what it loses. But there are two difficulties. One is the replacement problem: loss of the potential value of one life can be satisfactorily compensated for, from the utilitarian point of view, by the gain of the value of an entirely different life. But are human lives, in this way, like money—what matters being not the particular notes, only the total at the bottom of the ledger? The second is the slippery slope problem: if the loss of potential value makes abortion wrong, it makes very many other things wrong—contraception, abstinence, and in general any form at all of limiting the number of children when the potential utility of the extra life exceeds the disutility it brings with it. Can this be right? Can it be avoided?[60]

The same difficulty of transferring concepts that have been formed primarily with conscious, intelligent, active, and responsible adult humans in mind to a very different sort of subject appears again with animals. What is the value of an animal's life? How are we even to comprehend it? How are we to determine it? Utilitarianism faces a dilemma: either 'utility' is explained in terms of mental states common to humans and animals thereby easing the problem of extension of the concept to animals but making it less adequate for humans, or it is explained in some such terms as 'informed desire' thereby making it more plausible for humans but less easy to extend to animals. Much discussion has focused on whether animals are 'persons', because, as in the debate about abortion, 'persons' is seen as the vehicle with the important moral luggage. Persons are plausible bearers of rights; persons have the sort of life to which notions of 'value' or 'well-being' have some sort of application. The questions are good ones: what makes a being a bearer of rights?, what notion of welfare, if any, carries across species? Certainly one can distinguish 'member of the species *homo sapiens*' from 'persons', when 'person' is defined as a being who is rational and aware of himself as a distinct entity with a past and a future. Human idiots, infants, patients in irreversible comas fall into the first category but not the second; primates, dogs, cats and many other

---

[60]For non-utilitarian discussion of the problem see J. Thomson 'A Defence of Abortion', *Philosophy and Public Affairs*, 1977, 6; M. Tooley 'Abortion and Infanticide', *Philosophy and Public Affairs*, 1972, 2; J. Finnis 'The Right and Wrongs of Abortion', *Philosophy and Public Affairs*, 1973, 2; for various utilitarian approaches see R. Brandt 'The Morality of Abortion', *Monist*, 1972, 56; R. Hare 'Abortion and the Golden Rule', *Philosophy and Public Affairs*, 1975, 4; Glover *Causing Death and Saving Lives*, chap. 9–11; Singer *Practical Ethics*, chap. 6; Sumner *Abortion and Moral Theory*. On the closely related problem of euthanasia, see Glover *Causing Death and Saving Lives* chap. 14–15, J. Feinberg 'Voluntary Euthanasia and the Inalienable Right to Live', *Philosophy and Public Affairs*, 1978, 7; Singer *Practical Ethics* chap. 7.

animal species fall into the second category but not the first. But this is too crude an apparatus. It can rightly be argued that many animals are persons, on this definition.[61] But is this the notion of person that carries the important moral baggage? What moral baggage does it carry? How much, or what sort of, self-consciousness is needed before killing becomes wrong?[62] Might not the differences in rationality and self-consciousness even between the species that count as 'persons' be crucial to the morality of killing?

There has also been much discussion in the last ten years of our duties to aid the needy,[63] of deep issues that this raises about the distinction between obligation and supererogation[64] and between negative and positive duties,[65]; there has also been discussion of the moral

[61]It is argued by Singer *Practical Ethics* chap. 4–5.

[62]See also P. Singer 'All Animals Are Equal', *Philosophical Exchange*, 1974, 1; *Animal Liberation* (New York: Random House, 1975), 'Killing Humans and Killing Animals', *Inquiry*, 1979, 22; 'Utilitarianism and Vegetarianism', *Philosophy and Public Affairs*, 1980, 9; T. Regan and P. Singer (eds.) *Animal Rights and Human Obligations* (Englewood Cliffs: Prentice-Hall, 1976; Regan 'The Moral Basis of Vegetarianism', *Canadian Journal of Philosophy*, 1975, 5; 'Utilitarianism, Vegetarianism, and Animals Rights', *Philosophy and Public Affairs*, 1980, 9; 'Animal Rights, Human Wrongs', *Environmental Ethics*, 1980, 2; R. Godlovitch 'Animals and Morals', *Philosophy*, 1971, 46; S. Godlovitch, R. Godlovitch, and J. Harris (eds.) *Animals, Men and Morals* (London: Gollanz, 1971); J. Margolis 'Animals Have No Rights and Are Not Equal of Humans', *Philosophical Exchange*, 1974, 1; S. Clark *The Moral Status of Animals* (Oxford: Clarendon Press, 1977); J. Narveson 'Animal Rights', *Canadian Journal of Philosophy*, 1977, 7; J. Benson 'Duty and the Beast', *Philosophy*, 1978, 53; L. Francis and R. Norman 'Some Animals Are More Equal Than Others', *Philosophy*, 1978, 53; P. Devine 'The Moral Basis of Vegetarianism', *Philosophy*, 1978, 53; P. Wenz 'Act Utilitarianism and Animal Liberation', *Personalist*, 1979, 60; H. McCloskey 'Moral Rights and Animals', *Inquiry*, 1979, 22; R. Frey *Interests and Rights: The Case Against Animals* (Oxford: Clarendon Press, 1980). For a good bibliography on the subject see C. Magel and T. Regan 'A Select Bibliography on Animal Rights and Human Obligations', *Inquiry*, 1979, 22.

[63]See J. Narveson 'Aesthetics, Charity, Utility, and Distributive Justice', *Monist*, 1972, 56; P. Singer 'Famine, Affluence and Morality', *Philosophy and Public Affairs*, 1973, 1, and *Practical Ethics* chap. 8; G. Hardin *The Limits of Altruism* (Bloomington: University of Indiana Press, 1977); W. Aiken and H. LaFollette (eds.) *World Hunger and Moral Questions* (Englewood Cliffs: Prentice-Hall, 1977).

[64]See C. New 'Saints, Heroes and Utilitarians', *Philosophy*, 1974, 49; Hare 'Ethical Theory and Utilitarianism' pp. 128–129; M. Clark 'The Meritorious and the Mandatory', *Proceedings of the Aristotelian Society*, 1978–9, 79; R. Sikora 'Utilitarianism, Supererogation and Future Generations', *Canadian Journal of Philosophy*, 1979, 9; Brandt *Theory of the Good and the Right* pp. 276–277; T. McConnell 'Utilitarianism and Supererogatory Acts', *Ratio*, 1980, 22.

[65]See J. Harris 'The Marxist Conception of Violence', *Philosophy and Public Affairs*, 1974, 3; R. Trammell 'Saving Life and Taking Life', *Journal of Philosophy*, 1975, 72; R. Frey 'Some Aspects of the Doctrine of Double Effect', *Canadian Journal of Philosophy*, 1975, 5; J. Glover 'It Makes No Difference Whether or Not I Do It', *Proceedings of the Aristotelian Society*, 1975, 49; Glover 'Causing Death and Saving Lives' chap. 6–7; B. Russell 'On the Relative Strictness of Negative and Positive Duties', *American Philosophical Quarterly*, 1977, 14; J. Rachels 'Killing and Starving to Death', *Philosophy*, 1979, 54; B. Steinbock (ed.) *Killing and Letting Die* (Englewood Cliffs: Prentice-Hall, 1980). On the related question of whether, and how, the number of people harmed matters, see J. Taurek 'Should the Numbers Count?' *Philosophy and Public Affairs*, 1977, 6; D. Parfit 'Innumerate Ethics', *Philosophy and Public Affairs*, 1978, 7; G. Kavka 'The Numbers Should Count', *Philosophical Studies*, 1979, 36.

limits to warfare,[66] of population policy,[67] and of environmental planing.[68] In these discussions utilitarianism is always at the centre. This is the tribute philosophy cannot avoid paying it. It may not be the most loved but it is certainly still the most discussed moral theory of our time.

[66]See T. Nagel 'War and Massacre', *Philosophy and Public Affairs*, 1972, 1; R. Brandt 'Utilitarianism and the Rules of War', *Philosophy and Public Affairs*, 1972, 1; R. Hare 'Rules of War and Moral Reasoning', *Philosophy and Public Affairs*, 1972, 1; M. Walzer, 'The Problem of Dirty Hands,' *Philosophy and Public Affairs*, 1973, 2; G. Anscombe 'Mr. Truman's Degree' privately printed 1958, repr. *The Human World*, 1973; Glover *Causing Death and Saving Lives*, chap. 19.

[67]See H. Vetter 'Utilitarianism and New Generations', *Mind*, 1971, 80; J. Sterns 'Ecology and the Indefinite Unborn', *Monist*, 1972, 56; J. Narveson 'Moral Problems of Population', *Monist*, 1973, 57; M. Goldinger 'Is Population Control a Difficulty for the Utilitarian?', *Personalist*, 1973, 54; M. Bayles 'Harm to the Unconceived', *Philosophy and Public Affairs*, 1976, 5; B. Anglin 'The Repugnant Conclusion', *Canadian Journal of Philosophy*, 1977, 7; R. Sikora and B. Barry (eds.) *Obligations and Future Generations* (Philadelphia: Temple University Press, 1978); M. Bayles *Morality and Population Policy* (University of Alabama: University of Alabama Press, 1980); J. McMahan 'Problems of Population Theory', *Ethics*, 1981, 92. as well as works cited in note.

[68]See W. Blackstone (ed.) *Philosophy and Environmental Crisis* (Athens: University of Georgia, 1974); L. Tribe "Ways Not to Think about Plastic Trees: New Foundations for Environmental Law', *Yale Law Journal*, 1974, 88; R. Hare 'Contrasting Methods of Environmental Planning', in R. Peters (ed.) *Nature and Conduct* Royal Institute of Philosophy Lectures, vol. 8 (London: Macmillan, 1975); R. Nelson 'Ethics and Environmental Decision Making', *Environmental Ethics*, 1979, 1.

5

AMARTYA SEN

⤬

Poor, Relatively Speaking

⤬

1. Introduction

When on the 6th January 1941, amidst the roar of the guns of the second world war, President Roosevelt announced that "in the future days . . . we look forward to a world founded upon four essential freedoms", including "freedom from want", he was voicing what was soon to become one of the major themes of the post-war era. While the elimination of poverty all over the world has become a much-discussed international issue, it is in the richer countries that an immediate eradication seemed possible. That battle was joined soon enough after the war in those affluent countries, and the ending of poverty has been a major issue in their policy discussions.

There are, however, great uncertainties about the appropriate way of conceptualising poverty in the richer countries, and some questions have been repeatedly posed. Should the focus be on "absolute" poverty or "relative" poverty? Should poverty be estimated with a cut-off line that reflects a level below which people are — in some sense — "absolutely impoverished", or a level that reflects standards of living "common to that country" in particular? These questions — it will be presently argued — do not bring out the real issues clearly enough. However, a consensus seems to have emerged in favour of taking a "relative" view of poverty in the rich countries. Wilfred Beckerman and Stephen Clark put it this way in their important recent study of poverty and social security in Britain since 1961: "we have measured

101

poverty in terms of a 'relative' poverty line, which is generally accepted as being the relevant concept for advanced countries."[1]

There is indeed much merit in this "relative" view. Especially against the simplistic absolute conceptualisation of poverty, the relative view has represented an entirely welcome change. However, I shall argue that ultimately poverty must be seen to be primarily an absolute notion, even though the specification of the absolute levels has to be done quite differently from the way it used to be done in the older tradition. More importantly, the contrast between the absolute and the relative features has often been confused, and I shall argue that a more general question about ascertaining the absolute standard of living lies at the root of the difficulty. In particular, it will be claimed that *absolute* deprivation in terms of a person's *capabilities* relates to *relative* deprivation in terms of commodities, incomes and resources.

That is going to be my main theme, but before I get to that general issue, I ought to make clear the sense in which I believe that even the narrow focus on relative poverty has been valuable in the recent discussions on poverty. In the post-war years there was a premature optimism about the elimination of poverty in rich countries based on calculations using poverty lines derived from nutritional and other requirements of the kind used by Seebohm Rowntree in his famous poverty studies of York in 1899 and 1936, or by Charles Booth in his nineteenth century study of poverty in London. The post-war estimates using these given standards yielded a very comforting picture of the way things had improved over the years, and indeed in terms of old standards, the picture certainly looked greatly more favourable than in the darker pre-war days. For example, the third York survey of 1951, following Rowntree's earlier ones, indicated that using the same standard, the proportion of working class population in poverty appeared to have fallen from 31 per cent at the time of the last survey in 1936 to less than 3 per cent in the new survey of 1951.[2] This was partly the result of general economic growth and a high level of employment, but also the consequence of various welfare legislations following the Beveridge Report of 1942, covering family allowances, national insurance, national assistance and national health service. Deducting public transfers would have made the poverty ratio higher than 22 per cent rather than less than 3 per cent. The changed situation—despite some statistical problems—was indeed genuine, but it was much too slender a basis on which to declare victory in the war against poverty. While the Labour government did go to the electorate in 1950 with the emphatic claim in its Manifesto that "destitution has been banished",

[1]W. Beckerman and S. Clark *Poverty and Social Security in Britain Since 1961* (Oxford: Oxford University Press, 1982).

[2]S. Rowntree and G. Lavers *Poverty and the Welfare State* (London: Longmans, 1951) p. 40.

and that the government has "ensured full employment and fair shares of the necessities of life",[3] there was little real reason to be smug about eradication of poverty in Britain. There were lots of people who were in misery and clearly deprived of what they saw (as I shall presently argue, *rightly*) as necessities of life, and the battle against poverty was far from over.

It is in this context that the change of emphasis in the academic literature from an absolutist to a relativist notion of poverty took place, and it had the immediate effect of debunking the smug claims based on inadequate absolute standards. But instead of the attack taking the form of disputing the claim that the old absolute standards were relevant still, it took the investigation entirely in the relativist direction, and there it has remained through these years. The relativist response to the smugness was effective and important. Using what he regarded as the orthodox or conventional poverty line fixed at a level 40 per cent higher than the basic National Assistance scale, plus rent, Peter Townsend (1962) showed that as many as one in seven Britons were in poverty in 1960. Other important questions were also raised, e.g., by Dorothy Wedderburn (1962), and more detailed and comprehensive estimates soon followed, and the poverty battle was seen as wide open.[4] While I shall question the conceptualisation underlying this change, I certainly would not dispute the value of the relativist contribution in opening up the question of how poverty lines should be determined, as well as in preventing a premature declaration of victory by the old absolutist school.

2. A Thorough-going Relativity?

Peter Townsend, who — along with other authors such as Gary Runciman — has made pioneering and far-reaching contributions to the relativist view of poverty puts the case thus:

> Any rigorous conceptualisation of the social determination of need dissolves the idea of 'absolute' need. And a thorough-going relativity applies to time as well as place. The necessities of life are not fixed. They are continuously being adapted and augmented as changes take place in a society and in its products. Increasing stratification and a developing division of labour, as well as the growth of powerful new organisations, create, as well as reconstitute, 'need'. Certainly no standard of sufficiency could be revised only to take account of changes in prices, for that would ignore changes in the goods and services consumed as well as new obligations and expectations placed on members of the community. Lacking an alternate criterion, the best assumption

[3]Quoted in D. Bull *Family Poverty* (London: Duckworth, 1971) p. 13.

[4]See especially B. Able-Smith and P. Townsend *The Poor and the Poorest* (London: Bell, 1965) and A. Atkinson *Poverty in Britain and the Reform of Social Security* (Cambridge: Cambridge University Press, 1970).

would be to relate sufficiency to the average rise (or fall) in real incomes.[5]

The last remark—that the best assumption would be to relate sufficiency to "the average rise (or fall) in real incomes"—is obviously *ad hoc*. But the more general argument is undoubtedly quite persuasive. However, I think this line of reasoning suffers from two quite general defects. *First, absoluteness* of needs is not the same thing as their *fixity over time*. The relativist approach sees deprivation in terms of a person or a household being able to achieve *less than what others* in that society do, and this relativeness is not to be confused with *variation over time*. So the fact that "the necessities of life are not fixed" is neither here nor there, as far as the competing claims of the absolutist and relativist views are concerned. Even under an absolutist approach, the poverty line will be a function of *some* variables, and there is no *a priori* reason why these variables might not change over time.

The *second* problem is perhaps a more difficult one to sort out. There is a difference between achieving *relatively less than others*, and achieving *absolutely less because of falling behind others*. This general distinction, which I think is quite crucial to this debate, can be illustrated with a different type of interdependence altogether—that discussed by Fred Hirsch (1976) in analysing "positional goods". Your ability to enjoy an uncrowded beach may depend on your knowing about that beach when others do not, so that the *absolute* advantage you will enjoy—being on an uncrowded beach—will depend on your *relative* position—knowing something that others do not. You want to have that information, but this is not because you particularly want to do *relatively better than or as well as others*, but you want to do *absolutely well*, and that in this case requires that you must have some differential advantage in information. So your absolute achievement—not merely your relative success—may depend on your relative position in some other space. In examining the absolutist *vs.* the relativist approach it is important to be clear about the space we are talking about. Lumping together needs, commodities, etc., does not help to discriminate between the different approaches, and one of the items in our agenda has to be a closer examination of the relationship between these different spaces.

Before I come to that, let me consider a different approach to the relativist view—this one occurring in the important study of "poverty and progress in Britain" between 1953 and 1973 by Fiegehen, Lansley and Smith. They put the question thus:

[5]P. Townsend 'The Development of Research on Poverty', in Department of Health and Social Security, *Social Security Research: The Definition and Measurement of Poverty* (London: HMSO, 1979) pp. 17–18. See also his major study of poverty in the U.K. P. Townsend *Poverty in the United Kingdom* (London: Allen Lane and Penguin Books, 1979).

In part the renewed concern with 'want' reflected generally increased prosperity and the feeling that the standard of living which society guaranteed should be raised accordingly. This led to 'relative' concepts of poverty, by which the extent of poverty is judged not by some absolute historically defined standard of living, but in relation to contemporary standards. By such a moving criterion poverty is obviously more likely to persist, since there will always be certain sections of society that are badly off in the sense that they receive below-average incomes. Thus renewed interest in poverty stemmed to a considerable extent from a recognition that it is incumbent on society to assist the *relatively* deprived.[6]

One consequence of taking this type of a rigidly relativist view is that poverty cannot — simply cannot — be eliminated, and an anti-poverty programme can never really be quite successful. As Fiegehen, Lansley and Smith note, there will always be certain sections of society that are badly off in relative terms. That particular feature can be changed if the relative approach is differently characterized, e.g., checking the number below 60% of median income (the answer *can* be zero). But it remains difficult to judge, in any purely relative view, how successful an anti-poverty programme is, and to rank the relative merits of different strategies, since gains shared by all tend to get discounted. It also has the implication that a general decline in prosperity with lots of additional people in misery — say due to a severe recession or depression — need not show up as a sharp increase in poverty since the relative picture need not change. It is clear that somewhere in the process of refining the concept of poverty from what is viewed as the crudities of Charles Booth's or Seebohm Rowntree's old-fashioned criteria, we have been made to abandon here an essential characteristic of poverty, replacing it with some imperfect representation of *inequality* as such.

That poverty should in fact be viewed straightforwardly as an issue of inequality has, in fact, been argued by several authors. The American sociologists Miller and Roby have put their position thus:

Casting the issue of poverty in terms of stratification leads to regarding poverty as an issue of inequality. In this approach, we move away from efforts to measure poverty lines with pseudo-scientific accuracy. Instead, we look at the nature and size of the differences between the bottom 20 or 10 per cent and the rest of the society.[7]

---

[6]G. Fiegehen, P. Lansley and A. Smith *Poverty and Progress in Britain 1953–73* (Cambridge: Cambridge University Press, 1977) pp. 2–3.

[7]S. Miller and P. Roby 'Poverty: Changing Social Stratification', in P. Townsend (ed.) *The Concept of Poverty* (London: Heinemann, 1971). See also S. Miller, M. Rein, P. Roby and B. Cross 'Poverty, Inequality and Conflict', *Annals of the American Academy of Political Science*, 1967. Contrast Townsend's (*Poverty in the United Kingdom*) rejection of the identification of poverty with inequality (p. 57).

I have tried to argue elsewhere (Sen (1981), chapter 2) that this view is based on a confusion. A sharp fall in general prosperity causing widespread starvation and hardship must be seen by any acceptable criterion of poverty as an intensification of poverty. But the stated view of poverty "as an issue of inequality" can easily miss this if the *relative* distribution is unchanged and there is no change in "the differences between the bottom 20 or 10 per cent and the rest of the society". For example, recognising starvation as poverty is scarcely a matter of "pseudo-scientific accuracy"!

It can, however, be argued that such sharp declines are most unlikely in rich countries, and we can forget those possibilities. But that empirical point does nothing to preserve the basic adequacy of a conceptualisation of poverty which should be able to deal with a wide variety of counter-factual circumstances. Furthermore, it is not clear that such declines cannot really take place in rich countries. A measure of poverty should have been able to reflect the Dutch "hunger winter"[8] of 1944–45, when widespread starvation was acute. And it must not fail to notice the collapse that would surely visit Britain if Mrs. Thatcher's quest for a "leaner and fitter" British economy goes on much longer. The tendency of many of these measures to look plausible in situations of growth, ignoring the possibility of contraction, betrays the timing of the birth of these measures in the balmy sixties when the only possible direction seemed forward.

3. The Policy Definition

While one could easily reject a *fully* relativised view of poverty, making poverty just "an issue of inequality", it is possible to adopt a *primarily* relativised view without running into quite the same problems. The poverty line that has been most commonly used in recent studies of British poverty is the one given by the Official Supplementary Benefit scale,[9] and this scale has been consistently revised with attention being paid to the average level of British income. In fact, the scale has been revised upwards faster than the average income growth, and the poverty line in real terms did in fact double between July 1948 and November 1975.[10] Using this poverty line, adjusted for cost-of-liv-

---

[8]This famine was indeed spread very widely across the Dutch population, thereby making the relative extents of deprivation quite muddled: see W. Aykroyd *The Conquest of Famine* (London: Chatto and Windus, 1974) and Z. Stein, M. Susser, G. Saenger, and F. Marolla *Famine and Human Development: The Dutch Hunger Winter of 1944–1945* (London: Oxford University Press, 1975).

[9]See, for example Atkinson (*Poverty in Britain and the Reform of Social Security*), Bull, Fiegehen, Lansley and Smith, R. Berthoud, J. Brown, and S. Cooper *Poverty and the Development of Anti-Poverty Policy in the UK* (London: Heinemann, 1981), and Beckerman and Clark.

[10]Beckerman and Clark, *Poverty and Social Security in Britain Since 1961*, p. 4.

ing changes on a month to month basis, Beckerman and Clark (1982) have estimated that the number of persons in poverty in Britain went *up* by about 59 per cent between 1961–63 and 1974–76 (p. 3). This rise is not entirely due to the upward revision of the poverty line, and another important factor is the demographic change associated with an increase in the number of pensioners in the British population, but the upward trend of the poverty line is certainly a major influence in this direction.[11]

This practice of using the Supplementary Benefit scale as the poverty line is open to some obvious problems of its own. Not the least of this is the perversity whereby an increase in the attempt by the State to deal with poverty and low incomes by raising the Supplementary Benefit scale will tend to increase rather than diminish the measured level of poverty, by raising the poverty line. In this view, *helping* more is read as more help being *needed*. The most effective strategy for the government to adopt to reduce the number of the "poor", under this approach, is to *cut*, rather than *raise*, the level of assistance through Supplementary Benefits. This can scarcely be right.

Identifying the poverty line with the Supplementary Benefit scale belongs to a more general tradition, which the United States President's Commission on Income Maintenance in 1969 called the "policy definition" of poverty.[12] It is a level of income that is seen as something "the society feels some responsibility for providing to all persons". This approach too is, I believe, fundamentally flawed.[13] The problem is that the level of benefits is determined by a variety of considerations going well beyond reflecting the cut-off point of identified poverty. For one thing, it reflects what is feasible. But the fact that the elimination of some specific deprivation — even of starvation — might be seen, given particular circumstances, as unfeasible does not change the fact of that deprivation. Inescapable poverty is still poverty. Furthermore, the decisions regarding State assistance will reflect — aside from feasibility considerations — other pressures, e.g., pulls and pushes of politically important groups, policy objectives *other than* poverty removal (such as reduction of inequality). Attempts to read the poverty line from the assistance level are riddled with pitfalls. If Mrs. Thatcher decides today that the country "cannot afford" the present level of Supplementary

---

[11]Beckerman and Clark, pp. 3–4. A big factor in this increase in the Beckerman–Clark calculation is their procedure of adjusting the poverty line for cost-of-living increase every month in between the official adjustments of the Supplementary Benefit scale, so that those whose incomes were raised exactly to the Supplementary Benefit level through that scheme would shortly appear as being *below* the Beckerman–Clark poverty line as a result of the monthly adjustments.

[12]U.S. President's Commission on Income Maintenance *Poverty amid Plenty* (Washington, D.C.: U.S. Government Printing Office, 1969), p. 8.

[13]A. Sen *Poverty and Famines: An Essay on Entitlement and Deprivation* (Oxford: Oxford University Press, 1981) pp. 17–21.

Benefits and the scale must be cut, that decision in itself will not reduce poverty in Britain (through lowering the poverty line below which people count as poor).

4. The Absolutist Core

Neither the various relativist views, nor seeing poverty as "an issue in inequality", nor using the so-called "policy definition", can therefore serve as an adequate theoretical basis for conceptualising poverty. There is, I would argue, an irreducible absolutist core in the idea of poverty. One element of that absolutist core is obvious enough, though the modern literature on the subject often does its best to ignore it. If there is starvation and hunger, then—no matter what the *relative* picture looks like—there clearly is poverty. In this sense the relative picture—if relevant—has to take a back seat behind the possibly dominating absolutist consideration. While it might be thought that this type of poverty—involving malnutrition or hunger—is simply irrelevant to the richer countries, that is empirically far from clear, even though the frequency of this type of deprivation is certainly much less in these countries.

Even when we shift our attention from hunger and look at other aspects of living standard, the absolutist aspect of poverty does not disappear. The fact that some people have a lower standard of living than others is certainly proof of inequality, but by itself it cannot be a proof of poverty unless we know something more about the standard of living that these people do in fact enjoy. It would be absurd to call someone poor just because he had the means to buy only one Cadillac a day when others in that community could buy two of these cars each day. The absolute considerations cannot be inconsequential for conceptualising poverty.

The temptation to think of poverty as being altogether relative arises partly from the fact that the *absolute* satisfaction of some of the needs might depend on a person's *relative* position vis-à-vis others in much the same way as—in the case discussed earlier—the absolute advantage of a person to enjoy a lonely beach may depend upon his relative advantage in the space of knowledge regarding the existence and access to such beaches. The point was very well caught by Adam Smith when he was discussing the concept of necessaries in *The Wealth of Nations*:

> By necessaries I understand not only the commodities which are indispensably necessary for the support of life, but what ever the custom of the country renders it indecent for creditable people, even the lowest order, to be without. . . . Custom . . . has rendered leather shoes a necessary of life in England. The poorest creditable person of either sex would be ashamed to appear in public without them.[14]

[14]A. Smith *An Inquiry into the Nature and Causes of the Wealth of Nations* (London: Home University Library, 1776) pp. 351–2.

In this view to be able to avoid shame, an eighteenth century English-man has to have leather shoes. It may be true that this situation has come to pass precisely because the typical members of that community happen to possess leather shoes, but the person in question needs leather shoes not so much to be *less ashamed* than others—that rela-tive question is not even posed by Adam Smith—but simply not to be ashamed, *which as an achievement is an absolute one.*

5. Capabilities Contrasted with Commodities, Characteristics and Utilities

At this stage of this discussion I would like to take up a somewhat more general question, *viz.*, that of the right focus for assessing stan-dard of living. In my Tanner Lecture (given at Stanford University in 1979) and my Hennipman Lectures (given at the University of Amster-dam in 1982), I have tried to argue that the right focus is neither commodities, nor characteristics (in the sense of Gorman and Lancas-ter), nor utility, but something that may be called a person's capabil-ity.[15] The contrasts may be brought out by an illustration. Take a bicycle. It is, of course, a commodity. It has several characteristics, and let us concentrate on one particular characteristic, *viz.*, transportation. Having a bike gives a person the ability to move about in a certain way that he may not be able to do without the bike. So the transportation *characteristic* of the bike gives the person the *capability* of moving in a certain way. That capability may give the person utility or happiness if he seeks such movement or finds it pleasurable. So there is, as it were, a *sequence* from a commodity (in this case a bike), to characteristics (in this case, transportation), to capability to function (in this case, the ability to move), to utility (in this case, pleasure from moving).

It can be argued that it is the third category—that of capability to function—that comes closest to the notion of standard of living. The commodity ownership or availability itself is not the right focus since it does not tell us what the person can, in fact, do. I may not be able to use the bike if—say—I happen to be handicapped. Having the bike—or something else with that characteristic—may provide the basis for a contribution to the standard of living, but it is not in itself a constituent part of that standard. On the other hand, while utility reflects the use of the bike, it does not concentrate on the use itself, but on the mental reaction to that use. If I am of a cheerful disposition and enjoy life even without being able to move around, because I succeed in having my heart leap up every time I behold a rainbow in the sky, I am no doubt a happy person, but it does not follow that I have a high standard of

[15]A. Sen 'Equality of What?', in S. McMurrin (ed.) *The Tanner Lectures on Human Values* (Cambridge: Cambridge University Press, 1980); A. Sen 'The Standard of Living', Hennipman Lecture given on 22 April 1982. Also A. Sen *Choice, Welfare and Measure-ment* (Oxford: Oxford University Press, 1982) "Introduction", pp. 30–1.

living. A grumbling rich man may well be less happy than a contented peasant, but he does have a higher standard of living than that peasant; the comparison of standard of living is not a comparison of utilities. So the constituent part of the standard of living is not the good, nor its characteristics, but the ability to do various things by using that good or those characteristics, and it is that ability rather than the mental reaction to that ability in the form of happiness that, in this view, reflects the standard of living.

6. Absolute Capabilities and Relative Commodity Requirements

If this thesis of the capability focus of standard of living is accepted (and I believe the case for it is quite strong), then several other things follow. One of them happens to be some sorting out of the absolute-relative disputation in the conceptualisation of poverty. At the risk of oversimplification, I would like to say that poverty is an absolute notion in the space of capabilities but very often it will take a relative form in the space of commodities or characteristics.

Let us return to Adam Smith. The capability to which he was referring was the one of avoiding shame from the inability to meet the demands of convention.[16] The commodity needed for it, in a particular illustration that Smith considered, happened to be a pair of leather shoes. As we consider richer and richer communities, the commodity requirement of the same capability — avoiding this type of shame — increases. As Adam Smith (1776) noted, "the Greeks and Romans lived . . . very comfortably though they had no linen," but "in the present time, through the greater part of Europe, a creditable day-labourer would be ashamed to appear in public without a linen shirt" (pp. 351 – 2). In the commodity space, therefore, escape from poverty in the form of avoiding shame requires a varying collection of commodities — and it is this collection and the resources needed for it that happen to be relative *vis-à-vis* the situations of others. But on the space of the capabilities themselves — the direct constituent of the standard of living — escape from poverty has an absolute requirement, to wit, avoidance of this type of shame. Not so much having equal shame as others, but just not being ashamed, absolutely.

---

[16]This particular capability, emphasized by Adam Smith, clearly has a strong psychological component in a way that other capabilities that have been thought to be basic may not have, e.g., the ability to be well nourished or to move about freely or to be adequately sheltered (see Sen 'Equality of What?'). The contrast between capability and utility may, in some ways, be less sharp in the case of capabilities involving psychology, even though it would be impossible to catch the various psychological dimensions within the undifferentiated metric of utility no matter whether defined in terms of pleasure and pain, or choice, or desire fulfilment. In fact, the capability of being happy can be seen as just one particular capability, and utility — shorn of its claim to unique relevance — can be given some room *within* the general approach of capabilities. These issues have been further discussed in Sen *Choice, Welfare and Measurement*.

If we view the problem of conceptualising poverty in this light, then there is no conflict between the irreducible absolutist element in the notion of poverty (related to capabilities and the standard of living) and the "thoroughgoing relativity" to which Peter Townsend refers, if the latter is interpreted as applying to commodities and resources. If Townsend puts his finger wrong, this happens when he points towards the untenability of the idea of absolute needs. Of course, needs too can vary between one society and another, but the cases that are typically discussed in this context involve a different bundle of commodities and a higher real value of resources fulfilling the *same* general needs. When Townsend estimates the resources required for being able to "participate in the activities of the community", he is in fact estimating the varying resource requirements of fulfilling the same absolute need.

In a poor community the resources or commodities needed to participate in the standard activities of the community might be very little indeed. In such a community the perception of poverty is primarily concerned with the commodity requirements of fulfilling nutritional needs and perhaps some needs of being clothed, sheltered and free from disease. This is the world of Charles Booth or Seebohm Rowntree in nineteenth century or early twentieth century London or York, and that of poverty estimation today, say, in India. The more physical needs tend to dominate over the needs of communal participation, on which Townsend focuses, at this less affluent stage both because the nutritional and other physical needs would tend to have a more prominent place in the standard-of-living estimation and also because the requirements of participation are rather easily fulfilled. For a richer community, however, the nutritional and other physical requirements (such as clothing as protection from climatic conditions) are typically already met, and the needs of communal participation—while absolutely no different in the space of capabilities—will have a much higher demand in the space of commodities and that of resources. Relative deprivation, in this case, is nothing other than a relative failure in the commodity space—or resource space—having the effect of an absolute deprivation in the capability space.

The varying commodity requirements of meeting the same absolute need applies not merely to avoiding shame from failing to meet conventional requirements, and to being able to participate in the activities of the community, but also to a number of other needs. It has been pointed out by Theo Cooper in a regrettably unpublished paper (Cooper (1971)) that in West Europe or North America a child might not be able to follow his school programme unless the child happens to have access to a television. If this is in fact the case, then the child without a television in Britain or in Ireland would be clearly worse off—have a lower standard of living—in this respect than a child, say, in Tanzania without a television. It is not so much that the British or the Irish child has a brand new need, but that to meet the same need as the

Tanzanian child—the need to be educated—the British or the Irish child must have more commodities. Of course, the British child might fulfill the need better than the Tanzanian with the help of the television—I am not expressing a view on this—but the fact remains that the television is a necessity for the British child for school education in a way it is not for the Tanzanian child.

Similarly, in a society in which most families own cars, public transport services might be poor, so that a carless family in such a society might be *absolutely poor* in a way it might not have been in a poorer society. To take another example, widespread ownership of refrigerators and freezers in a community might affect the structure of food retailing, thereby making it more difficult in such a society to make do without having these facilities oneself.

It is, of course, not my point that there is no difference in the standards of living of rich and poor countries. There are enormous differences in the fulfilment of some of the most basic capabilities, *e.g.*, to meet nutritional requirements, to escape avoidable disease, to be sheltered, to be clothed, to be able to travel, and to be educated. But whereas the commodity requirements of these capability fulfilments are not tremendously variable between one community and another, such variability is enormous in the case of other capabilities. The capability to live without shame emphasized by Adam Smith, that of being able to participate in the activities of the community discussed by Peter Townsend, that of having self-respect discussed by John Rawls,[17] are examples of capabilities with extremely variable resource requirements.[18] And as it happens the resource requirements typically go up in these cases with the average prosperity of the nation, so that the relativist view acquires plausibility despite the absolutist basis of the concept of poverty in terms of capabilities and deprivation.

It is perhaps worth remarking that this type of *derived* relativism does not run into the difficulties noted earlier with thoroughgoing relativity of the kind associated with seeing poverty as "an issue of inequality". When the Dutch in the hunger winter of 1944–45 found themselves suddenly in much reduced circumstances, their commodity requirements of capability fulfilments did not go down immediately to reduce the bite of poverty, as under the rigidly relativist account. While the commodity requirements are sensitive to the opulence and the affluence of the community in general, this relationship is neither one of instant adjustment, nor is it a straightforward one to be captured simply by looking at the average income, or even the current Lorenz

---

[17]J. Rawls *A Theory of Justice* (Cambridge: Harvard University Press, 1971) pp. 440–6.

[18]Education is perhaps an intermediate case, where the resource variability is important but perhaps not as extreme as with some of these other capabilities related to social psychology.

curve of income distribution. Response to communal standards is a more complex process than that.

7. Primary Goods and Varying Requirements Between and Within Communities

I should also remark on a point of some general philosophical interest related to this way of viewing personal advantage and social poverty. The philosophical underpinning of the recent poverty literature has been helped enormously by John Rawls's far-reaching analysis of social justice. One respect in which Rawls differs sharply from the utility-based theories, e.g., utilitarianism, is his focus on what he calls "primary goods" rather than on utility in judging a person's advantage. Our focus on capability differs *both* from the utilitarian concern with just mental reactions and from the Rawlsian concern with primary goods as such, though the approach of capabilities is much influenced by Rawls's moral analysis. Making comparisons in the capability space is quite different from doing that either in the utility space (as done by utilitarians), or in the space of commodities or primary goods (even when this is done very broadly, as Rawls does). In this view the variables to focus on consist of such factors as *meeting* nutritional requirements rather than either the pleasure from meeting those requirements (as under utilitarianism), or the *income* or *food* needed to meet those requirements (as in the Rawlsian approach). Similarly, the capability approach focuses on meeting the need of self-respect rather than *either* the pleasure from having self-respect, *or* what Rawls calls "the social basis of self respect".[19] The capability approach differs from the traditional utility-based analysis as strongly as the Rawlsian approach does, but it continues to concentrate on human beings — their capabilities in this case — rather than moving with Rawls to incomes, goods and characteristics.[20] Rawls himself motivated his focus on primary goods, using arguments that rely on the importance of capabilities. What the capability approach does is to make that basis explicit and then it goes on to acknowledge the enormous variability that exists in the commodity requirements of capability fulfilment. In this sense, the capability approach can be seen as one possible *extension* of the Rawlsian perspective.

The extension makes a substantial practical difference not merely

[19]Rawls, pp. 60–5. Note, however, that Rawls vacillates between taking "the *bases* of self-respect" as a primary good (this is consistent with taking income as a primary good), and referring to "self-respect" itself as a primary good, which is closer to our concern with capabilities.

[20]I have discussed this contrast more extensively in A. Sen 'Equality of What?', *Choice, Welfare and Measurement* (Oxford: Blackwell, 1982) pp. 30–1; 'The Standard of Living'. See also J. Rawls 'Social Unity and Primary Goods', in A. Sen and B. Williams (eds.) *Utilitarianism and Beyond* (Cambridge: Cambridge University Press, 1982) pp. 168–9.

because the commodity requirements of capability fulfilment vary between one community and another, or one country and another, but also because there are differences *within* a given country or community in the mapping from commodities to capabilities. In a country with various racial groups, even the food requirements of nutritional fulfilment may vary a great deal from one group to another.[21] For example, in India the people in the state of Kerala have both the lowest level of average calorie intake in the country and the highest level of longevity and high nutritional fulfilment. While part of the difference is certainly due to distributional considerations and the availability of back-up medical services, the physiological differences in the calorie requirements of the Malayali in Kerala compared with, say, the larger Punjabi, is also a factor.

This type of *intra*-country or *intra*-community difference can be very important even in rich countries and even those with a basically homogeneous population. This is because of other variations, e.g., that of age. Of particular relevance in this context is the fact that a high proportion of those who are recognized as poor in the richer countries are also old or disabled in some way.[22] Inability to earn an adequate income often reflects a physical disadvantage of some kind, and this disadvantage is not irrelevant to the conversion of goods into capabilities. While the nutritional requirements may not increase with age or disability — may even decrease somewhat — the resource requirements of — say — movement, or of participation in the activities of the community, may be considerably larger for older or disabled people. The focus on absolute capabilities brings out the importance of these *intra*-community variations in the commodity space, going well beyond the *inter*-community variations emphasized in the typical relativist literature.

While it might not be easy to take full note of such intra-community variations in practical studies of poverty, it is important to have conceptual clarity on this question and to seek more sensitive practical measures in the long run. I should think the direction in which to go would be that of some kind of an efficiency-adjusted level of income with "income" units reflecting command over capabilities rather than over commodities. This will be, I do not doubt, quite a rewarding field of research.

---

[21]This is in addition to inter-individual and inter-temporal variations emphasized by P. Sukhatme *Nutrition and Poverty* (New Delhi: Indian Agricultural Research Institute, 1977), T. Srinivasan 'Malnutrition: Some Measurement and Policy Issues', mimeographed, World Bank, Washington, D.C., 1979, and others.

[22]See D. Wedderburn *The Aged in the Welfare State* (London: Bell, 1961) and Atkinson *Poverty in Britain and the Reform of Social Security*.

8. Concluding Remarks

I end with a few concluding statements. First, I have argued that despite the emerging unanimity in favour of taking a relative as opposed to an absolute view of poverty, there is a good case for an absolutist approach. The dispute on absolute vs. relative conceptualisation of poverty can be better resolved by being more explicit on the particular space (e.g., commodities, incomes, or capabilities) in which the concept is to be based.

Second, I have outlined the case for using an absolute approach to poverty related to the notion of *capability*. Capabilities differ both from commodities and characteristics, on the one hand, and utilities, on the other. The capability approach shares with John Rawls the rejection of the utilitarian obsession with one type of mental reaction, but differs from Rawls' concentration on primary goods by focusing on capabilities of human beings rather than characteristics of goods they possess.

Third, an absolute approach in the space of capabilities translates into a relative approach in the space of commodities, resources and incomes in dealing with some important capabilities, such as avoiding shame from failure to meet social conventions, participating in social activities, and retaining self-respect.

Fourth, since poverty removal is not the only object of social policy and inequality removal has a status of its own, taking an absolutist view of poverty must not be confused with being indifferent to inequality as such. While poverty may be seen as a failure to reach some absolute level of capability, the issue of inequality of capabilities is an important one—on its own right—for public policy.[23]

Fifth, while the inter-country and inter-community differences have been much discussed in the context of conceptualising poverty, the differences *within* a country and *within* a community need much more attention because of interpersonal variations in converting commodities into capabilities. This is particularly important since poverty is often associated with handicaps due to disability or age. This problem could perhaps be handled by using efficiency-income units reflecting command over capabilities rather than command over goods and services.

Finally, I have argued that the reasonableness of various axioms that aggregative measures of poverty may or may not be asked to satisfy depend (sometimes in an unobvious—certainly unexplored—way) on whether fundamentally a relative or an absolute approach is being adopted. This has practical implications on the choice of statistical measures to be used. It is important to know whether the poor, relatively speaking, are in some deeper sense absolutely deprived. It makes a difference.

[23]See Sen 'Equality of What?' and 'The Standard of Living'.

6

CAROLE PATEMAN

Feminist Critiques of the
Public – Private Dichotomy

THE DICHOTOMY BETWEEN the private and the public is central to almost two centuries of feminist writing and political struggle; it is, ultimately, what the feminist movement is about. Although some feminists treat the dichotomy as a universal, trans-historical and trans-cultural feature of human existence, feminist criticism is primarily directed at the separation and opposition between the public and private spheres in liberal theory and practice.

The relationship between feminism and liberalism is extremely close but also exceedingly complex. The roots of both doctrines lie in the emergence of individualism as a general theory of social life; neither liberalism nor feminism is conceivable without some conception of individuals as free and equal beings, emancipated from the ascribed, hierarchical bonds of traditional society. But if liberalism and feminism share a common origin, their adherents have often been opposed over the past two hundred years. The direction and scope of feminist criticism of liberal conceptions of the public and the private have varied greatly in different phases of the feminist movement. An analysis of this criticism is made more complicated because liberalism is inherently ambiguous about the 'public' and the 'private', and feminists and liberals disagree about where and why the dividing line is to be drawn between the two spheres, or, according to certain contemporary feminist arguments, whether it should be drawn at all.

Feminism is often seen as nothing more than the completion of the liberal or bourgeois revolution, as an extension of liberal principles and rights to women as well as men. The demand for equal rights has, of course, always been an important part of feminism. However, the attempt to universalise liberalism has more far-reaching consequences than is often appreciated because, in the end, it inevitably challenges liberalism itself.[1] Liberal feminism has radical implications, not least in challenging the separation and opposition between the private and public spheres that is fundamental to liberal theory and practice. The liberal contrast between private and public is more than a distinction between two kinds of social activities. The public sphere, and the principles that govern it, are seen as separate from, or independent of, the relationships in the private sphere. A familiar illustration of this claim is the long controversy between liberal and radical political scientists about participation, the radicals denying the liberal claim that the social inequalities of the private sphere are irrelevant to questions about the political equality, universal suffrage and associated civil liberties of the public realm.

Not all feminists, however, are liberals; 'feminism' goes far beyond liberal-feminism. Other feminists explicitly reject liberal conceptions of the private and public and see the social structure of liberalism as the political problem, not a starting point from which equal rights can be claimed. They have much in common with the radical and socialist critics of liberalism who rely on 'organic' theories (to use Benn and Gaus's terminology) but they differ sharply in their analysis of the liberal state. In short, feminists, unlike other radicals, raise the generally neglected problem of the patriarchal character of liberalism.

I. Liberalism and Patriarchalism

Benn and Gaus's account of the liberal conception of the public and the private illustrates very nicely some major problems in liberal theory. They accept that the private and the public are central categories of liberalism, but they do not explain why these two terms are crucial or why the private sphere is contrasted with and opposed to the 'public' rather than the 'political' realm. Similarly, they note that liberal arguments leave it unclear whether civil society is private or public but, although they state that in both of their liberal models the family is paradigmatically private, they fail to pursue the question why, in this case, liberals usually also see civil society as private. Benn and Gaus's account of liberalism also illustrates its abstract, ahistorical character and, in what is omitted and taken for granted, provides a good example of the theoretical discussions that feminists are now sharply criticising. The account bears out Eisenstein's claim that 'the ideology of public

---

[1]The subversive character of liberal-feminism has recently been uncovered by Z. Eisenstein, *The Radical Future of Liberal Feminism* (Longman, New York, 1981).

and private life' invariably presents 'the division between public and private life, . . . as reflecting the development of the bourgeois liberal state, not the patriarchal ordering of the bourgeois state'.[2]

The term 'ideology' is appropriate here because the profound ambiguity of the liberal conception of the private and public obscures and mystifies the social reality it helps constitute. Feminists argue that liberalism is structured by patriarchal as well as class relations, and that the dichotomy between the private and the public obscures the subjection of women to men within an apparently universal, egalitarian and individualist order. Benn and Gaus's account assumes that the reality of our social life is more or less adequately captured in liberal conceptions. They do not recognise that 'liberalism' is patriarchal-liberalism and that the separation and opposition of the public and private spheres is an unequal opposition between women and men. They thus take the talk of 'individuals' in liberal theory at face value although, from the period when the social contract theorists attacked the patriarchalists, liberal theorists have excluded women from the scope of their apparently universal arguments.[3] One reason why the exclusion goes unnoticed is that the separation of the private and public is presented in liberal theory as if it applied to all individuals in the same way. It is often claimed—by anti-feminists today, but by feminists in the nineteenth century, most of whom accepted the doctrine of 'separate spheres'—that the two spheres are separate, but equally important and valuable. The way in which women and men are differentially located within private life and the public world is, as I shall indicate, a complex matter, but underlying a complicated reality is the belief that women's natures are such that they are properly subject to men and their proper place is in the private, domestic sphere. Men properly inhabit, and rule within, both spheres. The essential feminist argument is that the doctrine of 'separate but equal', and the ostensible individualism and egalitarianism of liberal theory, obscure the patriarchal reality of a social structure of inequality and the domination of women by men.

In theory, liberalism and patriarchalism stand irrevocably opposed to

---

[2]Ibid., p. 223.

[3]J. S. Mill is an exception to this generalisation, but Benn and Gaus do not mention *The Subjection of Women*. It might be objected that B. Bosanquet, for example, refers in *The Philosophical Theory of the State* (Ch. X, 6), to 'the two persons who are [the] head' of the family. However, Bosanquet is discussing Hegel, and he shows no understanding that Hegel's philosophy rests on the explicit, and philosophically justified, exclusion of women from headship of a family or from participating in civil society or the state. Bosanquet's reference to 'two persons' thus requires a major critique of Hegel, not mere exposition. Liberal arguments cannot be universalised by a token reference to 'women and men' instead of 'men'. On Hegel see P. Mills, 'Hegel and "The Woman Question": Recognition and Intersubjectivity', in L. Clark and L. Lange (eds.), *The Sexism of Social and Political Theory* (University of Toronto Press, Toronto, 1979). (I am grateful to Jerry Gaus for drawing my attention to Bosanquet's remarks.)

each other. Liberalism is an individualist, egalitarian, conventionalist doctrine; patriarchalism claims that hierarchical relations of subordination necessarily follow from the natural characteristics of men and women. In fact, the two doctrines were successfully reconciled through the answer given by the contract theorists in the seventeenth century to the subversive question of who counted as free and equal individuals. The conflict with the patriarchalists did not extend to women or conjugal relations; the latter were excluded from individualist arguments and the battle was fought out over the relation of adult sons to their fathers.

The theoretical basis for the liberal separation of the public and the private was provided in Locke's *Second Treatise*. He argued against Filmer that political power is conventional and can justifiably be exercised over free and equal adult individuals only with their consent. Political power must not be confused with paternal power over children in the private, family sphere, which is a natural relationship that ends at the maturity, and hence freedom and equality, of (male) children. Commentators usually fail to notice that Locke's separation of the family and the political is also a sexual division. Although he argued that natural differences between men, such as age or talents, are irrelevant to their political equality, he agrees with Filmer's patriarchal claim that the natural differences between men and women entail the subjection of women to men or, more specifically, wives to husbands. Indeed, in Locke's statement at the beginning of the *Second Treatise* that he will show why political power is distinctive, he takes it for granted that the rule of husbands over wives is included in other (nonpolitical) forms of power. He explicitly agrees with Filmer that a wife's subordination to her husband has a 'Foundation in Nature' and that the husband's will must prevail in the household as he is naturally 'the abler and the stronger'.[4] But a natural subordinate cannot at the same time be free and equal. Thus women (wives) are excluded from the status of 'individual' and so from participating in the public world of equality, consent and convention.

It may appear that Locke's separation of paternal from political power can also be characterised as a separation of the private from the public. In one sense this is so; the public sphere can be seen as encompassing all social life apart from domestic life. Locke's theory also shows how the private and public spheres are grounded in opposing principles of association which are exemplified in the conflicting status of women and men; natural subordination stands opposed to free indi-

---

[4]J. Locke, *Two Treatises of Government*, 2nd edn, P. Lastlett (ed.) (Cambridge University Press, Cambridge, 1967), Bk. I, Ch. 47; Bk. II, Ch. 82. The conflict between the social contract theorists and the patriarchalists is more fully discussed in T. Brennan and C. Pateman, '"Mere Auxiliaries to the Commonwealth": Women and the Origins of Liberalism', *Political Studies*, XXVII (1979), pp. 183–200.

vidualism. The family is based on natural ties of sentiment and blood
and on the sexually ascribed status of wife and husband (mother and
father). Participation in the public sphere is governed by universal,
impersonal and conventional criteria of achievement, interests, rights,
equality and property—liberal criteria, applicable only to men. An
important consequence of this conception of private and public is that
the public world, or civil society, is conceptualised and discussed in
liberal theory (indeed, in almost all political theory) in abstraction
from, or as separate from, the private domestic sphere.

It is important to emphasise at this point that the contemporary
feminist critique of the public–private dichotomy is based on the same
Lockean view of the two categories; domestic life is as paradigmatically
private for feminists as it is in (this interpretation of) Locke's theory.
However, feminists reject the claim that the separation of the private
and the public follows inevitably from the natural characteristics of the
sexes. They argue that a proper understanding of liberal social life is
possible only when it is accepted that the two spheres, the domestic
(private) and civil society (public), held to be separate and opposed, are
inextricably interrelated; they are the two sides of the single coin of
liberal-patriarchalism.

If, at one theoretical level, feminists and liberals are in conflict over a
shared conception of the public and the private, at another level they
are at odds about these very categories. There is another sense in which
the private and public are far from synonymous with Locke's paternal
and political power. Precisely because liberalism conceptualises civil
society in abstraction from ascriptive domestic life, the latter remains
'forgotten' in theoretical discussion. The separation between private
and public is thus re-established as a division *within* civil society itself,
within the world of men. The separation is then expressed in a number
of different ways, not only private and public but also, for example,
'society' and 'state'; or 'economy' and 'politics'; or 'freedom' and 'coercion'; or 'social' and 'political'.[5] Moreover, in *this* version of the separation of private and public, one category, the private, begins to wear the
trousers (to adapt J. L. Austin's patriarchal metaphor for once in an
appropriate context). The public or political aspect of civil society

---

[5]Rawls's two principles of justice provide an example of this division. He states that the
principles 'presuppose that the social structure can be divided into two more or less
distinct parts'. He does not call these private and public, but the 'equal liberties of
citizenship' are usually called 'political' liberties and the 'social and economic inequalities' of the second part are usually seen as part of the 'private' sphere. In Rawls's final
formulation it is clear that the principles refer to civil society and that the family is
outside their scope. Part (b) of the second principle, equality of opportunity, cannot
apply to the family, and part (a), the difference principle, may not apply. A clever son,
say, may be sent to university at the expense of other family members. (I owe this last
point to my student Deborah Kearns.) John Rawls, *A Theory of Justice* (The Belknap Press
of Harvard University Press, Cambridge, Mass., 1971), pp. 61, 302.

tends to get lost, as, for example, Wolin points out in *Politics and Vision*.[6]

The uncertain position of the public sphere develops for very good reason; the apparently universal criteria governing civil society are actually those associated with the liberal conception of the male individual, a conception which is presented as that of *the* individual. The individual is the owner of the property in his person, that is to say, he is seen in abstraction from his ascribed familial relations and those with his fellow men. He is a 'private' individual, but he needs a sphere in which he can exercise his rights and opportunities, pursue his (private) interests and protect and increase his (private) property. If all men ('individuals') are so to act in an orderly fashion, then, as Locke is aware, a public 'umpire' (rather than a hidden — private? — hand), or a representative, liberal state, is required to make and enforce publicly known, equitable laws. Because individualism is, as Benn and Gaus remark, 'the dominant mode of liberal theory and discourse', it is not surprising either that the private and the public appear as the 'obvious' pair of liberal categories, or that the public gets stripped of its trousers and civil society is seen, above all else, as the sphere of private interest, private enterprise and private individuals.[7]

In the late twentieth century the relation between the capitalist economy and the state no longer looks like that between Locke's umpire and civil society and confusion abounds about the boundary between the private and public. But the confusion is unlikely to be remedied from within a theory which 'forgets' that it includes another boundary between private and public. One solution is to reinstate the political in public life. This is the response of Wolin or of Habermas in his rather opaque discussion of the 'principle' of the public sphere, where citizens can form reasoned political judgements.[8] Unlike these theorists, feminist critiques insist that an alternative to the liberal conception must also encompass the relationship between public and domestic life. The question that feminists raise is why the patriarchal character of the separation of a depoliticised public sphere from private life is so easily 'forgotten'; why is the separation of the two worlds

---

[6]Wolin, *Politics and Vision* (Little Brown, Boston, 1960).

[7]It is also the sphere of privacy. J. Reiman, 'Privacy, Intimacy, and Personhood', *Philosophy and Public Affairs*, 6 (1976), p. 39, links 'owning' one's body to the idea of a 'self' and argues this is why privacy is needed. My comments in the text do not explain why liberal theorists typically write of the private and the public rather than the political. An explanation could only be found in a full examination of liberal ambiguities about the public and the political, which takes us far from the purpose of this essay, although the problem arises again below in the context of the feminist slogan 'the personal is the political'.

[8]J. Habermas, 'The Public Sphere', *New German Critique*, VI, no. 3 (1974), pp. 49–55. However, Habermas, like other writers, ignores the fact that women are conventionally held to be deficient in reason and so unfit to participate in a public body.

located within civil society so that public life is implicitly conceptualised as the sphere of men?

The answer to this question can be found only by examining the history of the connection between the separation of production from the household and the emergence of the family as paradigmatically private. When Locke attacked (one aspect of) patriarchalism, husbands were heads of households but their wives played an active, independent part in numerous areas of production. As capitalism and its specific form of sexual as well as class division of labour developed, however, wives were pushed into a few, low-status areas of employment or kept out of economic life altogether, relegated to their 'natural', dependent, place in the private, familial sphere.[9] Today, despite a large measure of civil equality, it appears natural that wives are subordinate just because they are dependent on their husbands for subsistence, and it is taken for granted that liberal social life can be understood without reference to the sphere of subordination, natural relations and women. The old patriarchal argument from nature and women's nature was thus transformed as it was modernised and incorporated into liberal-capitalism. Theoretical and practical attention became fixed exclusively on the public area, on civil society — on 'the social' or on 'the economy' — and domestic life was assumed irrelevant to social and political theory or the concerns of men of affairs. The fact that patriarchalism is an essential, indeed constitutive, part of the theory and practice of liberalism remains obscured by the apparently impersonal, universal dichotomy between private and public within civil society itself.

The intimate relation between the private and the natural is obscured when, as in Benn and Gaus's account, the private and the public are discussed in abstraction from their historical development and also from other ways of expressing this fundamental structural separation within liberalism. I have already observed that, when the separation is located within civil society, the dichotomy between private and public is referred to in a variety of ways (and a full account of liberalism would have to explain these variations). Similarly, the feminist understanding of the private and the public, and the feminist critique of their separation and opposition, are sometimes presented in these terms, but the argument is also formulated using the categories of nature and culture, or personal and political, or morality and power, and, of course, women and men and female and male. In popular (and academic) consciousness the duality of female and male often serves to encapsulate or represent

[9]In the present context these remarks must be very condensed. For amplification see Brennan and Pateman, '"Mere Auxiliaries to the Commonwealth": Women and the Origins of Liberalism'; R. Hamilton, *The Liberation of Women: A Study of Patriarchy and Capitalism* (Allen & Unwin, London, 1978); H. Hartmann, 'Capitalism, Patriarchy and Job Segregation by Sex', *Signs*, 1, no. 3, Pt. 2 (Supp. Spring 1976) pp. 137–70; A. Oakley, *Housewife* (A. Lane, London, 1974), Chs. 2 and 3.

the series (or circle) of liberal separations and oppositions: female, or — nature, personal, emotional, love, private, intuition, morality, ascription, particular, subjection; male, or — culture, political, reason, justice, public, philosophy, power, achievement, universal, freedom. The most fundamental and general of these oppositions associates women with nature and men with culture, and several contemporary feminists have framed their critiques in these terms.

II. Nature and Culture

Patriarchalism rests on the appeal to nature and the claim that women's natural function of childbearing prescribes their domestic and subordinate place in the order of things. J. S. Mill wrote in the nineteenth century that the depth of the feelings surrounding the appeal to nature was 'the most intense and most deeply-rooted of all those which gather round and protect old institutions and customs'.[10] In the 1980s, when women in the liberal democracies have won citizenship and a large measure of legal equality with men, the arguments of the organised anti-feminist movement illustrate that the appeal to nature has lost none of its resonance. From the seventeenth century a question has been persistently asked by a few female voices: 'If all men are born free, how is it that all women are born slaves?'[11] The usual answer, vigorously presented by Mary Wollstonecraft in the *Vindication of the Rights of Women* in 1792, and today by feminist critics of the sexism of children's books, schooling and the media, is that what are called women's natural characteristics are actually, in Wollstonecraft's phrase, 'artificial', a product of women's education or lack of it. However, even the most radical changes in educational practice will not affect women's natural, biological capacity to bear children. This difference between the sexes is independent of history and culture, and so it is perhaps not surprising that the natural difference, and the opposition between (women's) nature and (men's) culture, has been central to some well-known feminist attempts to explain the apparently universal subordination of women. Arguments focusing on nature/culture fall into two broad categories, the anthropological and the radical feminist.[12]

In one of the most influential anthropological discussions, Ortner argues that the only way to explain why the value universally assigned

[10]J. S. Mill, *The Subjection of Women* in A. Rossi (ed.), *Essays on Sex Equality* (University of Chicago Press, Chicago, 1970), pp. 125–242, at p. 126.

[11]M. Astell, 'Reflections on Marriage' (published 1706), cited in L. Stone, *The Family, Sex and Marriage in England: 1500–1800* (Weidenfeld & Nicolson, London, 1977), p. 240.

[12]'Radical feminists' is the term used to distinguish the feminists who argue that the male–female opposition is the cause of women's oppression from 'liberal feminists' and 'socialist feminists'.

to women and their activities is lower than that assigned to men and their pursuits is that women are 'a symbol' of all 'that every culture defines as being of a lower order of existence than itself'.[13] That is, women and domestic life symbolise nature. Humankind attempts to transcend a merely natural existence so that nature is always seen as of a lower order than culture. Culture becomes identified as the creation and the world of men because women's biology and bodies place them closer to nature than men, and because their childrearing and domestic tasks, dealing with unsocialised infants and with raw materials, bring them into closer contact with nature. Women and the domestic sphere thus appear inferior to the cultural sphere and male activities, and women are seen as necessarily subordinate to men.

It is unclear whether Ortner is arguing that women's domestic activities symbolise nature, are part of nature or, rather, place women in a mediating position between nature and culture. She argues that the opposition between women/nature and men/culture is itself a cultural construct and not given in nature; 'Woman is not "in reality" any closer to (or further from) nature than man—both have consciousness, both are mortal. But there are certainly reasons why she appears that way.'[14] However, Ortner fails to give sufficient weight to the fundamental fact that men and women are social and cultural beings, or to its corollary that 'nature' always has a social meaning, a meaning that, moreover, varies widely in different societies and in different historical periods. Even if women and their tasks have been universally devalued, it does not follow that we can understand this important fact of human existence by asking questions in universal terms and looking for general answers formulated in terms of universal dichotomies. The distinction between domestic, private women's life and the public world of men does not have the same meaning in pre-modern European society as in present liberal-capitalism, and to see both the latter and hunter-gatherer societies from the perspective of a general opposition between nature and culture, or public and private, can lead only to an emphasis on biology or 'nature'. Rosaldo recently criticised arguments about women's subordination that, like Ortner's, implicitly rest on the question, 'How did it begin?' She points out that to seek a universally

---

[13]S. B. Ortner, 'Is Female to Male as Nature is to Culture?' in M. Z. Rosaldo and L. Lamphere (eds.), *Women, Culture and Society* (Stanford University Press, Stanford, 1974), p. 72. Ortner says nothing about the writers over the past two centuries who have glorified nature and seen culture as the cause of vice and inequality. However, the meaning of 'nature' in these arguments is extremely complex and the relationship of women to nature is far from clear. Rousseau, for instance, segregates women and men even in domestic life because women's natures are seen as a threat to civil life (culture). For some comments on this question see my '"The Disorder of Women": Women, Love and the Sense of Justice', *Ethics*, 91 (1980), pp. 20–34.

[14]Ortner, 'Is Female to Male as Nature is to Culture', p. 87.

applicable answer inevitably opposes 'woman' to 'man', and gives rise to a separation of domestic life from 'culture' or 'society' because of the 'presumably panhuman functions' thus attributed to women.[15]

The most thorough attempt to find a universal answer to the question of why it is that women are in subjection to men, and the most stark opposition between nature and culture, can be found in the writings of the radical feminists who argue that nature is the single cause of men's domination. The best known version of this argument is Firestone's *The Dialectic of Sex*, which also provides an example of how one form of feminist argument, while attacking the liberal separation of private and public, remains within the abstractly individualist framework which helps constitute this division of social life. Firestone reduces the history of the relation between nature and culture or private and public to an opposition between female and male. She argues that the origin of the dualism lies in 'biology itself—procreation',[16] a natural or original inequality that is the basis of the oppression of women and the source of male power. Men, by confining women to reproduction (nature), have freed themselves 'for the business of the world'[17] and so have created and controlled culture. The proposed solution is to eliminate natural differences (inequalities) between the sexes by introducing artificial reproduction. 'Nature' and the private sphere of the family will then be abolished and individuals, of all ages, will interact as equals in an undifferentiated cultural (or public) order.

The popular success of *The Dialectic of Sex* owes more to the need for women to continue to fight for control of their bodies and reproductive capacity than to its philosophical argument. The key assumption of the book is that women necessarily suffer from 'a fundamentally oppressive biological condition',[18] but biology, in itself, is neither oppressive nor liberating; biology, or nature, becomes either a source of subjection or free creativity for women only because it has meaning within specific social relationships. Firestone's argument reduces the social conceptions of 'women' and 'men' to the biological categories of 'female' and 'male', and thus denies any significance to the complex history of the relationship between men and women or between the private and public spheres. She relies on an abstract conception of a natural, biological female individual with a reproductive capacity which puts her at the mercy of a male individual, who is assumed to have a natural drive

[15]M. Z. Rosaldo, 'The Use and Abuse of Anthropology: Reflections on Feminism, and Cross-Cultural Understanding', *Signs*, 5, no. 3 (1980), p. 409. Compare D. Haraway, 'Animal Sociology and a Natural Economy of the Body Politic, Part I: A Political Physiology of Dominance', *Signs*, 4, no. 1 (1978), esp. pp. 24–25.

[16]S. Firestone, *The Dialectic of Sex* (W. Morrow, New York, 1970), p. 8.

[17]Ibid., p. 232. She also fails to distinguish 'culture' as art, technology etc. from 'culture' as the general form of life of humankind.

[18]Ibid., p. 255.

to subjugate her.[19] This contemporary version of a thorough Hobbesian reduction of individuals to their natural state leads to a theoretical dead-end, not perhaps a surprising conclusion to an argument that implicitly accepts the patriarchal claim that women's subordination is decreed by nature. The way forward will not be found in a universal dichotomy between nature and culture, or between female and male individuals. Rather, as Rosaldo argues, it is necessary to develop a feminist theoretical perspective that takes account of the social relationships between women and men in historically specific structures of domination and subordination; and, it might be added, within the context of specific interpretations of the 'public' and 'private'.

The long struggle to enfranchise women is one of the most important theoretical and practical examples of feminist attacks on the dichotomy between the private and public. Suffragist arguments show how the attempt to universalise liberal principles leads to a challenge to liberalism itself, and this is particularly well, if implicitly, illustrated in the writing of J. S. Mill. Despite the enormous amount of attention given to voting over the past thirty years, remarkably little attention has been paid by either theoretical or empirical students of politics to the political meaning and consequences of manhood and womanhood suffrage. In recent feminist literature, however, two different views can be found about the implications of the enfranchisement of women for the separation between the public and the private. There is disagreement whether the suffrage movement served to reinforce the sexual separation in social life or whether, rather despite itself, it was one means of undermining it. In the mid-nineteenth century, when feminism emerged as an organised social and political movement, the argument from nature had been elaborated into the doctrine of separate spheres; men and women, it was claimed, each naturally had a separate but complementary and equally valuable social place. The most striking difference between the early feminists and suffragists and contemporary feminists is that almost everyone in the nineteenth century accepted the doctrine of separate spheres.

The early feminists bitterly opposed the grossly unequal position of women but the reforms they struggled to achieve, such as an end to the legal powers of husbands that made their wives into private property and civil non-persons, and the opportunity to obtain an education so that single women could support themselves, were usually seen as means to equality for women who would remain within their own private sphere. The implicit assumption was that the suffrage, too, meant different things to men and women. This comes out clearly in one of the most passionately sentimental, and anti-feminist, statements

---

[19]I owe the last point to J. B. Elshtain, 'Liberal Heresies: Existentialism and Repressive Feminism' in M. McGrath (ed.), *Liberalism and the Modern Polity* (Marcel Dekker, New York, 1978), p. 53.

of the doctrine of separate spheres. In 'Of Queens' Gardens', Ruskin argues that,

> the man's duty, as a member of the commonwealth, is to assist in the maintenance, in the advance, in the defence of the state. The woman's duty, as a member of the commonwealth, is to assist in the ordering, in the comforting, and in the beautiful adornment of the state.[20]

Citizenship for women could thus be seen as an elaboration of their private, domestic tasks and one of the suffragists' main arguments was that the vote was a necessary means to protect and strengthen women's special sphere (an argument that gained weight at the end of the century as legislatures increasingly interested themselves in social issues related to women's sphere). Moreover, both the most ardent anti-suffragists and vehement suffragists agreed that women were weaker, but more moral and virtuous, than men. The anti-suffragists argued that, therefore, enfranchisement would fatally weaken the state because women could not bear arms or use force; the suffragists countered by claiming that women's superior morality and rectitude would transform the state and usher in a reign of peace. All this has led Elshtain to argue that it was precisely because the suffragists accepted the assumptions of the doctrine of separate spheres that they 'failed, even on their own terms'. Far from raising a challenge to the separation of the public and private, they merely 'perpetuated the very mystifications and unexamined presumptions which served to rig the system against them'.[21]

Much of Elshtain's argument is conducted in terms of the duality of morality and power, one way of formulating the separation of private and public when this is located *within* civil society. Liberal theorists often contrast the political sphere (the state), the sphere of power, force and violence, with the society (the private realm), the sphere of voluntarism, freedom and spontaneous regulation.[22] However, the argument about the implications of women's moral superiority, and Elshtain's use of the duality of morality and power, refer rather to the more fundamental separation of the private, domestic sphere from public life or civil society. The opposition between morality and power then counterposes physical force and aggression, the natural attributes of

[20]J. Ruskin, 'Of Queens' Gardens', in C. Bauer and L. Pitt (eds.), *Free and Ennobled* (Pergamon Press, Oxford, 1979), p. 17.

[21]J. B. Elshtain, 'Moral Woman and Immoral Man: A Consideration of the Public-Private Split and its Political Ramifications', *Politics and Society*, 4 (1974), pp. 453–61.

[22]A recent argument that relies on this contrast is J. Steinberg, *Locke, Rousseau and the Idea of Consent* (Greenwood Press, Westport, Conn., 1978), esp. Chs. 5–7. Emphasis on consent gives an appearance of morality to the private sphere, which is far less evident when, as is usually the case, self-interest is seen as the governing principle of (private) civil society. If the division within civil society is seen as freedom (as self-interest) opposing power, the location of morality within domestic life is more pointed but poses a serious problem of order for liberal public or civil society.

manliness, which are seen as exemplified in the military force of the state, against love and altruism, the natural attributes of womanhood, which are, paradigmatically, displayed in domestic life where the wife and mother stands as the guardian of morality.[23] Was the struggle for womanhood suffrage locked in the separation and dichotomies of patri-archal-liberalism, within the duality of morality and power (which, again, is one way of expressing the doctrine of separate spheres), to the extent suggested by Elshtain? To vote is, after all, a political act. In-deed, it has come to be seen as *the* political act of a liberal-democratic citizen, and citizenship is a status of formal civil or public equality.

A different assessment of the suffrage movement is presented in recent work by DuBois, who argues that the reason that both sides of the struggle for enfranchisement saw the vote as the key feminist demand was that the vote gave women

> a connection with the social order not based on the institution of the family and their subordination within it . . . As citizens and voters, women would participate directly in society as individuals, not indi-rectly through their subordinate position as wives and mothers.[24]

DuBois emphasises that the suffragists did not question women's 'pecu-liar suitability' for domestic life, but the demand for the vote consti-tuted a denial that women were naturally fit *only* for private life. The demand for the suffrage thus reached to the heart of the mutual accom-modation between patriarchalism and liberalism since to win the vote meant that, in one respect at least, women must be admitted as 'individ-uals'. This is why DuBois can argue that women's claim for a public, equal status with men, 'exposed and challenged the assumption of male authority over women'.[25] An important long-term consequence of women's enfranchisement, and the other reforms that have led to women's present position of (almost) formal political and legal equality with men, is that the contradiction between civil equality and social, especially familial, subjection, including the beliefs that help constitute it, is now starkly revealed. The liberal-patriarchal separation of the public and private spheres has become a political problem.

The dimensions of the problem are set out — very clearly with the benefit of hindsight — in John Stuart Mill's feminist essay *The Subjec-tion of Women* and his arguments for womanhood suffrage. Mill's essay shows that the assumption that an individual political status can be added to women's ascribed place in the private sphere and leave the

---

[23] An acute problem about 'nature' and women's 'nature' now emerges because women are seen both as natural guardians of morality and as naturally politically subversive: see my "Disorder of Women".

[24] E. DuBois, 'The Radicalism of the Woman Suffrage Movement', *Feminist Studies*, 3, no. 1/2 (1975), pp. 64, 66.

[25] E. DuBois, *Feminism and Suffrage* (Cornell University Press, Ithaca, N.Y., 1978), p. 46.

latter intact, or even strengthened, is ultimately untenable. Or, to make this point another way, liberal principles cannot simply be universalised to extend to women in the public sphere without raising an acute problem about the patriarchal structure of private life. Mill shows theoretically, as the feminist movement has revealed in practice, that the spheres are integrally related and that women's full and equal membership in public life is impossible without changes in the domestic sphere.

In the *Subjection*, Mill argues that the relation between men and women, or more specifically between husbands and wives, forms an unjustified and unjustifiable exception to the liberal principles of individual freedom and equality, free choice, equality of opportunity and allocation of occupations by merit that (he believes) govern other social and political institutions in nineteenth-century Britain. The social subordination of women is 'a single relic of an old world of thought and practice exploded in everything else'.[26] At the beginning of the essay Mill attacks the appeal to nature and argues that nothing can be known about the natural differences, if any, between women and men until evidence is available about their respective attributes within relationships and institutions where they interact as equals instead of as superiors and inferiors. Much of Mill's argument is directed against the legally sanctioned powers of husbands which placed them in the position of slave-masters over their wives. Legal reform should turn the family from a 'school of despotism' into a 'school of sympathy in equality' and a 'real school of the virtues of freedom'.[27] However, as recent feminist critics have pointed out, in the end he falls back on the same argument from nature that he criticises. Although Mill argues that in the prevailing circumstances of women's upbringing, lack of education and occupational opportunities, and legal and social pressures, they do not have a free choice whether or not to marry, he also assumes that, even after social reform, most women will still choose marital dependence. He states that it will generally be understood that when a woman marries she has chosen her 'career', just like a man entering a profession:

> she makes choice of the management of a household, and the bringing up of a family, as the first call upon her exertions . . . She renounces [all occupations] not consistent with the requirements of this.[28]

The question why, if marriage is a 'career', liberal arguments about (public) equality of opportunity have any relevance to women, is thus neatly begged.

[26]Mill, *Subjection*, p. 146.
[27]Ibid., pp. 174–75.
[28]Ibid., p. 179

Mill introduced the first measure for womanhood suffrage into the House of Commons in 1867. He advocated votes for women for the same two reasons that he supported manhood suffrage; because it was necessary for self-protection or the protection of interests and because political participation would enlarge the capacities of women. However, it is not usually appreciated that Mill's acceptance of a sexually ascribed division of labour, or the separation of domestic from public life, cuts the ground from under his argument for enfranchisement. The obvious difficulty for his argument is that women as wives will be largely confined to the small circle of the family so they will find it hard to use their votes to protect their interests. Women will not be able to learn what their interests are without experience outside domestic life. This point is even more crucial for Mill's argument about individual development and education through political participation. Mill, in what Benn and Gaus call his 'representative liberal text', refers to the development of a 'public spirit' by citizens.[29] In the *Subjection* he writes of the elevation of the individual 'as a moral, spiritual and social being' that occurs under 'the ennobling influence' of free government.[30] This is a large claim to make for the periodic casting of a ballot and Mill did not think that such consequences would arise from the suffrage alone. He writes that 'citizenship', and here I take him to be referring to universal suffrage, 'fills only a small place in modern life, and does not come near the daily habits or inmost sentiments'.[31] He goes on to argue that the (reformed) family is the real school of freedom. However, this is no more plausible than the claim about liberal democratic voting. A despotic, patriarchal family is no school for democratic citizenship; but neither can the egalitarian family, on its own, substitute for participation in a wide variety of social institutions (especially the workplace) that Mill, in his other social and political writings, argues is the necessary education for citizenship. How can wives who have 'chosen' private life develop a public spirit? Women will thus exemplify the selfish, private beings, lacking a sense of justice, who result, according to Mill, when individuals have no experience of public life.

Mill's ultimate failure to question the 'natural' sexual division of labour undermines his argument for an equal public status for women. His argument in the *Subjection* rests on an extension of liberal principles to the domestic sphere — which immediately brings the separation of the private and public, and the opposition between the principle of association in the two spheres into question. He would not have remained Benn and Gaus's 'exemplary' liberal theorist if he had not, at

[29]See S. I. Benn and R. F. Gaus *Public and Private in Social Life* (Croom Helm, London 1983) p. 53, referring to Mill's *Considerations on Representative Government*.
[30]Mill, *Subjection*, p. 237.
[31]Ibid., p. 174.

least in part, upheld the patriarchal-liberal ideology of the separation between public and private. On the other hand, by throwing doubt on the original Lockean separation of paternal and political power, and by arguing that the same political principles apply to the structure of family life as to political life, Mill also raises a large question about the status of the family. The language of 'slaves', 'masters', 'equality', 'freedom' and 'justice' implies that the family is a conventional not a natural association. Mill would not want to draw the conclusion that the family is political, but many contemporary feminists have done so. The most popular slogan of today's feminist movement is 'the personal is the political', which not only explicitly rejects the liberal separation of the private and public, but also implies that no distinction can or should be drawn between the two spheres.

IV. 'The Personal Is the Political'

The slogan 'the personal is the political' provides a useful point from which to comment on some of the ambiguities of the public and private in liberal-patriarchalism and also, in the light of some of its more literal feminist interpretations, to comment further on an alternative feminist conception of the political. Its major impact has been to unmask the ideological character of liberal claims about the private and public. 'The personal is the political' has drawn women's attention to the way in which we are encouraged to see social life in personal terms, as a matter of individual ability or luck in finding a decent man to marry or an appropriate place to live. Feminists have emphasised how personal circumstances are structured by public factors, by laws about rape and abortion, by the status of 'wife', by policies on childcare and the allocation of welfare benefits and the sexual division of labour in the home and workplace. 'Personal' problems can thus be solved only through political means and political action.

The popularity of the slogan and its strength for feminists arises from the complexity of women's position in contemporary liberal-patriarchal societies. The private or personal and the public or political are held to be separate from and irrelevant to each other; women's everyday experience confirms this separation yet, simultaneously, it denies it and affirms the integral connection between the two spheres. The separation of the private and public is both part of our actual lives and an ideological mystification of liberal-patriarchal reality.

The separation of the private domestic life of women from the public world of men has been constitutive of patriarchal-liberalism from its origins and, since the mid-nineteenth century, the economically dependent wife has been presented as the ideal for all respectable classes of society. The identification of women and the domestic sphere is now also being reinforced by the revival of anti-feminist organisations and the 'scientific' reformulation of the argument from nature by the socio-biologists.[32] Women have never been completely excluded, of course, from public life; but the way in which women are included is grounded, as firmly as their position in the domestic sphere, in patriarchal beliefs and practices. For example, even many anti-suffragists were willing for women to be educated, so that they could be good mothers, and for them to engage in local politics and philanthropy because these activities could be seen, as voting could not, as a direct extension of their domestic tasks. Today, women still have, at best, merely token representation in authoritative public bodies; public life, while not entirely empty of women, is still the world of men and dominated by them.

Again, large numbers of working class wives have always had to enter the public world of paid employment to ensure the survival of their families, and one of the most striking features of post-war capitalism has been the employment of a steadily increasing number of married women. However, their presence serves to highlight the patriarchal continuity that exists between the sexual division of labour in the family and the sexual division of labour in the workplace. Feminist research has shown how women workers are concentrated into a few occupational areas ('women's work') in low-paid, low-status and nonsupervisory jobs.[33] Feminists have also drawn attention to the fact that discussions of worklife, whether by *laissez-faire* liberals or Marxists, always assume that it is possible to understand economic activity in abstraction from domestic life. It is 'forgotten' that the worker, invariably taken to be a man, can appear ready for work and concentrate on his work free from the everyday demands of providing food, washing and cleaning, and care of children, only because these tasks are performed unpaid by his wife. And if she is also a paid worker she works a further shift at these 'natural' activities. A complete analysis and explanation of the structure and operation of capitalism will be forthcoming only when the figure of the worker is accompanied by that of the housewife.

Feminists conclude that the 'separate' liberal worlds of private and public life are actually interrelated, connected by a patriarchal structure. This conclusion again highlights the problem of the status of the 'natural' sphere of the family, which is presupposed by, yet seen as separate from and irrelevant to, the conventional relations of civil society. The sphere of domestic life is at the heart of civil society rather than apart or separate from it. A widespread conviction that this is so is

[32]On sociobiology see, e.g., E. O. Wilson, *Sociobiology: The New Synthesis* (Harvard University Press, Cambridge, Mass., 1975), and S. Goldberg, *The Inevitability of Patriarchy*, 2nd edn (W. Morrow, New York, 1974). For a critique, see, e.g., P. Green, *The Pursuit of Inequality* (Martin Robertson, Oxford, 1981), Ch. 5.

[33]See, e.g., for Australia, K. Hargreaves, *Women at Work* (Penguin Books, Harmondsworth, 1982); for England, J. West (ed.), *Women, Work and the Labour Market* (Routledge and Kegan Paul, London, 1982); for America, Eisenstein, *The Radical Future of Liberal Feminism*, Ch. 9.

revealed by contemporary concern about the crisis, the decline, the disintegration of the nuclear family that is seen as the bulwark of civilised moral life. That the family is a major 'social problem' is significant, for the 'social' is a category that belongs in civil society, not outside it, or, more accurately, it is one of the two sides into which civil society can be divided; the social (private) and the political (public). Donzelot has recently explored how the emergence of the social is also the emergence of 'social work' and a wide variety of ways of (politically) 'policing' the family, giving mothers a social status, and controlling children.[34] Feminists, too, have been investigating how personal and family life is politically regulated, an investigation which denies the conventional liberal claim that the writ of the state runs out at the gate to the family home. They have shown how the family is a major concern of the state and how, through legislation concerning marriage and sexuality and the policies of the welfare state, the subordinate status of women is presupposed by and maintained by the power of the state.[35]

These feminist critiques of the dichotomy between private and public stress that the categories refer to two interrelated dimensions of the structure of liberal-patriarchalism; they do not necessarily suggest that no distinction can or should be drawn between the personal and political aspects of social life. The slogan 'the personal is the political' can, however, be taken literally. For example, Millett, in *Sexual Politics*, implicitly rejects Locke's distinction between paternal and political power. In political science the political is frequently defined in terms of power, but political scientists invariably fail to take their definition to its logical conclusion. Millett agrees with the definition but, in contrast, argues that all power is political so that, because men exercise power over women in a multitude of ways in personal life, it makes sense to talk of 'sexual politics' and 'sexual dominion . . . provides [the] most fundamental concept of power'.[36] The personal becomes the political. This approach illuminates many unpalatable aspects of sexual and domestic life, in particular its violence, that too frequently remain hidden, but it does not greatly advance the critique of patriarchal-liberalism. As the radical feminist attempts to eliminate nature, as one side of the dichotomy, so Millett seeks to eliminate power, thus echoing the suffragist vision of a moral transformation of politics. But this does nothing

[34]J. Donzelot, *The Policing of Families* (Pantheon Books, New York, 1979). 'The most surprising thing is the status "the social" has won in our heads, as something we take for granted' (p. xxvi).

[35]On marriage see, e.g., D. L. Barker, 'The Regulation of Marriage: Repressive Benevolence' in G. Littlejohn et al. (eds.), *Power and the State* (Croom Helm, London, 1978); on rape see my 'Women and Consent', *Political Theory*, 8 (1980), pp. 149–68, and A. G. Johnson, 'On the Prevalence of Rape in the United States', *Signs*, 6, no. 1 (1980), pp. 136–46; on the welfare state see, e.g., E. Wilson, *Women and the Welfare State* (Tavistock, London, 1977).

[36]K. Millett, *Sexual Politics* (Hart-Davis, London, 1971), pp. 25, 26.

to question the liberal association (or identification) of the political
with power, or to question the association of women with the 'moral'
side of the duality.

Other feminists have also rejected the identification of the political
with power. Sometimes, by standing liberal-patriarchalism on its head,
it is merely claimed that, properly understood, political life is thus
intrinsically feminine.[37] More fruitfully, the feminist rejection of 'mas-
culine' power also rests on an alternative conception of the political. It
is argued that the political is the 'area of shared values and citizenship',[38] or that it 'includes shared values and civic concerns in which
power is only one aspect'.[39] These conceptions remain undeveloped in
feminist writings, but they are closely related to the arguments of the
critics of liberalism who deplore the depoliticisation of civil society or
liberalism's loss of distinctive sense of the political. For instance, Habermas argues for public, shared communication so that substantive
political problems can be rationally evaluated, and Wolin states that the
'public' and the 'common' are 'synonyms for what is political', so that
'one of the essential qualities of what is political . . . is its relationship
to what is "public"'.[40] These critics and some feminists agree that what
is not personal is public—and that what is public is political. The
implication is that there is no division within civil society, which is the
realm of the public, collective, common political life of the community.
The argument is usually developed, however, without any consideration of how this conception of the public-political sphere is related to
domestic life, or any indication that such a problem arises. The feminists have posed, but have not yet answered, this fundamental question.
What can be said is that although the personal is not the political, the
two spheres are interrelated, necessary dimensions of a future, democratic feminist social order.

V. *Conditions for a Feminist Alternative to Liberal-Patriarchalism*

Feminist critiques of the liberal-patriarchal opposition of private and
public raise fundamental theoretical questions, as well as the complex
practical problems of creating a radical social transformation. But one
objection to feminist arguments denies that our project is even sensible. Wolff has recently claimed, from a position sympathetic to feminism, that overcoming the separation of the two spheres presents an
inherently insoluble problem. To 'struggle against the split' is pointless;

[37]N. McWilliams, 'Contemporary Feminism, Consciousness Raising and Changing
Views of the Political' in J. Jaquette (ed.), *Women in Politics* (Wiley, New York, 1974), p.
161.
[38]Ibid.
[39]L. B. Iglitzin, 'The Making of the Apolitical Woman: Femininity and Sex-Stereotyp-
ing in Girls' in Jaquette, *Women in Politics*, p. 34.
[40]J. Habermas, 'The Public Sphere', and Wolin, *Politics and Vision*, pp. 9, 2.

the best that can be achieved is ad hoc adjustments to the existing order. The separation of public and private derives from two 'equally plausible and totally incompatible conceptions of human nature'. One is that of 'man [sic] as essentially rational, atemporal, ahistorical', and the second is of 'man as essentially time bound, historically, culturally and biologically conditioned'.[41] To argue that everyone should be treated in the public world as if the facts of sex, class, colour, age and religion do not count, is to insist that we should deny the most basic human facts about ourselves and thus accentuate the inhumanity and alienation of the present. But Wolff's two conceptions are not of a single 'human' nature, and they are far from equally plausible; they represent the liberal-patriarchal view of the true natures of (private) women and (public) men. Human beings *are* time bound, biological and culturally specific creatures. Only from a liberal individualist perspective (one failing to see itself as a patriarchalist perspective) that abstracts the male individual from the sphere where his wife remains in natural subjection, then generalises this abstraction as public man, can such an opposition of 'human' nature, of women and men, private and public, appear philosophically or sociologically plausible.

Feminists are trying to develop a theory of a social practice that, for the first time in the western world, would be a truly general theory — including women and men equally — grounded in the interrelationship of the individual to collective life, or personal to political life, instead of their separation and opposition. At the immediately practical level, this demand is expressed in what is perhaps the most clear conclusion of feminist critiques; that if women are to participate fully, as equals, in social life, men have to share equally in childrearing and other domestic tasks. While women are identified with this 'private' work, their public status is always undermined. This conclusion does not, as is often alleged, deny the natural biological fact that women not men *bear* children; it does deny the patriarchal assertion that this natural fact entails that only women can *rear* children. Equal parenting and equal participation in the other activities of domestic life presuppose some radical changes in the public sphere, in the organisation of production, in what we mean by 'work', and in the practice of citizenship. The feminist critique of the sexual division of labour in the workplace and in political organisations of all ideological persuasions, and its rejection of the liberal-patriarchal conception of the political, extends and deepens the challenge to liberal-capitalism posed by the participatory demo-

---

[41]R. P. Wolff, 'There's Nobody Here but Us Persons' in C. Gould and M. Wartofsky (eds.), *Women and Philosophy* (Putnam's, New York, 1976), pp. 137, 142–43. Wolff also objects to the feminist struggle against the separation of private and public because it builds normative assumptions about human nature into the advocacy of new forms of social institutions — an oddly misplaced objection in the light of the assumption about women's and men's nature embodied in patriarchal-liberalism.

cratic and Marxist criticism of the past two decades, but also goes well beyond it.

The temptation, as Wolff's argument shows, is to suppose that if women are to take their place as public 'individuals' then the conflict is about the universalisation of liberalism. But that is to ignore the feminist achievement in bringing to light the patriarchal character of liberalism and the ambiguities and contradictions of its conception of the private and public. A full analysis of the various expressions of the dichotomy between the private and the public has yet to be provided, together with a deeper exploration than is possible in this essay of the implications of the double separation of domestic life from civil society and the separation of the private from public within civil society itself. Feminist critiques imply a dialectical perspective upon social life as an alternative to the dichotomies and oppositions of patriarchal-liberalism. It is tempting, as shown by feminists themselves, either to replace opposition by negation (to deny that nature has any place in a feminist order) or to assume that the alternative to opposition is harmony and identification (the personal is the political; the family is political). The assumptions of patriarchal-liberalism allow only these two alternatives, but feminist critiques assume that there is a third.

Feminism looks toward a differentiated social order within which the various dimensions are distinct but not separate or opposed, and which rests on a social conception of individuality, which includes both women and men as biologically differentiated but not unequal creatures. Nevertheless, women and men, and the private and the public, are not necessarily in harmony. Given the social implications of women's reproductive capacities,[42] it is surely Utopian to suppose that tension between the personal and the political, between love and justice, between individuality and communality will disappear with patriarchal-liberalism.

The range of philosophical and political problems that are encompassed, implicitly or explicitly, in feminist critiques indicates that a fully developed feminist alternative to patriarchal-liberalism would provide its first truly 'total critique'.[43] Three great male critics of abstractly individualist liberalism already claim to have offered such a critique, but their claim must be rejected. Rousseau, Hegel and Marx each argued that they had left behind the abstractions and dichotomies

[42]See R. P. Petchesky, 'Reproductive Freedom: Beyond "A Woman's Right to Choose",' *Signs*, 5, no. 4 (1980), pp. 661–85.

[43]I have taken the phrase from R. M. Unger, *Knowledge and Politics* (Free Press, New York, 1975). Unger's claim to have provided a total critique of liberalism must also be rejected. He fails to see that the antinomies of theory and fact, reason and desire, and rules and values are, at the same time, expressions of the patriarchal antinomy between man and woman. He states (p. 59) that 'the political form of the opposition of formal reason to arbitrary desire is the contrast between public and private existence'—but it is also the opposition between the 'nature' of men and women.

of liberalism and retained individuality within communality. Rousseau and Hegel explicitly excluded women from this endeavour, confining these politically dangerous beings to the obscurity of the natural world of the family; Marx also failed to free himself and his philosophy from patriarchal assumptions. The feminist total critique of the liberal opposition of private and public still awaits its philosopher.

PART II
THE ELIGIBLE: WHAT WOULD
WE CHOOSE?

THE THREE ESSAYS here are designed to illustrate different styles of contractarian thought. In the terms of our introduction, Rawls has a noninteractive view of the contract he invokes: each party to the contract makes his decision unilaterally and, being all rational and all subject to the same conditions, each makes the same decision. Gauthier and Habermas both view the contract as an interactive affair, involving conversation and accommodation between the parties. But whereas Gauthier sees it as an economic matter of bargaining, with each openly seeking his own advantage, Habermas sees it as a political enterprise in which each addresses what he takes to be considerations of the common good.

7

JOHN RAWLS

The Basic Structure as Subject

I

AN IMPORTANT ASSUMPTION of my book *A Theory of Justice*[1] is that the basic structure of society is the primary subject of justice. By the basic structure is meant the way in which the major social institutions fit together into one system, and how they assign fundamental rights and duties and shape the division of advantages that arises through social cooperation. Thus the political constitution, the legally recognized forms of property, and the organization of the economy, all belong to the basic structure. I held that the first test of a conception of justice is whether its principles provide reasonable guidelines for the classical questions of social justice in this case.

In my book I did not consider in any detail why the basic structure is to be taken as the primary subject. I left this to be gathered from various remarks made while discussing other matters. Here I shall try to remedy this lack. Of course, it is perfectly legitimate at first to restrict inquiry to the basic structure. We must begin somewhere, and this starting point may turn out to be justified by how everything works out. But certainly we would like to find a more illuminating answer than this; and moreover one that draws upon the special features of the basic structure in contrast with other social arrangements, and connects these features with the particular role and content of the principles of

[1]Cambridge, Mass., 1971.

justice themselves. I aim to present an explanation that meets these conditions.

Now a social contract is an agreement (1) between all rather than some members of society, and it is (2) between them as members of society (as citizens) and not as individuals who hold some particular position or role within it. In the Kantian form of this doctrine, of which the conception of justice as fairness is an example, (3) the parties are regarded as, and also regard themselves as, free and equal moral persons; and (4) the content of the agreement is the first principles that are to regulate the basic structure. We take as given a short list of conceptions of justice developed by the tradition of moral philosophy and then ask which of these the parties would acknowledge, when the alternatives are thus restricted. Assuming that we have a clear enough idea of the circumstances necessary to insure that any agreement reached is fair, the content of justice for the basic structure can be ascertained, or at least approximated, by the principles that would be agreed to. (Of course, this presupposes the reasonableness of the tradition; but where else can we start?) Thus pure procedural justice is invoked at the highest level: the fairness of the circumstances transfers to fairness of the principles adopted.

I wish to suggest the following: first that once we think of the parties to a social contract as free and equal (and rational) persons, then it is natural to take the basic structure as the primary subject. Second, that in view of the distinctive features of this structure, the initial agreement, and the conditions under which it is made, must be understood in a special way that distinguishes this agreement from all others; and doing this allows a Kantian view to take account of the fully social nature of human relationships. And finally, that while a large element of pure procedural justice transfers to the principles of justice, these principles must embody an ideal form for the basic structure in the light of which ongoing institutional processes are to be constrained and the accumulated results of individual transactions continually corrected.

II

Several lines of reasoning point to the basic structure as the primary subject of justice. One is the following: suppose we begin with the initially attractive idea that society should develop over time in accordance with free agreements fairly arrived at and fully honored. Straightway we need an account of when agreements are free and the social circumstances under which they are reached are fair. In addition, while these conditions may be fair at an earlier time, the accumulated results of many separate ostensibly fair agreements, together with social and historical contingencies, are likely as time passes to alter institutions and opportunities so that the conditions for free and fair agreements no longer hold. The role of the basic structure is to secure just background conditions against which the actions of individuals and associations take place. Unless this structure is appropriately regulated and corrected, the social process will cease to be just, however free and fair particular transactions may look when viewed by themselves.

We recognize this fact when we say, for example, that the distribution resulting from voluntary market transactions (even should all the ideal conditions for competitive efficiency obtain) is not, in general, fair unless the antecedent distribution of income and wealth as well as the structure of the system of markets is fair. The existing wealth must have been properly acquired and all must have had fair opportunities to earn income, to learn wanted skills, and so on. Again, the conditions necessary for background justice can be undermined, even though nobody acts unfairly or is aware of how the conjunction of contingencies affects the opportunities of others. There are no feasible rules that it is practicable to impose on economic agents that can prevent these undesirable consequences. These consequences are often so far in the future, or so indirect, that the attempt to forestall them by restrictive rules that apply to individuals would be an excessive if not impossible burden. Thus we start with the basic structure and try to see how this system itself should make the corrections necessary to preserve background justice.

III

A second reflection points in the same direction. Consider the situation of individuals engaged in market transactions. We have seen that certain background conditions are necessary for these transactions to be fair. But what about the nature of individuals themselves: how did they get to be what they are? A theory of justice cannot take their final aims and interests, their attitude to themselves and their life, as given. Everyone recognizes that the form of society affects its members and determines in large part the kind of persons they want to be as well as the kind of persons they are. It also limits people's ambitions and hopes in different ways, for they will with reason view themselves in part according to their place in it and take account of the means and opportunities they can realistically expect. Thus an economic regime is not only an institutional scheme for satisfying existing desires and aspirations but a way of fashioning desires and aspirations in the future.

Nor, similarly, can we view the abilities and talents of individuals as fixed natural gifts, even if there is an important genetic component. These abilities and talents cannot come to fruition apart from social conditions and as realized they always take but one of many possible forms. An ability is not, for example, a computer in the head with a definite measurable capacity unaffected by social circumstances. Among the elements affecting the realization of natural capacities are social attitudes of encouragement and support and the institutions concerned with their training and use. Thus even a potential ability at any given time is not something unaffected by existing social forms and particular contingencies over the course of life up to that moment. So not only our final ends and hopes for ourselves but our realized abilities and talents reflect, to a large degree, our personal history, opportunities, and social position. What we might have been had these things been different, we cannot know.

Finally, both of the preceding considerations are strengthened by the fact that the basic structure most likely contains significant social and economic inequalities. These I assume to be necessary, or else highly advantageous, in maintaining effective social cooperation; presumably there are various reasons for this, among which the need for incentives is but one. Even if these inequalities are not very great, they seem bound to have a considerable effect and so to favor some over others depending upon their social origins, their realized natural endowments, and the chance coincidences and opportunities that have come their way. The basic structure includes inequalities between certain starting-places, so to speak, and this feature, together with the earlier observations, prompts us to take this structure as the primary subject.

IV

In the conception of justice as fairness the institutions of the basic structure are viewed as just provided they (reasonably) satisfy the principles that free and equal moral persons, in a situation that is fair between them, would adopt for the purpose of regulating that structure. The main two principles read as follows: (1) Each person has an equal right to the most extensive scheme of equal basic liberties compatible with a similar scheme of liberties for all. (2) Social and economic inequalities are permissible provided that (a) they are to the greatest expected benefit of the least advantaged; and (b) attached to positions and offices open to all under conditions of fair equality of opportunity.

Let us consider how the special features of the basic structure affect the conditions of the initial agreement and hence the content of these principles. Now by assumption the basic structure is the all-inclusive social system that determines background justice; so any fair situation between individuals conceived as free and equal moral persons must be one that suitably evens out the contingencies within this system. Agreements reached when people know their present place in an ongoing society would be influenced by disparate social and natural contingencies. The principles adopted would then be selected by the historical course of events that took place within that structure. We would not have gotten beyond social happenstance in order to find an independent standard.

It is also clear why, when we interpret the parties as free and equal moral persons, they are to reason as if they know very little about themselves (referring here to the restrictions of the veil of ignorance). For to proceed otherwise is still to allow the disparate and deep contingent effects of the social system to influence the principles adopted; and this is true even if the parties have no particular information about themselves but only general facts about their own society (which is perhaps all that a condition of impartiality requires). When we as contemporaries are influenced by a general description of the present state of society in agreeing how we are to treat each other, and those generations that come after us, we have not yet left out of account the accidents of the basic structure. And so one arrives at the thicker rather than the thinner veil of ignorance: the parties are to be understood so far as possible solely as moral persons, that is, in abstraction from all those contingencies that the basic structure over time has shaped and influenced; and to be fair between them, the initial situation must situate them equally for as moral persons they are equal: the same essential properties qualify each.

Finally, the social contract must be regarded as hypothetical. Of course, any actual agreement is liable to the distortions just noted; but in any case, historically valid compacts, were such to exist, would have but limited force and could not serve as the basis of a general theory. Equally decisive is the fact that society is a system of cooperation that extends over time: it is cooperation between generations and not just cooperation among contemporaries. If we are to account for the duties and obligations between generations, there is no clear way to do this in a contract view without interpreting the initial agreement as hypothetical. The correct principles for the basic structure are those that the members of any generation (and hence all generations) would agree to as the ones their generation is to follow and as the principles they would want other generations to have followed and to follow subsequently, no matter how far back or forward in time.

Once we note the distinctive role of the basic structure and abstract from the various contingencies within it to find an appropriate conception of justice to regulate it, something like the notion of the original position seems inevitable. It is a natural extension of the idea of the social contract when the basic structure is taken as the primary subject of justice.

V

The essential point is the distinctive role of the basic structure: we must distinguish between particular agreements made and associations formed within this structure, and the initial agreement and membership in society as a citizen. Consider first particular agreements: typically these are based on the parties' known (or probable) assets and abilities, opportunities and interests, as these have been realized within background institutions. We may assume that each party, whether an individual or an association, has various alternatives open to them, that they can compare the likely advantages and disadvantages of these alternatives, and act accordingly. Under certain conditions someone's contribution to a joint venture, or to an on-going association, can be estimated: one simply notes how the venture or association would fare without that person's joining, and the difference measures their worth to the venture or association. The attractiveness of joining to the individual is similarly given by a comparison with their opportunities. Thus particular agreements are reached within the context of existing and foreseeable configurations of relationships as these have been and most likely will be realized within the basic structure; and it is these configurations that give meaning to contractual calculations.

The context of a social contract is strikingly different, and must allow for three facts, among others: namely, that membership in our society is given, that we cannot know what we would have been like had we not belonged to it (perhaps the thought itself lacks a sense), and that society as a whole has no ends or ordering of ends in the sense that associations and individuals do. The bearing of these facts is clear once we try to view the social contract as an ordinary agreement and ask how deliberations leading up to it would proceed. Since membership in their society is given, there is no question of the parties comparing the attractions of other societies. Moreover, there is no way to identify potential contribution to society as an individual not yet a member of it; for this potentiality cannot be known and is, in any case, irrelevant to their present situation. Not only this, but from the standpoint of society as a whole *vis-à-vis* any one member, there is no set of agreed ends by reference to which the potential social contributions of an individual could be assessed. Associations and individuals have such ends, but not a well-ordered society; although it has the aim of giving justice to all its citizens, this is not an aim that ranks their expected contributions and on that basis determines their social role. The notion of an individual's contribution to society as itself an association falls away. It is necessary, therefore, to construe the social contract in a special way that distinguishes it from other agreements.

In the conception of justice as fairness this is done by constructing the notion of the original position. This construction must reflect the fundamental contrasts just noted and it must supply the missing elements so that an appropriate agreement may be reached. Consider in turn the points in the preceding paragraph. First, the parties in the original position suppose that their membership in the society is given. This presumption reflects the fact that we are born into our society and within its framework realize but one of many possible forms of our person; the question of entering another society does not arise. The task is to agree on principles for the basic structure of the society of one's birth. Second, the veil of ignorance not only establishes fairness between equal moral persons, but by excluding information about the parties' actual interests and abilities, it represents the fact that apart from our place and history in a society, even our potential abilities cannot be known and our interests and character are still to be formed. Thus, the initial situation suitably recognizes that our nature apart from society is but a potential for a whole range of possibilities. Third and finally, there is no social end except that established by the principles of justice themselves, or else authorized by them; but these principles have yet to be adopted.

Nevertheless, although the calculations that typically influence agreements within society have no place, other aspects of the original position provide the setting for rational deliberation. Thus the alternatives are not opportunities to join other societies, but instead a list of conceptions of justice to regulate the basic structure of one's own society. The parties' interests and preferences are given by their desire for primary goods. Their particular final ends and aims indeed are already formed, although not known to them; and it is these already formed interests that they seek to protect by ranking conceptions on the basis of their preference (in the original position) for primary goods. Finally, the availability of general social theory gives a sufficient basis for estimating the feasibility and consequences of the various conceptions of justice. These aspects of the original position allow us to carry through the idea of the social contract despite the unusual nature of this agreement.

VI

I now point out three ways in which the social aspect of human relationships is reflected in the content of the principles of justice themselves. First, the difference principle (which governs economic and social inequalities) does not distinguish between what is acquired by individuals as members of society and what would have been acquired by them had they not been members. Indeed, no sense can be made of the notion of that part of an individual's social benefits that exceed what would have been their situation in another society or in a state of nature. We can, if we like, in setting up the argument from the original position, introduce the state of nature in relation to the so-called no-agreement point.[2] This point can be defined as general

---

[2]See A Theory of Justice (op. cit.), pp. 136, 147; see also p. 80.

egoism and its consequences, and this can serve as the state of nature. But these conditions do not identify a definite state. All that is known in the original position is that each of the conceptions of justice available to the parties has consequences superior to general egoism. There is no question of determining anyone's contribution to society, or how much better off each is than they would have been had they not belonged to society and then adjusting the social benefits of citizens by reference to these estimates. Although we may draw this kind of distinction for agreements made within society, the requisite calculations for principles holding for the basic structure itself have no foundation. Neither our situation in other societies, nor in a state of nature, has any role in comparing conceptions of justice. And clearly these notions have no relevance at all in the application of the principles of justice.

Second, and related to the preceding, the two principles of justice regulate how entitlements are acquired in return for contributions to associations, or to other forms of cooperation, within the basic structure. As we have seen, these contributions are estimated on the basis of particular configurations of contingencies, which are influenced in part by individual efforts and achievements, in part by social accident and happenstance. Contributions can only be locally defined as contributions to this or that association in this or that situation. Such contributions reflect an individual's worth (marginal usefulness) to some particular group. These contributions are not to be mistaken for contributions to society itself, or for the worth to society of its members as citizens. The sum of an individual's entitlements, or even of their uncompensated contributions to associations within society, is not to be regarded as a contribution to society. To this kind of contribution we can give no meaning; there is no clear or useful notion of an individual's contribution to society that parallels the idea of individual contributions to associations within society. Insofar as we compare the worth of citizens at all, their worth in a well-ordered society is always equal; and this equality is reflected in the system of basic equal liberties and fair opportunities, and in the operations of the difference principle.

Third and last, recall that in a Kantian view the parties are regarded as free and equal moral persons. Now freedom means a certain form of social institutions, namely, a certain pattern of rights and liberties; and equality in turn means, for example, that certain basic liberties and opportunities are equal and that social and economic inequalities are regulated by principles suitably expressive of equality. Moral persons are those with a conception of the good (a system of final ends) and a capacity to understand a conception of justice and to follow it in their life. Of course, we cannot define free and equal moral persons as those whose social relations answer to precisely the principles that are agreed to in the social contract. For then we should have no argument for these principles. But it is no accident that once the parties are described in terms that require some social expression, the first principles of justice are themselves institutional and apply to the public structure of society. The content of the two principles fulfills this expectation. And this is in contrast, for example, with utilitarianism which takes as basic the capacity for pleasure and pain, or for certain valuable experiences. Nevertheless, the social manner in which the parties are described does not mean a lapse into some kind of holism; what results is a conception of a well-ordered society regulated by the two principles of justice.

VII

Now I come to the last point: namely, why it is that, although society may reasonably rely on a large element of pure procedural justice in determining distributive shares, a conception of justice must incorporate an ideal form for the basic structure in the light of which the accumulated results of on-going social processes are to be limited and corrected.

First a remark about pure procedural justice: the two principles make considerable use of this notion. They apply to the basic structure and its system for acquiring entitlements; within appropriate limits, whatever distributive shares result are just. A fair distribution can be arrived at only by the actual working of a fair social process over time in the course of which, in accordance with publicly announced rules, entitlements are earned and honored. These features define pure procedural justice. Therefore, if it is asked in the abstract whether one distribution of a given stock of things to definite individuals with known desires and preferences is more just than another then there is simply no answer to this question.[3]

Thus the principles of justice, in particular the difference principle, apply to the main public principles and policies that regulate social and economic inequalities. They are used to adjust the system of entitlements and earnings and to balance the familiar everyday standards and precepts which this system employs. The difference principle holds, for example, for income and property taxation, for fiscal and economic policy. It applies to the announced system of public law and statutes and not to particular transactions or distributions, nor to the decisions of individuals and associations, but rather to the institutional background against which these take place. There are no unannounced and unpredictable interferences with citizens' expectations and acquisitions. Entitlements are earned and honored as the public system of rules declares. Taxes and restrictions are all in principle foreseeable,

---

[3]On pure procedural justice, see *Theory of Justice*, pp. 64, 66, 72ff, 79, 84–89, 274–280, 305–315.

and holdings are acquired on the known condition that certain corrections will be made. The objection that the difference principle enjoins continuous and capricious interference with private transactions is based on a misunderstanding.

Again, the two principles of justice do not insist that the actual distribution reflect any observable pattern, say equality, nor any measure computed from the distribution, such as a certain Gini coefficient (as a measure of the degree of equality). What is enjoined is that (permissible) inequalities make a certain functional contribution over time to the expectations of the least favored. The aim, however, is not to eliminate the various contingencies from social life, for some such contingencies seem inevitable. Thus even if an equal distribution of natural assets seemed more in keeping with the equality of free persons, the question of redistributing these assets (were this conceivable) does not arise, since it is incompatible with the integrity of the person. Nor need we make any specific assumptions about how great these natural variations are; we only suppose that, as realized in later life, they are influenced by many kinds of contingencies. Institutions must organize social cooperation so that they encourage constructive efforts. We have a right to our natural abilities and a right to whatever we become entitled to by taking part in a fair social process. The two principles of justice define the relevant fair process and so whatever distributive shares result are fair.

At the same time, these principles specify an ideal form for the basic structure in the light of which pure procedural processes are constrained and corrected. Among these constraints are the limits on the accumulation of property (especially if private property in productive assets exists) that derive from the requirements of the fair value of political liberty and fair equality of opportunity, and the limits based on considerations of stability and excusable envy, both of which are connected to the essential primary good of self-respect.[4] We need such an ideal to guide the corrections necessary to preserve background justice. As we have seen, even if everyone acts fairly as defined by rules that it is both reasonable and practicable to impose on individuals, the upshot of many separate transactions will undermine background justice. This is obvious once we view society, as we must, as involving cooperation over generations. Thus even in a well-ordered society, adjustments in the basic structure are always necessary. What we have, in effect, is an institutional division of labor between the basic structure and rules applying directly to particular transactions. Individuals and associations are left free to advance their ends more effectively within the framework of the basic structure secure in the knowledge that

[4]See *ibid.*, pp. 224–227, 277f; 534–537; 543–546.

elsewhere in the social system the necessary corrections to preserve background justice are being made.

The essential point, then, is that the need for a structural ideal to specify constraints and to guide corrections does not depend upon injustice. Even with strict compliance with all reasonable and practical rules, such adjustments are continually required. The fact that actual political and social life is often pervaded by much injustice merely underlines this necessity. A procedural theory that contains no structural principles for a just social order would be of no use in our world, where the political goal is to eliminate injustice and steer change towards a fair basic structure. The notion of a well-ordered society provides the requisite structural principles and specifies the overall direction of political action. There is no rational basis for preventing or eliminating injustice if such an ideal form for background institutions is rejected.

VIII

I conclude with some general remarks. I have tried to show that once we think of the members of society as free and equal moral persons, it is natural for a social contract view to take the basic structure of society as the primary subject of justice. Yet in view of the distinctive features of this structure, the initial agreement must be characterized in such a way that: (a) it brings out the difference between this agreement and all other agreements; and (b) it enables us to take account of the fully social nature of human relationships. Throughout my aim has been to set the stage for a reply to idealism.

The problem is this: to develop a viable Kantian conception of justice the force and content of Kant's doctrine must be detached from its background in transcendental idealism and given a procedural interpretation by means of the construction of the original position. It must then be shown that this construction, which draws upon the idea of the social contract, is not subject to the cogent objections that idealists raised against the contract doctrine of their day. Thus Hegel thought that this doctrine confused society and the state with an association of private persons; that it permitted the general form and content of public law to be determined by the contingent and specific private interests of individuals; that it could find no place for the fact that it is not optional (up to us) whether or not we belong to society. For Hegel the social contract was an illegitimate and unwitting extension of ideas at home in and limited to (what he called) civil society.[5]

[5]See *Philosophy of Right*, tr. by T. M. Know (Oxford, 1942), pp. 58f, 156f, 186.

I have tried to show how the conception of justice as fairness avoids these and similar objections. The procedural interpretation of Kant's view not only satisfies the canons of a reasonable empiricism, but its use of the idea of the social contract meets Hegel's criticisms. At the same time, since it proceeds from a suitably individualistic basis, it presents the details of a moral conception that can take appropriate account of social values without falling into organicism.[6]

[6]I am indebted to Joshua Cohen, Joshua Rabinowitz, and T. M. Scanlon for valuable discussions on the topic of this paper. In Sections 5 and 6 I indicate the lines of a reply to David Gauthier's illuminating critique "Justice and Natural Endowment," *Social Theory and Practice*, vol. 3 (1974), pp. 3–26. I regret that lack of space forbids a fuller exposition. I am grateful to Burton Dreben for many improvements.

8

DAVID GAUTHIER

Bargaining Our Way Into Morality: A Do-It-Yourself Primer

1. "THE THEORY OF justice," according to John Rawls, "is a part, perhaps the most significant part, of the theory of rational choice."[1] Let us reflect on the significance of this claim.

Choice is the endeavour to realize one among several alternative possible states of affairs. The *rationality* which may be exhibited in choice is conceived in *maximizing* terms. A numerical measure is applied to the alternative possibilities, and choice among them is rational if and only if one endeavours to realize that possibility which has been assigned the greatest number. This measure is associated with *preference*; the alternative possible state of affairs is ordered preferentially, and the numerical measure, which is termed *utility*, is so established that greater utility indicates greater preference. The complications of this procedure need not concern us here.[2] What is important is that rational choice is conceived as *preference-based* choice, so that the rationally chosen state of affairs is the most preferred among the alternative possibilities.

John Rawls' claim, therefore, is that the theory of justice is the most significant part of the theory of preference-based choice. But this claim must seem quite implausible. Justice is a moral virtue — indeed, some would claim that justice is the central moral virtue.[3] The theory of

---

[1]John Rawls, *A Theory of Justice*, Cambridge, Mass., 1971, p. 16.

[2]For further discussion of preference and utility, see R. D. Luce and Howard Raiffa, *Games and Decisions*, Wiley, New York, 1957, Ch. 2.

[3]Cf. Aristotle, *Ethica Nicomachea*, 1129b25ff.

justice must be a part, and perhaps the most significant part, of the theory of morality. How can morality be part of preference-based choice?

The point of morality is surely to *override* preference. Were we to suppose that one should always endeavour to realize his or her most preferred state of affairs, then what need would we have for moral concepts? Why use the language of morality, of duties and obligations, of rights and responsibilities, when one might appeal directly to each person's greatest interest?

You offer me a choice among pieces of cake. I, greedily but perfectly rationally, basing my choice strictly on my preferences, select the largest piece. "That isn't fair," someone complains. "Of course not," I reply. My concern was not to be fair. My concern was to get the largest piece of cake—and I did. Surely here the appeal to *fairness*, to a consideration related to justice, is intended to override, or at least to constrain, preference-based choice. If you suppose that I should have chosen with fairness in mind, then you believe that I should not have acted simply to gratify my greed, even though my preference was for the largest piece of cake. You believe that I should have considered, not only my own desires, but also the desires of others.

Do examples such as this show that Rawls is wrong to treat the theory of justice as part of the theory of rational choice? Not at all. I shall argue that his claim is sound. Not that I agree with Rawls' theory of justice—that is quite another matter.[4] But justice provides a fundamental link between morality and preference, a link which, I believe, we are able to formulate in a precise and definitive way.

Indeed, I shall go farther than Rawls. In coming to understand how justice links morality and preference, one also realizes that our framework of moral concepts is seriously outmoded. Morality has been traditionally conceived as embracing the entire range of justifiable constraints on preference-based choice. But this range will be seen, in the light of my argument, to include at least two distinct, and apparently disparate, parts. One part, which I shall treat under the heading of *distributive justice*,[5] proves to be a constraint on preference-based choice which is based on the *structure* of some of the situations in which we make choices. This constraint is generated internally, within the theory of rational choice. That a *constraint* on preference can be justi-

---

[4]For some of my disagreements with Rawls, see my paper "Justice and Natural Endowment: Toward a Critique of Rawls' Ideological Framework," *Social Theory and Practice*, 3, 1974, pp. 3–26.

[5]Why *distributive* justice? Because my concern is with justice in contexts in which a distribution of benefits and costs is part of the object of choice. In my view, distributive justice contrasts with acquisitive justice; the first constrains modes of cooperation, the second constrains the baseline from which cooperation proceeds. The Lockean proviso (see n. 19 *infra*) concerns acquisitive justice, and falls in the realm of speculation which is not my concern in this paper.

fied by an *appeal* to preferences may appear paradoxical, but I shall endeavour to remove the air of paradox as we proceed. And as the upshot of my argument I shall insist that distributive justice is not problematic in principle; it may be removed from the area of speculative enquiry, and established securely within rational choice. The age-old philosophical problems about the rationality of morality are *solved* for the case of distributive justice.

But the firm foundation provided for the constraints on preference-based choice required by distributive justice does not extend to those other constraints which are embraced in our traditional conception of morality. This is why our framework of moral concepts is outmoded. We must distinguish those constraints on preferences which can be justified by an appeal to preference itself from other, external constraints. The latter remains, at least for the present, within the area of speculative enquiry. And here the philosophical problems about the rationality of morality press with renewed vigour.

2. My positive aim in this paper is to show you how we bargain our way into that part of morality which constitutes distributive justice. The bargain is based on our preferences; its outcome is an agreement which constrains our preferences; thus paradox is removed. But before doing this, I want to assure you that in my argument, I permit no sleight-of-hand with the conception of preference, and no question-begging assumptions about the conception of rationality.

I greedily take the largest piece of cake, and you reprimand me for not thinking of the others. Now you might claim that deep down, in my heart of hearts, I really do prefer to consider my fellows. You ask me to reflect. How would I feel were I in their shoes — or had I their appetites? And so forth. Humpty-Dumpty supposed that by paying words extra, we could make them mean what we like.[6] If we pay preference extra, perhaps it will line up with morality. The principles of justice will then reflect our real preferences, requiring us to choose what we really, reflectively, deep-down prefer. Humpty-Dumpty might say this. But Humpty-Dumpty is proverbially confused.

My aim is to *ground* the theory of distributive justice in the theory of rational choice. In doing this, I generate a part of moral theory from a theory which itself raises no moral issues. But if we insist that our real preferences are moral preferences, then the theory of rational choice is converted into a part of moral theory, and the non-moral grounding of distributive justice is sacrificed. Rather than showing how moral considerations of justice can be generated from non-moral considerations of choice, we should be showing how seemingly non-moral considerations of choice are actually morally based. Paying preference extra, to

---

[6]Cf. Lewis Carroll, *Through the Looking-Glass*, Ch. VI. "When I make a word do a lot of work like that," said Humpty Dumpty, "I always pay it extra."

make it mean what we like, turns our starting-point upside down — like Humpty-Dumpty after the fall.

Thus I shall not talk about "real" preferences — except to refer to what we actually and quite straightforwardly prefer. I *really* prefer the largest piece of cake. But, one might now say, nevertheless I have good *reason* to consider the preferences of others. Indeed, one might say, I have as much reason to consider their preferences as to consider my own. So what I should *rationally* choose is, not that state of affairs which I personally should most prefer, but rather that state of affairs which would best satisfy *everyone's* preferences. And that choice would, of course, be just.

Here the sleight-of-hand concerns reason. Rational choice, as I characterized it initially, assumes an essentially subjectivistic and instrumental conception of rationality. What is now urged is that this conception is inadequate. What is rational, it is claimed, must be rational for everyone. On the subjective view, this is taken to imply only that if *I* choose rationally on the basis of *my* preferences, then *you* choose rationally on the basis of *your* preferences. But it may be alleged that if *I* choose rationally on the basis of *any* preferences, then *you* choose rationally on the basis of those *same* preferences. On this objective view, the basis of rational choice must include everyone's preferences, or no one's, unless there are intrinsic differences among preferences (or preferrers) such that some count, and some do not.

The objectivistic conception of rationality might seem an ally in my attempt to ground the theory of distributive justice in the theory of rational choice. If objectivity requires that choice be based on everyone's preferences, then fairness seems implicit in the requirements of objective reason. But is objectivity correctly conceived as a requirement of, or a part of, rationality? Although I can not consider this question here, I shall say, quite dogmatically, that I find in every defense of the objectivistic conception of rationality a surreptitious, if not explicit, appeal to moral considerations.[7] The theory of objectively rational choice is thus a part of moral theory, and so can not provide a non-moral grounding of distributive justice.

I do not deny that rationality has implications for morality; indeed, I hope to show what those implications are. But I do deny that rationality is a moral conception. And so I can not appeal to an objectivistic account of rationality which itself depends on moral presuppositions, but only to a subjectivistic, instrumental account which is clearly non-moral. A person acts rationally insofar as he or she seeks to maximize expected utility, where utility is a measure of individual preference. I neither need, nor will accept, any stronger premiss.

---

[7]The test case here would be the discussion of objective reasons in Thomas Nagel, *The Possibility of Altruism*, Oxford, 1970, Chs. X, XII.

3. The link which justice provides between morality and rational choice is discovered by reflection on a phenomenon long of concern to economists, but only recently receiving explicit attention from philosophers. The perfectly competitive market, the ideal of economic theory, is frequently marred by the presence of external inefficiencies. Here is a simple example of an inefficiency.

Several factories must each choose a method of waste disposal. Suppose that air is a free good, so that each factory may discharge effluents into the atmosphere without payment or restriction. Each may then find that it minimizes disposal costs by using the atmosphere as a sink for its wastes. But each factory may also suffer from the pollution occasioned by the effluents discharged. Indeed, it may be that the total cost to all factories, of atmospheric pollution caused by their wastes, exceeds the total net benefit in discharging those wastes into the atmosphere, rather than employing the least costly non-polluting method of disposal. The use of the atmosphere as a sink then constitutes an external inefficiency — *external*, in that each user displaces the costs of pollution onto others, and *inefficient*, in that the total costs of pollution exceed the total increase in disposal costs which would be required by an alternative non-polluting method of waste disposal. But no factory has any incentive to adopt such an alternative; each correctly minimizes its own costs by discharging its effluents into the atmosphere.

An external inefficiency creates a severe problem for rational choice. We may show this by considering an ideal case, in which each person involved in a situation is able to choose his or her course of action in the light of the actions selected by others.[8] Then, if the persons are rational, each will select that course of action which he or she expects will maximize his or her own utility, given the actions selected by the others. Each action will then be a *best reply* by the agent to the other's actions. If in any situation the action of each is a best reply to the actions of the others, then the set of actions is a *best reply* set.

In the presence of an external inefficiency, the outcome of any best reply set of actions is *sub-optimal*, which is say that there is at least one other outcome possible in the situation which would better satisfy the preferences of *every person*.[9] Thus rational choice, given an external inefficiency, leads to an outcome which is *mutually disadvantageous*, in

---

[8]It may seem that if each person is to choose his or her course of action in the light of the actions chosen by the others, a regress is involved. But in fact the requirement may be operationalized quite straightforwardly. Suppose that each person were to announce his or her proposed action to the others, that after each announcement any other person might announce a new or changed proposal, and that no one were to act until, everyone having made some proposal, no one had announced any change.

[9]Strictly, an outcome is sub-optimal if there is at least one other possible outcome which would better satisfy the preferences of some persons without lessening the satisfaction of any.

comparison with some other outcome which the persons could achieve if at least some were to choose differently.

In our example, each factory's best reply to the adoption of waste disposal methods by the others, is to discharge its own wastes into the atmosphere. But if each were to adopt some non-polluting alternative, then all would benefit. It may therefore seem that there is a straightforward solution to this problem created by the external inefficiency —a *cooperative* solution based on mutual *agreement*. All of the factories should agree to the least costly non-polluting method of waste disposal. It may then be urged that each factory's *true* best reply to the others consists in such mutual agreement, and since its outcome is optimal, the inefficiency disappears and there is no problem for rational choice.

Alas, matters are not so simple and straightforward. First, although a non-polluting method of waste disposal reduces total net costs, yet each factory need not benefit. Some factories may suffer greatly from the pollution caused by others, or may find some non-polluting method of waste disposal only slightly more costly than using the atmosphere as a sink, but other factories may suffer very little from pollution, or may find the increased costs of any alternative disposal method very great. Thus an agreement to adopt a non-polluting method of waste disposal, although beneficial on balance, may increase net costs for some factories. To avoid this, the agreement must provide for transfer payments, from those factories which would otherwise benefit most from non-pollution to those which would otherwise not benefit at all. But the amount of compensation is not easily determined. In general, many possible arrangements will leave each factory better off than if all pollute, so that reaching a specific agreement, which each would rationally choose, raises difficulties not only in practice, but for the theory of choice.

Furthermore, although the outcome of an agreement not to pollute may be optimal, and although the outcome of an agreement which includes transfer payments may be mutually advantageous, yet *adherence* to any agreement need not be the best reply course of action for any factory. Each factory would most prefer that all others cease using the atmosphere as a sink, while it continues polluting. Hence each will be tempted to defect from any agreement, however beneficial the agreement may be. Adherence to an agreement not to pollute, and to compensate any who would not otherwise benefit, is not, in the absence of penalties for violation, the most preferred course of action for any factory, whether the other factories adhere to the agreement, or violate it. Mutual violation thus makes up the best reply set of actions.

External inefficiencies thus raise two problems for rational choice. First, how are we to formulate a specific, optimal, mutually advantageous agreement, or mode of cooperation, for overcoming an inefficiency, which each person affected will consider it rational to accept?

Second, how are we to ensure that rational persons will comply with an agreement so formulated and accepted? These problems may be related, in that we may suppose that compliance with an agreement is rational if acceptance of the agreement is also rational. But this is not evident, and I shall return to the problem of rational compliance in section 6.

4. Let us now focus on the problem of formulating a rational agreement. An agreement consists of a set of actions, one for each person party to it. I assume for the present that compliance is assured, so that no restriction to best reply sets of actions is involved. Now we may say that an agreement takes effect if and only if each party selects the same set of actions. Hence we may represent the problem of formulating agreement as a problem of rational choice — the problem of choosing among alternative possible states of affairs, each the outcome of a set of actions, one for each person involved, subject to the condition that the choice takes effect only if all parties select the same alternative.

This problem arises for anyone who may find him or herself in situations so structured that external inefficiencies arise, or in other words, so structured that no best reply set of actions is optimal. Although not all situations involving interaction among persons have this structure, there can be no assurance against finding oneself in such situations, as long as each individual's preference orderings among alternative possibilities are independent of the orderings of others. So this is a general problem which we all face. Its resolution is not to be found in the particular circumstances in which an individual finds him or herself. Rather its answer must be a general policy applicable to all such circumstances — and, obviously, applicable to all individuals. The policy which any person should adopt, who seeks to cooperate with his or her fellows in the face of external inefficiencies, is and must be identical with the policy every other person should adopt. The content of an agreed set of actions will of course vary with persons, their capacities, preferences, and circumstances, but the form which their agreement takes will be perfectly general.

Consider then the reasoning of a supposedly rational agent — myself — faced with this problem of rational choice. Given an external inefficiency, I must be willing to enter into some agreement with my fellows. Its expected utility to me must exceed the expected utility of failing to agree, which is the utility of my best reply to the actions I should expect others to perform in the absence of agreement. Its expected utility cannot exceed the greatest utility which would be compatible with others receiving only minimally more than they would in the absence of agreement. Thus a utility range is defined, with its lowest point the utility of no agreement, and its highest point the maximum utility compatible with others receiving their "no-agreement" utility. Each person will define such a utility range for him or herself, and only sets of actions which assure everyone a utility within his or her range will be candidates for agreement.

In choosing among candidates some compromise will be required. I must recognize that I am involved in a *bargaining situation*, and must make some *concession*.[10] How do I decide the magnitude of the concession which my agreement to some set of actions would require? The answer is implicit in the conception of a utility range. The lowest point of my range represents my point of *total concession*, in which I gain nothing from agreement. The highest point represents *no concession*, in which I gain everything. Any intermediate point may be represented as a proportion of my total concession. Not only will this measure my concession; it will relate it to the concessions of others. Two persons make *equal concessions* in a situation if and only if each concedes the *same proportion* of his or her total concession.

Each set of actions which is a candidate for agreement may be represented also as a set of concessions, one for each person. Each such set must have a largest member—*the maximum* concession required for agreement to be reached on that set. Some possible set of concessions must have a largest member which is *no* greater than the largest member of any alternative set. This is the *minimax* concession—the smallest, or minimum, among all possible largest, or maximum concessions.

If there is to be agreement, then someone must make a concession at least equal to the minimax. Now if it is not rational for me to make such a concession, then, since the policy which is rational for me is rational for everyone, it is not rational for any person to make such a concession, and there can be no rational agreement. But it is rational for me to enter into an agreement; hence it must be rational for me to make a minimax concession. Furthermore, since agreement can be reached without any person making a larger concession, and since it cannot be rational for me to make a greater concession than necessary, it cannot be rational for me to make a concession larger than the minimax. Hence it is rational for me to enter into any agreement requiring at most the minimax concession from me. Since everyone reasons similarly, bargaining among rational persons proceeds on the *principle of minimax concession*. And this solves the problem of rational choice occasioned by external inefficiencies.

We have now characterized a *rational bargain*. I must next argue that the principle of minimax concession captures our conception of distri-

---

[10]Discussions of bargaining theory may be found in J. F. Nash, "The Bargaining Problem," *Econometrica*, 18, 1950, pp. 155–162; E. Kalai and M. Smorodinsky, "Other Solutions to Nash's Bargaining Problem," *Econometrica*, 43, 1975, pp. 513–518; and my paper "The Social Contract: Individual Decision or Collective Bargain!," in C. A. Hooker, J. J. Leach, and E. F. McClennen (eds.), *Foundations and Applications of Decision Theory*, Vol. II, Reidel, Dordrecht and Boston, 1978, pp. 47–67. The account I provide here of a rational bargain parallels a solution offered by Kalai and Smorodinsky.

butive justice, in characterizing a bargain which is fair as well as rational. And I must also argue that the principle constitutes a constraint on preference-based choice, even though it is, as I have shown, itself the outcome of a preference-based choice. Thus I must show that in acting on the principle of minimax concession, we enter into bargains which are fair, and which constrain preference — or in other words, we bargain our way into morally binding arrangements.

One word of warning is in place before proceeding. Although we may literally bargain our way into moral constraints in some contexts, references to bargains and agreements are to be understood hypothetically. We face externalities and, if we are rational, we cooperate to overcome them. We may then assess our mode of cooperation *as if* it were the outcome of a bargain. But we need suppose no actual bargain or agreement.

5. Under what conditions is a state of affairs *distributively just?* The presence of more than one person (or perhaps of more than one sentient being) gives rise to a "distribution" of utilities, but this is not sufficient to raise issues of justice. If a state of affairs is said to be just or unjust, there must be at least one alternative to it, the variation in the utility-levels of different persons among alternatives must be at least partially interdependent, and the selection among alternatives must be at least partially a matter of human choice. These conditions are required if any comparison of the utilities received by different persons is to have moral significance. For distributive justice to have significance, distributive considerations must be relevant to the choice among the alternatives. If that choice is adequately represented by a best reply set of actions, then although the choice has distributive effects, these are of no concern to the choosers. It is, therefore, only when all best reply sets lead to sub-optimal outcomes, so that there are mutual advantages to be found in agreement or cooperation among persons, that considerations of distributive justice arise. Other moral considerations may arise in other contexts, but in restricting distributive justice to the context of mutually advantageous cooperation, we are following in the footsteps of Hobbes, Hume, and Rawls.[11]

This restriction on the scope of considerations of distributive justice suggests that a state of affairs is just, if and only if those involved in it would justly have agreed to the set of actions bringing it about. We must make any reference to agreement hypothetical, since as I have pointed out, much of our social interaction which is at least partially cooperative involves no actual agreement or bargain. But we may replace our question about the justice of states of affairs by one about the justice of agreements, provided we recognize that "Would we

[11]Cf. discussions in Thomas Hobbes, *Leviathan*, Ch. 15; David Hume, *An Enquiry Concerning the Principles of Morals*, Sec. III, Pt. I; John Rawls, *A Theory of Justice*, pp. 126–130.

agree . . . ?" rather than "Did we agree . . . ?" is the appropriate way to introduce reference to such agreements.

The justice of an agreement may be supposed to have two dimensions—one concerning the manner of agreement, the other concerning the matter or content of agreement. But we cannot strictly distinguish these dimensions since in the case of hypothetical agreement, manner reduces to matter. We might say that, *ceteris paribus*, an agreement is just in manner if and only if it is genuinely voluntary. But the nearest approximation to what is voluntary in the case of hypothetical agreement, must be what is rationally acceptable. And so rationality and justice are inextricably intertwined in our account.

But we may still reflect on the matter of agreement. And here, although rationality and justice are still intertwined, the connection is less direct. For we may say, quite without reference to rationality, that a non-optimal agreement, in depriving someone of benefit unnecessarily, without gain to anyone else, is unfair to the person so deprived. It is unfair for me to be allowed to profit at another's expense, no doubt, but it is equally unfair to me not to be allowed to profit, if no one is worsened thereby. Thus optimality is a requirement of fairness, and so of justice, as well as a requirement of rationality.

And this is not all. It is unfair to profit at another's expense. How is this unfairness expressed in the context of agreement? Each person's utility range represents his or her possible gain. The expected utility of any proposed agreement may be represented as a proportion of that gain, and so represented, constitutes the *relative advantage* of the agreement to the person. Now one profits at another's expense insofar as one's own relative advantage can arise only if he or she accepts, not merely a lesser relative advantage, but one less than anyone need accept. Thus one would arrive at a fair agreement by maximizing the minimum relative advantage received by anyone. But the measure of relative advantage is such that for any agreement, the sum of one's relative advantage and one's concession equal unity. Thus maximin relative advantage is equivalent to minimax concession. And so the requirements of fairness and rationality coincide. A hypothetical agreement which is just in manner and fair in matter is a rational agreement.

The justice of an agreement has been characterized *relatively* to the set of possible agreements. In other words, a state of affairs is distributively just (or unjust) in relation to alternatives. The set of possible agreements is itself defined relatively to the expected outcome of no agreement. Thus the justice or injustice of a state of affairs is determined against a baseline which provides a certain expected utility to each person, but which itself is not characterized as just or unjust. Any assessment, either of the range of possibilities, or of the baseline, falls outside the scope of considerations of distributive justice, except insofar as the assessment refers to other cooperative arrangements treated in terms of hypothetical agreement. Such assessment thus constitutes part of the realm of speculative enquiry from which distributive justice is freed by its identification with rational choice.

6. Why does a rational bargain, or a mode of cooperation which could be rationalized in terms of a bargain, involve a moral constraint on action? An objector might plausibly argue that insofar as the point of a bargain is to benefit all parties to it, morality has no place. Agreement and cooperation simply constitute an extension of rational prudence.

The apparent strength of this objection rests on ignoring the problem of compliance. This problem has received attention from earlier theorists of justice; although my concern here is not to discuss texts, a quotation from Hume may be illuminating. Hume, I should note, holds a general view of morality strongly opposed to the one I have assumed; he supposes it to further, rather than to constrain, each individual's pursuit of his own interests.[12] But on this view he finds that justice presents a problem:

"Treating vice with the greatest candour, . . . there is not, in any instance, the smallest pretext for giving it the preference above virtue, with a view of self-interest; except, perhaps, in the case of justice, where a man, taking things in a certain light, may often seem to be a loser by his integrity. . . . a sensible knave, in particular incidents, may think that an act of iniquity or infidelity will make a considerable addition to his fortune, without causing any considerable breach in the social union and confederacy. That *honesty is the best policy*, may be a good general rule, but is liable to many exceptions; and he, it may perhaps be thought, conducts himself with most wisdom, who observes the general rule, and takes advantage of all the exceptions."

"I must confess that, if a man think that this reasoning much requires an answer, it would be a little difficult to find any which will to him appear satisfactory and convincing."[13]

Hume states the problem of compliance very clearly. Grant that it is rational — or, to use his terminology, preferred with a view to self-interest — to agree on a particular mode of cooperation in situations in which otherwise external inefficiencies would prevent an optimal outcome. Grant that one should adhere to such agreements as a general rule, so that one avoids penalties, maintains one's reputation, and sets others a good example. Yet it is nevertheless advantageous to act on whatever opportunities will prove maximally profitable to oneself, including opportunities to violate one's agreements. And so it is in some cases rational to violate agreements, even though it is unjust.

---

[12]". . . what theory of morals can ever serve any useful purpose, unless it can show, by a particular detail, that all the duties which it recommends, are also the true interest of each individual?" *An Enquiry Concerning . . . Morals*, Sec. IX, Pt. II.

[13]*An Enquiry Concerning . . . Morals*, Sec. IX, Pt. II.

I reject this conclusion. Adherence to one's agreements does indeed in some situations constitute a genuine constraint on preference-based choice. Were this not so, adherence would not be morally significant. But it is not contrary to reason to adhere, insofar as one is adhering to what is or would be a rational bargain. If one is to overcome inefficiencies by bargaining, then one must be able to expect everyone to adhere to the bargained outcome. It is advantageous to overcome inefficiencies, advantageous to do this by bargaining, advantageous therefore to be able to expect adherence to the outcome, and so, I maintain, *rational* to adhere to the outcome. Rationality is transmitted from making an agreement, to keeping the agreement.

Elsewhere I discuss this matter at greater length, arguing that the conclusion I have just reached requires a modification in the maximizing conception of rationality—a modification which, however, it is rational to choose.[14] Thus rationality and morality are brought into harmony. Adherence to a rational bargain, one resting on the principle of minimax concession, is just, and justice is both a requirement of reason, rightly understood, and an imperative of morality, constraining our preference-based choices.

The principle of minimax concession is thus both the object of rational choice for any person faced with external inefficiencies, and a ground of moral constraint. Characterizing all rational bargains and all modes of rational cooperation, it may itself be conceived as the outcome of a meta-bargain—of a supreme hypothetical agreement among all human beings who must interact in situations in which best reply sets of actions are sub-optimal. In accepting the principle of minimax concession, we bargain our way, not into particular moral arrangements, but into morality itself—or at least, into that part of morality constituted by distributive justice.

7. The principle of minimax concession is applied against a baseline situation, and a range of possibilities which must each be mutually advantageous in relation to that baseline. In effect, both the characteristics and the existing circumstances of the persons involved are taken for granted; they provide a framework which determines whether the principle of justice has any application. As Hume noted, the relation between human beings and other creatures who, though rational, lack power to express effectively any resentment against human behaviour, does not involve the restraints of justice. Humans may act as they will, and "as no inconvenience ever results from the exercise of a power, so firmly established in nature, the restraints of justice and property, being totally *useless*, would never have place in so unequal a confederacy."[15] Hume insisted that animals in relation to humans, barbarous

---

[14]Cf. my paper "Reason and Maximization," *Canadian Journal of Philosophy*, 4, 1975, especially pp. 426–430.

[15]*An Enquiry Concerning . . . Morals*, Sec. III, Pt. I.

Indians in relation to civilized Europeans, and in many nations the female sex in relation to the male, are in a position of inferiority such that questions of justice and injustice simply do not arise.

Hobbes, who saw in morality a rational response to the horrendous external inefficiencies of the state of nature, and Rawls, who supposed the principles of justice to be the objects of rational choice in circumstances "under which human cooperation is both possible and necessary" have both insisted that one must reason from an initial situation of equality.[16] But this is no part of the present account—or of Hume's theory. Human beings are equally rational, and so all must choose the same principle to regulate their interaction. The worry that one might tailor principles to his or her particular advantage can be seen to be unfounded, once the formal constraints on choice are properly understood. The real worry is that the principle applies to whatever situations do arise, so that, although we bargain our way into moral constraints, we do so from a purely amoral stance. When we eliminate from our account all factors which do not fall within the domain of rational choice—when we eliminate, for example, either Rawls' specially favoured or Hobbes' specially disfavoured no agreement point—we find that distributive justice is an extremely weak constraint on preference-based choice.

An example—quite fictitious, of course—will help to clarify my point. Suppose a planet, the land mass of which consists of two large islands, widely separated by stormy seas. On each, human life—or life close enough to human for our purposes—has developed in complete independence and ignorance of the other. On one island, the Purple People have developed an ideally just society. Knowing the extent of their natural resources, they have adopted policies governing population, conservation, and development, to ensure, as far as they are able, that the worst-off person shall benefit, relative to his or her personal characteristics and the possible modes of social cooperation, as much as possible, not only in the present generation, but throughout their forseeable future. On the other island, the Green People live in totally chaotic squalor. Taking no thought for the morrow, they have propagated their kind and squandered their resources so that they are on the brink of catastrophic collapse. At this point in their respective histories, an exploration party from the Purple People discovers the Green People, and reports back on their condition.

Consensus among the Purple People is reached on the following points. First, any contact between Purple and Green will require Pur-

---

[16]"If Nature . . . have made men equal, that equalitie is to be acknowledged: or if Nature have made men unequal; yet because men think that themselves equal, will not enter into conditions of Peace, but upon Equal terms, such equalitie must be admitted." *Leviathan*, Ch. 15. "It seems reasonable to suppose that the parties in the original position are equal." *A Theory of Justice*, p. 19. The words quoted in the text are from p. 126.

ple's initiative, since the Greens lack means of both transportation and communication across the ocean. Second, the combined resources of the two islands cannot support the combined populations at the level achieved by the Purple society. Third, maximization of the average absolute level of planetary well-being would require a massive but technologically feasible transfer of resources from Purples to Greens. And fourth, the Purple People have the capacity to eliminate the Green People, without any possibility of significant retaliation.

Four parties develop among the Purple People. The first, whom I shall call Utilitarians, demand that the Purples give up their comfortable way of life to rescue the Greens from impending catastrophe and maximize overall well-being. The second group proposes that existing levels of well-being in the two societies be taken as a baseline, and the possibilities of mutually advantageous interchange be explored, in line with the principle of minimax concession.[17] This policy, members of the group urge, will maximize the minimum gain relative to existing circumstances, and so will be just. The third group argues that the strains of the continuing inequality between Purple and Greens envisaged in the policy proposed by the second group will outweigh any advantages from interchanges, and urge therefore that no contact be established with the Greens. Finally, the fourth group, whom I shall call Hobbists, argues that the others mistakenly identify the baseline with the existing situation rather than with the outcome of no agreement. Whatever the Greens may seek to do, the best action for the Purples is to eliminate the Greens and appropriate their resources. There is no place for mutually advantageous agreement, and so for consideration of justice.

Let us reflect on these proposals. In my view, many existing moral theories accept far too strong constraints on the maximization of individual utility. Advocates of such theories would find themselves committed to the individually and socially sacrificial policies of the Utilitarian Purples. But not one of us acts on the counterpart of such policies. It is, however, a long step between supposing that one would be literally mad if one took utilitarianism seriously *in practice*, and supposing that we should accept only that part of morality which can be salvaged with our theory of distributive justice. For we should then be committed to the annihilative policies of the Hobbist Purples, since they recognize that the Purples have no reason to cooperate in any way with the Greens, but rather every reason to eliminate them and acquire their resources.

Of course, it is possible that humanitarian feelings would not only hold the Purple People back from the Hobbist policy, but would make

---

[17]I shall leave the second and third parties unnamed. I do however believe that the second party could fairly be called Humean, but I cannot defend this claim here.

that policy actually less satisfying than one of the alternatives. But surely we should want to say that it would be *wrong* for the Purples to annihilate the Greens, even if the Purples take no interest whatsoever in the Greens' interests, or feel no emotional concern at all. The Greens, we might even say, have rights, which would be violated were the Purples to annihilate them.[18] There are moral constraints which the Purples should recognize, stronger than any which are generated by mutual advantage.

Either the Purple People should cooperate with the Greens, taking their present situations as the baseline, or they should leave them alone. Which they should do depends, in my view, on empirical, psychological considerations about the strains of a continuing, unequal relationship. This is an issue in moral psychology, but not directly in moral philosophy. But to defend this position, I require something akin to Nozick's well-known Lockean proviso, as a constraint on the baseline from which mutual advantage is to be determined.[19] In the absence of such a constraint, I see no defense against the Hobbist who insists that the inequality in power between Purples and Greens makes any moral relationship, any moral constraint, irrational.

Thus I come to both an optimistic and a pessimistic conclusion. The optimistic conclusion is that the argument which I have presented grounds a part, and a not unimportant part, of traditional morality, on a strictly rational footing. Using only the weak conceptions of value as individual preference-satisfaction, and of rationality as maximizing preference-satisfaction, I have established the rationality of distributive justice, as that constraint on preference-based choice required by minimax concession.

The pessimistic conclusion is that no similar argument will put the remainder, or any important part of the remainder, of traditional morality on a similarly rational footing. I have not shown this, but we may easily see that the only constraints on preference-based choice which are compatible with our conceptions of value and reason must be those which it is mutually advantageous for us to accept, and these are simply the constraints required by minimax concession. Having abandoned all religious or metaphysical props for morality, we are left with no justification for principles some of which, at least, we are unwilling to abandon.

Related to these conclusions are two opposed views of our society. The optimistic view is that modern Western society is, so far, unique in

---

[18]The reader may (should) be reminded of: "Individuals have rights, and there are things no person or group may do to them (without violating their rights)." Robert Nozick, *Anarchy, State and Utopia*, Basic Books, New York, 1974, p. ix.

[19]"Locke's proviso . . . is meant to ensure that the situation of others is not worsened." *Anarchy, State and Utopia*, p. 175. Clearly the Hobbist policy would worsen the situation of the Greens.

its recognition that the sole purposes for which coercive authority is justified among human beings are, first, to overcome the force and fraud which are the great external inefficiencies in the state of nature, thus making possible the emergence of the free, competitive market, and second, to assure the efficacy of those modes of cooperation which are required to avoid those public bads and attain those public goods which the free activity of the market will not provide. Until corrupted by the utilitarian and egalitarian ideas which have led to the welfare state, our society was beginning, for the first time in human history, to make it possible for human affairs to be guided by reason and justice.

The pessimistic view is that modern Western society has abandoned every justification for coercive authority and for constraints on preference-based choice save that which stems from consideration of mutual advantage, thereby opening the way to the dissolution of all those genuinely social bonds among human beings which are the necessary cement of any viable public order. That there is a rational resolution of the problem of compliance is of little concern to human beings for whom reason is the slave of the passions, and who, freed from traditional constraints, face a rapid decline into the state of nature conceived as the war of every person against every person.[20]

There is a schizophrenia in these conclusions which I find haunting the core of my moral and political theory. Perhaps we exceed both our hopes and our fears in bargaining our way into morality.

[20]Cf. my paper "The Social Contract as Ideology," *Philosophy and Public Affairs*, 6, 1977, especially pp. 159–164.

9

PHILIP PETTIT

Habermas on Truth and Justice

1. Introduction

THE PROBLEM WHICH motivates this paper bears on the relationship between Marxism and morality. It is not the well-established question of whether the Marxist's commitments undermine an attachment to ethical standards, but the more neglected query as to whether they allow the espousal of political ideals. The study and assessment of political ideals is pursued nowadays under the title of theory of justice, the aim of such theory being to provide a criterion for distinguishing just patterns of social organization from unjust ones. The main rivals in the field represent justice respectively as legitimacy, welfare and fairness.[1] Marxism does not put forward a distinctive conception of justice itself and the question is whether the Marxist is free to choose as he thinks fit among the candidates on offer.

There is a sting in the question. The various conceptions of justice elaborated in the literature of political philosophy are all of them paradigms of that sort of thinking castigated by Marxists as bourgeois or ideological, undialectical or unhistorical. This indeed is no accident, for the method whereby the argument between the conceptions is advanced seems particularly vulnerable to such criticism: it is invariably characterized as depending at crucial points on an appeal to intuition about matters of justice, and intuition of this kind is surely susceptible

---

[1] See my *Judging Justice: An Introduction to Contemporary Political Philosophy* (London: Routledge & Kegan Paul, 1980).

to the influences of social formation with which Marx among others has made us familiar.[2]

In face of this depressing state of affairs the Marxist might think of disallowing altogether the investigation of the nature of justice. And yet that is scarcely an attractive option. For if the demands of justice are not something that we can sensibly think of construing in an objective manner, then what is it that vindicates the Marxist criticism of existing social structures? It will not do for the Marxist to invoke the march of history, for the fact that present structures are doomed, if indeed they are so, does nothing to show that their demise should be applauded or hastened.

The Marxist, it appears, is in a dilemma.[3] If he countenances the enterprise of political philosophy, the investigation of the nature of justice, he must weaken the received theory of social formation. If he does not countenance it, he must give up all claim to the rational criticism of social arrangements and play the role of blind collaborator to the historical process. My own view is that his best recourse is to adopt the first horn and reconsider the nature of ideology, but in this essay I would like to examine the approach to the problem which Jürgen Habermas has sponsored in his recent writing.

Habermas is the principal representative today of that tradition of Marxist thinking known as critical theory. This tradition goes back to the Frankfurt Institute of Social Research which was founded in 1923: its main exponents in earlier years were Theodore Adorno and Max Horkheimer but it also encompassed such thinkers as Walter Benjamin, Erich Fromm and Herbert Marcuse.[4] Habermas has wrought a powerful transformation of Marxist thinking in his work of the last twenty years, although one which maintains many of the emphases of his heritage in critical theory. He rates on any estimate as one of the most important Marxist theorists writing today.

The key to Habermas's reworking of Marxism is his importation from the hermeneutic tradition of a distinction between the interventionist disposition that we adopt towards systems which we seek to control and the interactive one that we take up *vis-à-vis* persons with whom we

---

[2]See *Judging Justice*, Chapter 4.

[3]The problem is nicely described in a passage from Alasdair MacIntyre, *Against the Self-Images of the Age* (London: Duckworth, 1971), 92–93. 'Marx originally indicted capitalist values as well as capitalist methods. His belief that any appeal to the exploiters on a moral basis was bound to embody the illusion of common standards of justice governing human behaviour made him suspicious of all moralizing. But when Eduard Bernstein attempted to find a Kantian basis for socialism, the defenders of Marxist orthodoxy Karl Kautsky and Rosa Luxembourg were forced to reopen the question of the nature of the moral authority of the Marxist appeal to the working class. This question, as the experience of Luxembourg and of Lukács, of Trotsky and of Guevara shows, was never satisfactorily answered.'

[4]See Paul Connerton (ed.), *Critical Sociology* (Harmondsworth: Allen Lane, 1976), and Martin Jay, *The Dialectical Imagination* (London: Heinemann, 1973).

wish to communicate. What he has done, in a nutshell, is to elaborate the significance for Marxist theory and praxis of accepting that this distinction is a valid one. At the level of praxis he has emphasized that if one thinks of revolution on the model of the party steering the proletariat, or if one sees social organization as ideally tending towards finer bureaucratic rationalization, one condones a treatment of human beings which sees them only as systems to be technically controlled. At the level of theory he has stressed that only an interest in securing such technical control licenses the deterministic ambitions of historical materialism, and that a more liberal sense of the cognitive interests which theory ought to serve, in particular social theory, makes possible a richer interpretation and development of the historical materialist tradition.[5]

But what Habermas has to say on these general matters I must leave aside. I want to consider in this paper only the response which he has underwritten to the dilemma posed above. He has recently put forward a consensus theory of justice which is meant to slip between the horns of that dilemma, indicating a valid basis for social criticism and yet escaping the charge of ideological distortion. The feature of the consensus theory which turns the necessary trick is what I shall call its agnosticism. The theory gives us a criterion of justice, identifying the just social scheme as that which would attract rational consensus, but it denies that the criterion can be applied with certainty in an imperfect world, holding that we cannot now know what would command rational agreement. The criterion is one which the Marxist critic may claim, with due diffidence, to be applying; he is gambling on what people would opt for in a rational consensus. However, it is not a criterion which can raise ideological worries, for by leaving us in an agnostic position about what scheme would satisfy the condition it defers appropriately to the constraints of social formation.

My discussion of Habermas's theory will divide naturally into two parts. Habermas rejects the view that evaluative matters, and in particular matters having to do with justice, are any less objective and decidable than empirical ones.[6] He does not go so far as to say that evaluative statements are true or false in the same way as empirical, but he does think that the method whereby empirical truth is established provides a

---

[5]For a comprehensive introduction to Habermas's thought see Thomas McCarthy, *The Critical Theory of Jürgen Habermas* (London: Hutchinson, 1978). Richard Bernstein has a useful shorter account in *The Restructuring of Social and Political Theory* (London: Methuen, 1976). Books of Habermas which have appeared in English are: *Towards a Rational Society* (London: Heinemann, 1971), *Knowledge and Human Interests* (London: Heinemann, 1972), *Theory and Practice* (London: Heinemann, 1974) and *Legitimation Crisis* (London: Heinemann, 1976). For a bibliography see McCarthy.

[6]'Wahrheitstheorien' in *Wirklichkeit und Reflexion: Walter Schulz zum 60 Geburtstag* (Pfullingen: Neske, 1973), 226–227. We speak of justice where Habermas uses the word 'Richtigkeit'.

model for the corresponding evaluative procedure.[7] Thus in the first part of this discussion I shall consider his approach to empirical truth and in the second I shall look at his parallel treatment of the evaluative counterpart to truth, something that might be called evaluative adequacy: the phrase however is not one that we shall need, for where the adequacy of political evaluations is under discussion we may equally well speak of justice, this being what such adequacy betokens. As we shall see, Habermas defends what he calls a consensus theory of truth and it is this which gives him his model for a consensus theory of justice.[8]

2. The Consensus Theory of Truth

Truth, according to Habermas, is something which a speaker implicitly claims for any assertion that he makes.[9] In being bold enough to speak, the speaker invites us to believe that what he says is intelligible, that he is sincere in saying it, that he is not speaking out of turn, at least not in any serious sense of that phrase, and that he is speaking the truth: these are the four validity claims, as Habermas calls them, of any assertion.[10] Although it is said to be the job of a universal pragmatics of speech to isolate these claims, the case for the truth claim is readily made. Any assertion 'p' is equivalent to the assertion '"p" is true' and, this being general knowledge, a speaker who says that 'p' must expect to be taken to believe, and in that sense must implicitly claim, 'p' is true.[11]

It is a feature of communication that a speaker must be prepared to back up the claims which he implicitly makes if he is challenged by his

---

[7]'Wahrheitstheorien', 219. It is doubtful whether Habermas has any good reason for not speaking of evaluative truth. For a discussion of the case for ascribing truth-value to evaluate assertions see David Wiggins 'Truth, Invention and the Meaning of Life', *Proceedings of the British Academy* 26 (1976), and my own 'Evaluative "Realism" and Interpretation' in S. Holtzmann and C. Leich (eds), *Wittgenstein: To Follow a Rule* (London: Routledge & Kegan Paul, 1981).

[8]The main source on Habermas's theory of truth, and indeed also on his theory of justice, is the still untranslated paper 'Wahrheitstheorien'; this will henceforth be referred to as 'W' and any quotations from it will be in my own translation. McCarthy provides a faithful commentary on Habermas's views on truth and justice in the book mentioned under reference 5. For a critical commentary on his theory of truth see Mary Hesse, 'Habermas's Consensus Theory of Truth', *Proceedings of the Philosophy of Science Association 1978*, 2 (1979). Reprinted in Mary Hesse, *Revolutions and Reconstructions in the Philosophy of Science* (Hassocks: Harvester, 1980).

[9]Habermas also holds that there is a truth claim implicit in non-assertoric speech acts, as there is held to be a claim of each of the other sorts mentioned later. See 'Was heisst Universalpragmatik?' in K. O. Apel (ed.), *Sprachpragmatik und Philosophie* (Frankfurt: Suhrkamp, 1976). What he has in mind seems to be a claim to the truth of the existential presuppositions of such acts.

[10]On the four claims see 'Was heisst Universalpragmatik?'. The claim to intelligibility is not so much a claim as an assumption. The other claims might be suitably rendered as claims to knowledge, honesty and authority.

[11]See W 213–215: notice Habermas's supposition that every assertion is true or false.

hearers. The attempt to redeem the truth claim of an assertion gives rise to what Habermas calls theoretical discourse. In such discourse arguments are advanced for and against the truth of the proposition in question. The structure of the arguments is described by Habermas on a model derived from Stephen Toulmin.[12] The contentious proposition, say 'Harry is a British subject', will be traced by the speaker to a piece of *evidence* or data, such as 'Harry was born in Bermuda'. If the force of this evidence is questioned an attempt will be made to provide a *warrant* for the connection: this will take the form of a rule such as 'A man born in Bermuda will generally be a British subject'. Finally under yet further pressure an effort will be made to supply this warrant with a *backing*: say an account of certain legal provisions which explain why the rule in question holds.

But if truth is the topic of debate in theoretical discourse, what does it consist in? Habermas reasons that any answer to this question must maintain the connection between truth and argument: it must make truth out to be something operational, something that can be decided among partners in discourse. 'We call those statements true for which we are able to argue.'[13] On the basis of this consideration he rejects the assimilation of truth either to the subjective experience of certainty or to correspondence with objective fact. The first move would break the connection between truth and argument because certainty is a private experience and, while it may generally attend the acceptance of certain simple observation reports, it is not systematically responsive to the argument which guides propositional assent.[14] The assimilation to correspondence would also break the link between truth and argument, Habermas says, because, if they are taken seriously, the facts in correspondence with which truth allegedly consists must be admitted to be transcendent and inaccessible entities: they are not identifiable after all with the events and objects which form the data of our experience.[15]

At this point it would appear that there are two options open to Habermas. He might maintain the operational character of truth through identifying the property methodologically, by reference to the procedure of verification, or sociologically, by reference to the circumstance licensing assent. The methodological approach is part of the heritage of logical positivism and it would identify truth with that property which belongs to propositions and theories that satisfy certain confirmation tests. This identification may be understood analytically or not, depending on whether truth is defined as the ability to pass the

[12]W 241ff. See Stephen Toulmin, *The Uses of Argument* (Cambridge: Cambridge University Press, 1964).

[13]W 219.

[14]W 223–226. Cf. 'A Postscript to *Knowledge and Human Interests*' in *Philosophy of the Social Sciences* 3 (1973), 170.

[15]W 215–219.

tests or is taken as the property, whatever it is, which explains that ability: depending on whether it is said to be necessarily or contingently connected with test-passing. Habermas has no truck with it however, in either sense.[16] He is not explicit about his reasons for rejecting the account but one may conjecture that he would object to it on the grounds that there is no plausible set of confirmation tests which would pick out just those theories that we take to be true. What he has to say on the underdetermination of theory-choice by observation and induction suggests that he would go along with the presently fashionable view that there is no canonical procedure of verification, or even of falsification, by reference to which truth might be identified.[17]

The sociological approach to the identification of truth is that which Habermas prefers. This says that truth is that property which belongs to propositions and theories that are capable of commanding consensus. 'I may ascribe a predicate to an object if and only if every other individual who could enter into discussion with me would ascribe the same predicate to the same object. In order to distinguish true from false statements, I refer to the judgment of others — in fact to the judgment of all others with whom I could ever undertake a discussion (among whom I include counterfactually all the partners in discussion that I could find if my life history were co-extensive with the history of mankind). The condition for the truth of statements is the potential agreement of all others. Every other person would have to be able to convince himself that I ascribed the predicate "p" correctly to the object x and would have to be able then to agree with me. Truth means the promise of achieving a rational consensus.'[18]

As with the methodological criterion of truth, the sociological allows of being construed in an analytical or non-analytical manner. We may pose a question parallel to that raised in Plato's *Euthyphro*, where it is asked whether the gods will something because it is good, or whether it is good because they will it. The question is whether a proposition secures rational consensus because it is true, or whether it is true because it secures rational consensus. The identification of truth is analytical in the second event, truth consisting in the ability to command consensus, it is non-analytical in the first, truth being that which explains the attainment of the consensus.

One reason for thinking that Habermas must intend his sociological theory of truth to be understood non-analytically is that he is a fallibilist and thinks that we can never be certain that we have attained the truth; if rational consensus is attained and truth is analytically tied to the

[16]W 239.
[17]W 247. See Thomas Kuhn, *The Structure of Scientific Revolutions*, 2nd edn (Chicago: Chicago University Press, 1970), and Paul Feyerabend, *Against Method* (London: New Left Books, 1975).
[18]W 219.

achievement of such consensus then it would appear that fallibilistic doubts are out of place. This consideration is not compelling however because Habermas says that we cannot ever be certain that a consensus is properly rational, in which case we could never be certain that truth had been reached even if it was defined by the ability to command rational consensus.[19]

But there is a second consideration which also prompts the non-analytical reading of Habermas's criterion. This is that Habermas obviously thinks of propositions that attract rational consensus as having a property which accounts for that distinction: if nothing else, this is the property of offering reasons which move people to give the proposition their assent. 'The truth of a proposition stated in discourses means that everybody can be persuaded by reasons to recognize the truth claim of the statement as being justified.'[20] This truth is best taken as consisting for Habermas in the inherent reasonableness of the statement: as he says himself, borrowing an English phrase, in its 'warranted assertibility'.[21] The property is not defined by the ability of the proposition to command consensus but serves rather to explain that ability.

As so far explicated Habermas's theory of truth is not anything very unusual. Like many contemporary approaches it is nurtured on C. S. Peirce's identification of truth with permanent credibility: 'The opinion which is fated to be agreed to by all who investigate is what we mean by the truth'.[22] Its origin is the rejection of two illusions commonly assaulted in contemporary philosophy: the metaphysical illusion that a proposition or theory might be rationally quite satisfying and yet fail to be true[23]; and the methodological illusion, that it is possible to spell out in the form of procedural tests those things that make a proposition or theory rationally satisfying.[24] Reject both of these illusions and it is more or less inevitable that one will identify truth sociologically as the property which belongs to those claims that are found rationally satisfying. Habermas rings a change on this familiar theme; he does not force any great novelty upon us.

Things alter however as Habermas advances the specification of his consensus theory of truth. The further specification comes in two stages and at the second of these some very distinctive claims are put

[19]See W 258 and *Kultur und Kritik* (Frankfurt: Suhrkamp, 1973), 381.

[20]'A Postscript to *Knowledge and Human Interests*', 170.

[21]W 240.

[22]C. S. Peirce, 'How to Make Our Ideas Clear' in P. P. Wiener (ed.), *C. S. Peirce: Selected Writings* (New York: Dover, 1958), 133. For an interesting comment on the value of Peirce's definition see Nelson Goodman, *Ways of Worldmaking* (Sussex: Harvester Press, 1978), 123–124. Richard Bernstein discusses Habermas's interpretation of Peirce in his introduction to the German edition of his book on *Praxis and Action: Praxis and Handeln* (Frankfurt: Suhrkamp, 1975).

[23]For criticism of this illusion see Hilary Putnam, 'Realism and Reason' in *Meaning and the Moral Sciences* (London: Routledge & Kegan Paul, 1978).

[24]See the works of Kuhn and Feyerabend mentioned under reference 17.

forward. The first stage consists in an account of the sort of discursive argument which a proposition should be able to survive if it is to count as warranting assertion. What Habermas says, and it is surely uncontentious, is that the argument should be radical in the sense of allowing questioning at every level: not just questioning of the evidence invoked to support the proposition, but of the warrant buttressing the evidence, and of the backing which reinforces the warrant; ultimately it must even tolerate interrogation of the very conceptual scheme within which the original claim was put forward. 'An argumentatively achieved consensus is a sufficient criterion for the resolution of a discursive validity claim if and only if freedom of movement between the argumentative levels is guaranteed by the formal properties of the discourse.'[25]

So far, again, so good. But now Habermas makes a move which is at once obscure and contentious. He puts forward the thesis, as he describes it himself, that the formal properties of discourse which guarantee the required freedom of movement, the necessary interrogative space, are those realized when the discourse is conducted in an ideal speech situation.[26] For such a situation to be brought about a number of things must happen: these are summed up in the general symmetry requirement, as he calls it, that participants enjoy a fair distribution of chances to speak; more specifically they mean that each participant can open or continue any line of discussion, that each can put forward any assertion or call any into question, that the participants are equally free in their relations with one another to express their most intimate feelings, and that they are equally free to make demands on each other and offer each other help.[27]

The move to the ideal speech situation is contentious because it is by no means obvious that to bring about such a situation would be to ensure interrogative space in the ensuing discourse; if the participants are lazy thinkers no amount of democratization will guarantee that their interrogation is radical. What I wish to explore however is not the contentious nature of this final step in Habermas's presentation, but rather its obscurity. Even if the ideal speech situation is what would be required to maintain interrogative space in discourse between a number of people, it is unclear why Habermas needs to go into such matters. It is not enough to know that truth is that property which would cause a proposition to be accepted by anyone, even when the proposition is subjected to radical interrogation? Why does one have to be told how to ensure that the interrogation is radical in the case where a

---

[25]W 255. Compare the model of theory selection presented in Mary Hesse, 'Models of Theory Change' in P. Suppes et al., Logic, Methodology and Philosophy of Science (Amsterdam, 1973).
[26]W 255.
[27]W 255–256. Cf. 'Was heisst Universalpragmatik?'.

number of people open discussion with one another, rather than each thinking the matter out on his own?

The question is useful because it admits of an enlightening answer. The notion of consensus may be understood in either of two senses, the one a distributive sense, as I shall say, the other a collective one. A proposition admits of distributive consensus if and only if each person assents to it, whether or not after discussion with others and whether or not in awareness of what others think. A proposition admits of collective consensus on the other hand if the people involved discuss it as a group and come to a unanimous decision about it. Up to the last stage in his presentation it seemed that Habermas identified truth as the property of propositions which were rationally capable of distributive consensus: the property of propositions to which anyone would rationally have to give assent, i.e. have to give assent after radical interrogation. At the last stage however he reveals that he conceives of the consensus for which any true proposition must have the potential as a collective consensus. Thus he gives himself the problem of stating conditions that guard against a failure of collective reason, a foreclosure of radical questioning: this, since it is notorious that in collectivities people quickly succumb to pressures of conformity and co-ordination.

There is no obvious reason why Habermas should have to concern himself with the problem of how to maintain interrogative space, the free movement between levels of argument, in the search for collective consensus. His sociological account identifies truth as the property which belongs to those propositions to which anyone would rationally have to agree. 'The condition for the truth of statements is the potential agreement of all others.'[28] This perfectly reasonable account supposes only distributive consensus. It is quite gratuitous to add the requirement that the agreement must be achieved in collective discussion and it is therefore quite unnecessary for an upholder of the theory to investigate how best to guard against collective irrationality. Only the first step in Habermas's specification of his theory of truth is to the point; to be rational a person's assent must indeed be able to stand the test of radical argument. There is no reason to say that the assent must be forthcoming as part of a collective consensus achieved in an ideal speech situation; it may coincide with the judgment that would appear on such an occasion, but that is neither here nor there. The discourse in which Habermas says that questions of truth are raised is normally an interpersonal affair and it may be this which leads him to put a collective construction on the consensus required by his theory. But, as Habermas himself admits, discourse may also be internalized, it may only involve a single thinking subject.[29]

---

[28]W 219. See reference 18.
[29]See *Theory and Practice*, 28.

In conclusion, a question: does anything turn on the construal of consensus in a collective rather than a distributive manner? Well, to be sure of the truth of a proposition I must be convinced, presumably from the weight of reasons in its favour, that the proposition would rationally command everyone's agreement; such consensus, rather than subjective certainty or correspondence with objective facts, is the hallmark of truth. Now if the consensus is understood distributively this might be taken to put truth more readily within my grasp than it would be if the consensus required were collective. Having become convinced by radical argument in my own case that a proposition deserves assent I may take it, by analogy, that anyone would respond to the considerations offered in similar manner; thus, if consensus is understood distributively, I may assume that the proposition is true. This line of thought might be held not to work so easily if consensus is construed collectively, for the collective requirement might be taken to introduce a dimension of inscrutability. Who, it might be asked, is to say what judgment on the proposition people would come to collectively? Group dynamics are sufficiently obscure to make the question telling. It appears then that the collective construal of consensus has the effect, at most, of making truth less accessible than the distributive construal would do, although it is doubtful if even this effect is achieved: the extra trouble which Habermas takes on himself may be lacking, not just in argumentative support, but also in strategic purpose.

3. The Consensus Theory of Justice

With this account of Habermas's consensus theory of truth we may turn to consider the theory of justice that he models on it. Our goal, it will be recalled, is to see whether his theory of justice succeeds in slipping between the horns of the dilemma that we constructed in the introduction. Does it manage at once to provide a valid basis for social criticism and to evade the charge of ideological distortion? More sharply, does the criterion of justice which it supplies fulfil the task of telling us what justice is, while leaving us in an agnostic position as to what justice demands? It will be noticed that the consensus theory of truth performs something like this feat, for it tells us what truth is but it does not enable us unproblematically to distinguish true theories from false. The difficulty of applying the criterion to identify true theories is that the theories in question are empirical ones and identification must await the presentation of all relevant evidence. It does not primarily have to do with the problem of foreseeing which theories will attract consensus, even collective consensus: this point will come up again later.

For Habermas, although he is not explicit about the matter, there are two independent parallels between the case of truth and that of justice.

The first, and we have already drawn attention to it, is that to debate justice is to discuss the adequacy of political evaluations—judgments of justice—and such adequacy is the evaluative counterpart to the truth of empirical statements. Thus just as truth is examined in theoretical discourse, so we may expect a discursive consideration of justice. The other parallel suggests a similar conclusion. We mentioned that for Habermas someone making an assertion presses, not just a truth claim, but a claim to be intelligible, a claim to be sincere, and a claim not to be speaking out of turn: as he says, a claim to *Richtigkeit*, i.e. appropriateness, rightness or justice. This latter claim, he says, resembles the truth claim in demanding discursive redemption and so, on a second count, justice is put in parallel to truth.[30]

In fairness to Habermas a word more must be offered on this second way of drawing the parallel between justice and truth, for the parallel may seem to engage questions of justice only very marginally. The main point to be made is that justice is implicitly claimed not only by someone making an assertion, but also by someone giving an order, putting a request, offering advice, and so on.[31] The redemption of such justice claims may be expected to lead quite far afield. A claim is vindicated when it can be backed up by a norm, a norm which proves itself to be justifiable, whether or not it is institutionalized in the society.[32] The investigation of the validity of such norms will cover the entire spectrum of social life for every norm is engaged in some speech act: 'at least one justified recommendation (or as the case may be, one just command) must correspond to any norm which ought to have validity under given circumstances'.[33]

Where theoretical discourse is the forum for the consideration of truth, Habermas describes the forum for looking into justice as practical discourse. In practical discourse he thinks that we find the same abstract structure of argument as we found in theoretical. The discourse is inaugurated when the justice of some speech act is called into question: or, as we may also say, when the adequacy of the corresponding evaluation is challenged. The ensuing argument will look to *prima facie* evidence, overarching warrant and ultimate backing. In the practical case the evidence will take the form of a legitimating ground, the warrant that of a general norm or principle and the backing the form of an excursus on the beneficial features of the norm. Thus the justice of my telling you to repay money that you borrowed might be vindicated by my recalling that you promised to repay it (ground), by my invoking the norm that promises ought to be kept (warrant) and ultimately by

[30]W 220ff. See reference 10.
[31]W 227–228.
[32]W 228–229.
[33]W 229.

my expounding on the benefits secured by the realization of such a norm (backing).[34]

But granted that there are all these similarities, what makes for the distinction between practical and theoretical discourse? According to Habermas the crucial difference is that whereas in theoretical discourse the bridge between backing and warrant is usually inductive, the backing consisting in observation reports that support the general laws invoked as warrant, the bridge in the practical case is provided by the principle of universalization. His idea is that a practical warrant consists in a norm, a practical backing in an account of the interests served by the norm, and that the interests support the norm in so far as they are impartially served by it: that is, in so far as the norm would be chosen by someone who took those interests universally into account, and did not look only to his own welfare. 'Induction serves as a bridge principle for justifying the logically discontinuous passage from a finite number of singular statements (data) to a universal statement (hypothesis). Universalization serves as a bridge principle for justifying the passage to a norm from descriptive comments (on the consequences and side-effects of the application of norms for the fulfilment of commonly accepted needs).'[35]

In passing it may be remarked that the distinction drawn by Habermas between practical and theoretical discourse, although he conceives of it as a difference of form,[36] depends on the acceptance of substantial assumptions. It is by no means uncontentious to claim that the justification of a norm can be pursued only by reference to interests that it fairly serves, needs that it impartially fulfils. Someone committed to a natural rights approach might say that the satisfaction of interests and needs has nothing to do with the assessment of a norm, that the norm is to be judged by whether or not it meets certain general constraints.[37] Habermas offers no argument for the line that he takes. He notes in passing that 'norms regulate legitimate chances of need satisfaction'[38], but that this is so does not establish that the norms should be judged by the satisfaction they produce.

Putting these matters aside, we are now in a position to understand Habermas's claim that the justice of norms is assessed in practical discourse, as the truth of propositions, specifically empirical propositions, is examined in theoretical. The effect of the claim is to force on us a consensus theory of justice in parallel to the consensus theory of truth. For all the considerations which motivate the latter theory are taken by Habermas also to apply in the justice case. 'If justice can

---

[34]W 242–244.
[35]W 245.
[36]W 226–227 and 239.
[37]See my *Judging Justice*, mentioned under reference 1, Chapters 8–10.
[38]W 251.

qualify as a discursively resoluble validity claim, side by side with truth, then it follows that just norms must allow of being grounded in the same way as true propositions.'[39] The upshot is that we are to think of justice as something that permits only indirect characterization: it is the property which belongs to norms that would rationally command anyone's assent. This characterization is to be understood, once again, in a non-analytical fashion so that the justice of the norms explains their ability to attract assent, rather than being defined by it: the norms are not just because they secure a rational consensus; on the contrary, they secure a rational consensus because they are just.

This characterization of justice is one with which it is difficult to quarrel, although it is far from clear that none other is available. In the truth case Habermas offered arguments against the direct analysis of truth by reference to certainty or correspondence, and he also gave us reason for opposing an indirect analysis in methodological terms. Thus an indirect sociological account seemed to be the only one in the offing. In the justice case similar considerations are ignored and we are unceremoniously invited to assume that the most enlightening account of justice approaches it along a sociological route parallel to that which access was gained to truth. The assumption is not irresistible but I propose to go along with it for the time being.

As in the case of truth, Habermas specifies his initial statement of his consensus theory of justice in two further stages. At a first stage, and once again the comment is unobjectionable, he says that the argument which a just norm is expected to be able to survive, the argument which is meant to elicit universal assent, must be of a radical kind that allows questioning at every level. It must permit questioning of evidence, warrant and backing and even allow the encompassing moral framework to be submitted to examination. The remark quoted earlier is intended to apply to the consideration of justice as much as it is to that of truth. 'An argumentatively achieved consensus is a sufficient criterion for the resolution of a discursive validity claim if and only if freedom of movement between the argumentative levels is guaranteed by the formal properties of the discourse.'[40]

It is the second stage of specification, in this case as in the other, which causes problems. Once again Habermas assumes that the consensus by reference to which justice is identified must be a collective consensus, although there is no obvious reason why a distributive consensus will not do. That assumption made, he then concerns himself with the question of how to guarantee that in collective discussion the required freedom of movement between different levels of argument, the necessary interrogative space, will be preserved. His answer is: by

[39]W 226.
[40]W 255.

realization of those conditions that define the ideal speech situation. But there is no reason given why he should have to go into this matter and it is not even certain that any difference is made by the assumption that the consensus required to identify justice is a collective one. As we saw with truth, it might be taken that the assumption makes justice less scrutable, the outcome of a collective consensus being taken to be more difficult to foresee than that of a distributive one; but this point is not readily decidable, since we cannot be certain that group dynamics would make the collective judgment different from the distributive one.

So much then by way of characterization of Habermas's consensus theory of justice. The question which we now have to ask is whether it fulfils the task of telling us what justice is, while leaving us in an agnostic position as to what justice demands. So far as the arguments presented up to this point go the answer must be that it does not. The theory would allow me to deduce that others would respond in a similar way if radical argument in my own case showed me that a particular norm deserved recognition; thus, taking consensus in the distributive sense, it would permit me to regard the norm as just. As we have seen there is no reason to construe the consensus demanded in a collective sense but even if there were it is not certain that the same line of thought would fail. And even if it did fail, group dynamics being such as to render the point of collective agreement unpredictable, it would seem to fail for reasons which suggest that we ought to have stuck with distributive consensus in the first place. For if group dynamics interfere to make people agree to something collectively that each on his own would have been moved by radical argument to reject, that would seem to indicate that they are a force of distortion rather than enlightenment.

It appears then that to accept Habermas's theory of justice is not to have agnosticism thrust upon one. Peirce would not have wanted his theory of truth to stop scientists from putting forward hypotheses: he did not entertain the prospect of their sitting back and waiting to see what opinions were fated to be agreed upon; indeed the same holds, presumably, for Habermas. By parity of argument there is no reason why the consensus view of justice should inhibit anyone from speculating and arguing about questions of political right, laying down that this norm is compelling, the other objectionable, and so on. But that being so, one may wonder whether the dilemma that we originally posed has been successfully evaded. For it now seems that Habermas is committed to the validity of our investigating matters of justice when the Marxist theory of ideology to which he subscribes would castigate the enterprise as irremediably distorted: this, at least, on the assumption that the investigation licensed by the consensus theory of justice will follow the familiar lines of established political philosophy, an assumption which Habermas does nothing to belie.

At the beginning of this section I mentioned that the consensus theory of truth does secure a sort of agnostic result, for while it tells us what truth is, it does not give us a standard by reference to which we can begin to work out which theories are true and which false. The reason is that in order to begin to judge theories for their truth-value we need to have all the relevant empirical data available and this condition is patently unfulfilled so long as scientific research goes on. No parallel consideration applies however in the case of justice, since the arguments by which we are moved to make our judgments, and by which we think that anyone should be moved, are not vulnerable in the same way to the effect of novel empirical discovery. Thus someone who accepts the consensus theory can have no reason not to go right ahead with the enterprise of making up his mind between such rival criteria of justice as those which define it respectively as legitimacy, welfare and fairness.

Our case against Habermas might seem ready to be closed. The consensus theory of justice, whatever we think about it in other respects, does not meet the constraint of leaving us in an agnostic position on questions of justice; it licenses a variety of speculation which Marxists have traditionally dismissed as ideological. But the case cannot be closed quite yet for Habermas has other arguments to offer in favour of the conclusion that the consensus view of justice forces agnosticism upon us. These arguments are independent of the parallel with the consensus theory of truth and I shall deal with them in the remainder of this section. There are three arguments in all and they respectively invoke considerations of agreement, accessibility and autonomy: none, I shall urge, is irresistible.

The argument from agreement is by no means explicit in Habermas's work but it is suggested by the following remark. 'It is obvious that practical questions, which are posed with a view to the choice of norms, can only be decided through a consensus between all of those concerned and all of those potentially affected.'[41] This comment is made by way of drawing a contrast between the resolution of questions of justice and the settlement of questions of truth. It suggests that because the selection of a norm as just means the choice of a rule of behaviour which will affect others as well as oneself, one must wait on the consensus of others before the selection is made; otherwise one is scarcely treating them as equals. The situation is meant to contrast sharply with that of selecting a proposition or theory as true, where the choice made will only affect one's own beliefs and behaviour. If the reasoning is valid, what it indicates is that the attempt to work out on one's own the shape that the just society ought to have is both presumptuous and pointless: presumptuous, because it means that one assumes the role of a dictator who is ready to order other people's lives for them; and pointless, because it is unlikely to yield the social constitution which people would jointly decide upon.

This argument for the required agnosticism will not work, for the reason that it depends on a confusion of two procedures: on the one hand, the more or less cognitive exercise in which answers are sought to questions such as 'Is this or that sort of arrangement just or not?'; and on the other, the organizational enterprise in which responses are elicited to issues of the form 'Shall we follow this or that constitutional pattern?' There are those who deny the distinction between the two procedures: anyone who thinks that evaluation is undetermined, being ultimately a matter of decision for example, is free to reject it. But Habermas does not belong to this 'decisonist' party, as we have already seen. 'I suspect that the justification of the validity claims contained in the recommendation of norms of action and norms of assessment can be just as discursively tested as the justification of the validity claims implied in assertions.'[42] Thus he must admit that it is one thing for an individual to resolve the cognitive question of what sort of norms are just and another for him to take part in the normative organization of a society.[43]

Once this distinction is admitted however the force of the argument from agreement is dissipated. It is not presumptuous to try to work out one's views on cognitive questions of justice, simply because they affect one's opinions on how society ought to be organized and determine the broad lines that one would follow in organizational deliberations. If it were presumptuous to do this then so would it be to attempt to clarify one's mind on economic matters, since one's economic views must have a similar influence on one's organizational disposition. And neither is it pointless to try to elaborate one's beliefs about matters of justice in advance of multilateral deliberations on the organization of society. On detailed questions of arrangement the outcome of such deliberations must be impossible to predict but on broad issues of justice, assuming that reason prevails, the line taken must coincide with that which one's personal reflection selects as rational.

The second ancillary argument for the agnostic construal of Habermas's consensus theory of justice may be called the argument from accessibility. This is suggested in the following remark, although it is not explicitly developed. 'Norms regulate legitimate chances of need satisfaction and the interpreted needs are a matter of inner nature to which each person has a privileged access, in so far as he has a non-deceitful relationship with himself.'[44] This remark is made in the same

---

[42]W 226.
[43]Such a distinction is more or less explicit in *Theory and Practice*, 32ff.
[44]W 251.

context as that which presents the argument from agreement and it also is meant to mark a contrast between the consensus theory of justice and the consensus theory of truth. The idea behind it is that since justice can only be determined by reference to something on which each person is authority in his own case, there is no sense in trying to work out one's picture of the just society in advance of multilateral deliberation and consensus, whether of a distributive or collective kind. Once again support is proffered for the agnostic construal of Habermas's theory of justice.

In this remark Habermas makes a substantial assumption about the sort of reasoning appropriate for settling issues of judgment, an assumption on which we commented earlier. The assumption is contentious and neither is it intrinsically connected with the consensus theory of justice: one might have a different view of the sort of reasoning suitable for political matters and still hold by the essential core of the consensus theory. But even if we let the assumption pass, we must be unpersuaded by this second argument. We might baulk at the strongly anti-behaviourist assumption that each person has a privileged awareness of his own needs, so long as he is not self-deceived, but this is not the objection that I have in mind. The reason we must be unpersuaded by the argument is that the point which it makes could be applauded by certain non-agnostic political philosophers: for example, by a particular kind of utilitarian.

The utilitarian believes that the just social scheme is that which produces the greatest happiness among the people living under it. One species of utilitarian, whose procedure I have characterized in detail elsewhere,[45] argues that people are happiest when the satisfaction of their wants or needs is maximized, and that we must use an interview technique based on the economic theory of utility and decision to establish which of the alternative schemes available is likely to secure this result. A political philosopher of this hue could have no objection to the point which is made in the argument from accessibility. The argument would not inhibit him from going ahead with his interviews and his calculations, always trying to guard against the self-deception of his subjects, in the attempt to determine the outline of the just society. Thus the argument fails to reinforce the agnostic construal of the consensus theory of justice. It would do so only if it was impossible to get at a person's politically relevant needs other than by letting him cast a vote for his preferred scheme and only if, in addition, there was no possibility of eliciting a suitable vote in a poll. The first condition is, as a matter of empirical fact, unfulfilled and the second would be realized only if it were the case, which it patently is not, that collective discussion is required for the eliciting of suitable votes and, what is

---

[45]See my *Judging Justice*, mentioned under reference 1, Chapter 13.

more, collective discussion under some unobtainable circumstances such as those of the ideal speech situation. (Notice that were the first condition fulfilled and the second not, then the argument would fail to be compatible with a utilitarian procedure but it would continue to be consistent with a well-known alternative in political philosophy: the majoritarian criterion, according to which the just scheme is that which secures the greatest number of votes.)

The third ancillary argument for the agnostic construal of the consensus theory of justice urges upon us the virtue of leaving judgments of justice to the wisdom of parties seeking collective agreement under the conditions of the ideal speech situation; it suggests that only such parties are in a position to make reliable judgments, and this for a reason that should caution us against trying to work out what they would decide. Specifically, it is claimed that collective consensus under ideal conditions of communication ensures, whether or not uniquely, that the interests satisfied by the scheme chosen are those of autonomous agents, in particular that they are real interests and interests held in common. 'If under these conditions a consensus about the recommendation to accept a norm arises argumentatively, that is, on the basis of hypothetically proposed, alternative justifications, then this consensus expresses a "rational will". Since all those affected have, in principle, at least the chance to participate in the practical deliberation, the "rationality" of the discursively formed will consists in the fact that the reciprocal behavioural expectations raised to normative status afford validity to a *common* interest ascertained *without deception.'* [46]

Let us take first the point that the ideal conditions of communication guarantee that people's real interests, that is, their interests as interpreted without distortion or deception, are satisfied by the scheme chosen. Habermas foresees that under those conditions people are forced by the glare of unconstrained communication to bring their needs clearly to light. 'Even the interpretations of needs in which each individual must be able to recognize what he wants become the object of discursive will-formation.' [47] He contrasts this situation favourably with that which is countenanced on any approach that takes people's interests as given and then tries to satisfy them impartially, pursuing universalizability. 'The principle of justification of norms is no longer the monologically applicable *principle* of universalizability but the communally followed *procedure* of discursive redemption of normative validity claims.' [48] Needs are interpreted and established under the subtle influence of interaction,[49] and the approach favoured by Ha-

---

[46] *Legitimation Crisis*, henceforth LC, 108. The italics are in the original.

[47] LC 108.

[48] *Zur Rekonstruktion des Historischen Materialismus* (Frankfurt: Suhrkamp, 1976), 85. Cf. *Theory and Practice*, 150–151.

[49] *Theory and Practice*, 151.

bermas does not take this formative process as finished but presses it rather towards perfection. 'It carries on the process of the insertion of drive potentials into a communicative structure of action—that is, the socialization process—"with will and consciousness".'[50]

The second point made in the argument from autonomy is that the ideal conditions of communication filter out, not only people's real interests, but also interests which are genuinely common or 'generalizable'. Habermas is not entirely clear about what he means by such interests. They are described as 'needs that can be communicatively shared'[51] and are contrasted with 'particular desires and private satisfactions or sufferings'.[52] Presumably they include universal self-regarding desires which each can fulfil compatibly with respecting similar desires in others. An example might be the desire which each of us has for freedom from arbitrary arrest, a desire which contrasts in its noncompetitive nature with something like the desire for social position. They must certainly also include society-regarding desires which each person naturally has or comes to develop. An example of this sort of aspiration would be the desire for a peaceful or cohesive community. Both these kinds of desires are capable of being communicatively shared in the sense that each person can avow and pursue them consistently with welcoming their avowal and pursuit by others. The second point in the argument from autonomy is that under the conditions of the ideal speech situation such needs are filtered out from particular, divisive concerns, so that the scheme chosen is given a satisfactory base. 'The interest is common because the constraint-free consensus permits only what all can want.'[53]

What are we to make of this final argument? Well, the second point is hardly a telling one, since there is no reason to think that we cannot work out which interests are common and which particular in advance of seeing what happens under ideal conditions of communication. Habermas himself insists that the distinction between these two sorts of interests is argumentatively based and not a matter of arbitrary decision.[54] In that case there seems to be no obstacle to our going through people's concerns and rationally establishing where the line ought to be drawn.

The first point in the argument is less easy to deal with since we may well agree that one of the faults with an approach such as that of impartial utilitarianism is that it takes people's interpretations of their needs as given. This might push us into attempting to identify the just scheme by reference to other factors such as natural rights, a possibility

[50]LC 89.
[51]LC 108.
[52]'A Postscript to *Knowledge and Human Interests*', 171.
[53]LC 108.
[54]LC 108.

that Habermas does not consider, but if we think that justice ought to
be judged on the basis of the satisfaction of human needs or wants we
may be understandably downcast by the lack in question. In that case
we must be at least responsive to the claim that debate in the ideal
speech situation would bring to the surface people's real wants, unde-
ceived and undistorted.

And yet, ought we even then to be persuaded to espouse agnosticism
and put down justice as something on which we cannot trust our own
judgments, although we know the circumstances under which judgments would be trustworthy? The cost of going that way is enormous,
in that it entails a self-denying ordinance in the area of political philosophy. And moreover, there are two considerations that counsel against
it. The first is that while our interpretations of our needs, and the
desires which they sponsor, are certainly subject to the influence of
social formation, there is no ground for believing that they are indefinitely malleable. Thus we might reasonably hope that a social scheme
which satisfied people's existing wants would not diverge radically
from that which would satisfy their enlightened ones; and if we are
unconvinced of this then we might plausibly have a go at working out
what people would come to want under enlightenment and then pre-
scribe that the just scheme is that which satisfies those hypothetical
desires. The second consideration that counsels against the agnostic
conclusion is that it is doubtful in any case whether the ideal conditions
of communication would automatically guarantee clairvoyance on the
part of those seeking political consensus. Habermas does not offer us
any detailed argument on the point, and we may well remain unconvinced, taking the only guarantee of self-knowledge to be radical reflection, and thinking it possible that people in ideal communication
might yet escape this experience.[55]

But there is a doubt raised by the argument from autonomy which, in
conclusion, I would like to confess. It sometimes seems in Habermas's
comments that he is mooting a model of human needs other than that
which is generally taken for granted, and if this model is sound, then his
argument has more weight than we have allowed. The generally accepted model, which might be described as a biological one, assumes
that human needs remain recognizable across cultural variations in
their expression. The model mooted by Habermas is better characterized as an artistic one, for it suggests that at least some of the needs
which a just society should fulfil appear under the right conditions, as if
out of nowhere: that like the need that one finds satisfied in a novel
form of art, they are undetectable in advance of their appropriate
objects. If we think that many significant human needs are of this kind,

---

[55]Notice that Habermas mentions self-reflection and artistic experience as sources of
enlightenment about one's real needs in *Zur Rekonstruktion des Historischen Materialismus*, 344–345.

then we may expect people under ideal conditions of communication to develop interests of which we can have no inkling, interests that are without precedents or parallels. In that case we must be less short with Habermas's final argument for the agnostic construal of his conception of justice. It will be certain that under the existing order of things we are not in a position to work out what regime will satisfy our real interests, for it will be guaranteed that we are without the resources to recognize at least some of the interests in question.

The artistic model of human needs may attract some derision as a piece of romantic mysticism, but it is deserving of serious consideration. We cannot give it such attention here and we must be content just to note that our case against Habermas's agnosticism depends on the assumption of the more commonly accepted biological model. If we speak confidently of having established our point of view, we do so with this weakness put aside. A fuller defence of our claims must raise the question of the nature of human needs, and the rationality of respecting needs in ourselves and others which we are presently incapable of identifying. My own hope is that such a defence is available, for I fear that putting justice out of cognitive reach may ultimately mean inhibiting social criticism, and indulging the seductive idea that someday everything will be changed, changed utterly.

4. Conclusion

It appears then that neither the parallel with the consensus theory of truth, nor the three ancillary arguments that we have considered, secure for Habermas the agnostic construal of his consensus theory of justice; this, assuming the biological model of needs. Even when justice is identified in the indirect sociological fashion that he proposes it is presented as something which we may legitimately hope to investigate; none of the considerations brought forward by Habermas can deny us the right to that ambition. But if the investigation of the nature of justice is licensed, and nothing is said to suggest that it will be radically different from the sort of inquiry traditional in political philosophy, then a seal of approval is given to a mode of theorizing which has always attracted the Marxist criticism of being ideologically contained. Habermas has not slipped between the horns of the dilemma which we posed in the introduction. His consensus theory of justice, conceived for the purpose of grounding social criticism, involves him willy-nilly in countenancing the enterprise of political philosophy, and it means therefore that he must modify the Marxist theory of ideology which would deny the validity of that pursuit.

If my argument is sound then we must welcome Habermas into the company of contemporary political philosophers such as John Rawls, Robert Nozick and Ronald Dworkin. These thinkers unashamedly pursue the articulation of the demands of justice and, while Habermas may wish to express reservations on the plausibility of the project, his commitments force him to take his part in it. But where should we place him in the constellation of positions taken up by contemporary political philosophers? Interesting to note, his consensus theory does not of itself force him into any particular position. Just as one might accept Peirce's account of truth, or indeed Habermas's own, and adopt any of an indefinite number of rival scientific theories, so the acceptance of a consensus account of justice leaves one free to spell out the requirements of justice in any of the many competing ways. However, Habermas does have substantive opinions on the nature of justice and these appear in his remarks to the effect that the just system is that which impartially and maximally satisfies people's real needs. What one would like to see in his future work is a defence of this criterion against competitors and a detailed elaboration of its consequences: the sort of elaboration which, I have argued, he has no good reason not to try to provide.

PART III
THE FEASIBLE: WHAT CAN WE GET?

THE FIRST OF these three essays, by Elster, is an examination of different models of what the state should be like, mainly from the point of view of feasibility considerations. It is a useful taxonomy of models of the state as well as an illustration of feasibility analysis at work. The paper by Buchanan offers an account of the viewpoint of public choice theory, with the suggestion that many political theories are hopelessly optimistic about what we can feasibly expect from the agents of an extensive state apparatus. The final essay by Hayek may help explain why economists, rightly or wrongly, think so well of the market: the idea is that it promises, unlike more centralized arrangements, to be sensitive to relevant information about people's preferences; it promises to be a feasible institution, able reliably to fulfill the expectations that make it attractive.

10

JON ELSTER

The Market and the Forum:
Three Varieties of Political Theory

I WANT TO compare three views of politics generally, and of the democratic system more specifically. I shall first look at social choice theory, as an instance of a wider class of theories with certain common features. In particular, they share the conception that the political process is instrumental rather than an end in itself, and the view that the decisive political act is a private rather than a public action, viz. the individual and secret vote. With these usually goes the idea that the goal of politics is the optimal compromise between given, and irreducibly opposed, private interests. The other two views arise when one denies, first, the private character of political behaviour and then, secondly, goes on also to deny the instrumental nature of politics. According to the theory of Jürgen Habermas, the goal of politics should be rational agreement rather than compromise, and the decisive political act is that of engaging in public debate with a view to the emergence of a consensus. According to the theorists of participatory democracy, from John Stuart Mill to Carole Pateman, the goal of politics is the transformation and education of the participants. Politics, on this view, is an end in itself—indeed many have argued that it represents the good life for man. I shall discuss these views in the order indicated. I shall present them in a somewhat stylized form, but my critical comments will not I hope, be directed to strawmen.

I

Politics, it is usually agreed, is concerned with the common good, and notably with the cases in which it cannot be realized as the aggregate outcome of individuals pursuing their private interests. In particular, uncoordinated private choices may lead to outcomes that are worse for all than some other outcome that could have been attained by coordination. Political institutions are set up to remedy such *market failures*, a phrase that can be taken either in the static sense of an inability to provide public goods or in the more dynamic sense of a breakdown of the self-regulating properties usually ascribed to the market mechanism.[1] In addition there is the redistributive task of politics — moving along the Pareto-optimal frontier once it has been reached.[2] According to the first view of politics, this task is inherently one of interest struggle and compromise. The obstacle to agreement is not only that most individuals want redistribution to be in their favour, or at least not in their disfavour.[3] More basically consensus is blocked because there is no reason to expect that individuals will converge in their views on what constitutes a just redistribution.

I shall consider social choice theory as representative of the private-instrumental view of politics, because it brings out supremely well the logic as well as the limits of that approach. Other varieties, such as the Schumpeterian or neo-Schumpeterian theories, are closer to the actual political process, but for that reason also less suited to my purpose. For instance, Schumpeter's insistence that voter preferences are shaped and manipulated by politicians[4] tends to blur the distinction, central to my analysis, between politics as the aggregation of given preferences and politics as the transformation of preferences through rational discussion. And although the neo-Schumpeterians are right in emphasiz-

---

[1] J. Elster, *Logic and Society* (Chichester: Wiley, 1978) refers to these two varieties of market failure as suboptimality and counterfinality, respectively, linking them both to collective action.

[2] This is a simplification. First, as argued in P. Samuelson ('The evaluation of real national income', *Oxford Economic Papers*, 1950, 2: 1–29), there may be political constraints that prevent one from attaining the Pareto-efficient frontier. Secondly, the very existence of several points that are Pareto-superior to the *status quo*, yet involve differential benefits to the participants, may block the realization of any of them.

[3] P. Hammond ('Why ethical measures need interpersonal comparisons', *Theory and Decision*, 1976, 7: 263–74) offers a useful analysis of the consequences of selfish preferences over income distributions, showing that 'without interpersonal comparisons of some kind, any social preference ordering over the space of possible income distributions must be dictatorial'.

[4] J. Schumpeter (*Capitalism, Socialism and Democracy* (London: Allen & Unwin, 1961)) p. 263: 'the will of the people is the product and not the motive power of the political process'. One should not, however, conclude (as does J. Lively (*Democracy* (Oxford: Blackwell, 1975, p. 38)) that Schumpeter thereby abandons the market analogy, since in his view (Schumpeter, *Business Cycles* (New York: McGraw-Hill, 1939, p. 73)) consumer preferences are no less manipulable (with some qualifications stated in J. Elster, *Explaining Technical Change* (Cambridge: Cambridge University Press, 1983, Chap. 5)).

ing the role of the political parties in the preference-aggregation process,[5] I am not here concerned with such mediating mechanisms. In any case, political problems also arise within the political parties, and so my discussion may be taken to apply to such lower-level political processes. In fact, much of what I shall say makes better sense for politics on a rather small scale — within the firm, the organization or the local community — than for nationwide political systems.

In very broad outline, the structure of social choice theory is as follows.[6] (1) We begin with a *given* set of agents, so that the issue of a normative justification of political boundaries does not arise. (2) We assume that the agents confront a *given* set of alternatives, so that for instance the issue of agenda manipulation does not arise. (3) The agents are supposed to be endowed with preferences that are similarly *given* and not subject to change in the course of the political process. They are, moreover, assumed to be causally independent of the set of alternatives. (4) In the standard version, which is so far the only operational version of the theory, preferences are assumed to be purely ordinal, so that it is not possible for an individual to express the intensity of his preferences, nor for an outside observer to compare preference intensities across individuals. (5) The individual preferences are assumed to be defined over all pairs of individuals, i.e. to be complete, and to have the formal property of transitivity, so that preference for A over B and for B over C implies preference for A over C.

Given this setting, the task of social choice theory is to arrive at a social preference ordering of the alternatives. This might appear to require more than is needed: why not define the goal as one of arriving at the choice of one alternative? There is, however, usually some uncertainty as to which alternatives are really feasible, and so it is useful to have an ordering if the top-ranked alternative proves unavailable. The ordering should satisfy the following criteria. (6) Like the individual preferences, it should be complete and transitive. (7) It should be Pareto-optimal, in the sense of never having one option socially preferred to another which is individually preferred by everybody. (8) The social choice between two given options should depend only on how the individuals rank these two options, and thus not be sensitive to changes in their preferences concerning other options. (9) The social preference ordering should respect and reflect individual preferences, over and above the condition of Pareto-optimality. This idea covers a variety of notions, the most important of which are

[5]See in particular A. Downs, *An Economic Theory of Democracy* (New York: Harper, 1957).

[6]For fuller statements, see K. Arrow (*Social Choice and Individual Values* (New York: Wiley, 1963)), A. Sen (*Collective Choice and Social Welfare* (San Francisco: Holden-Day, 1970)) and J. Kelly (*Arrow Impossibility Theorems* (New York: Academic Press, 1978)), as well as the contribution of Aanund Hylland in *Foundations of Social Choice Theory* (Cambridge: Cambridge University Press, 1985).

anonymity (all individuals should count equally), *nondictatorship* (*a fortiori* no single individual should dictate the social choice), *liberalism* (all individuals should have some private domain within which their preferences are decisive), and *strategy-proofness* (it should not pay to express false preferences).

The substance of social choice theory is given in a series of impossibility and uniqueness theorems, stating either that a given subset of these conditions is incapable of simultaneous satisfaction or that they uniquely describe a specific method for aggregating preferences. Much attention has been given to the impossibility theorems, yet from the present point of view these are not of decisive importance. They stem largely from the paucity of allowable information about the preferences, i.e. the exclusive focus on ordinal preferences.[7] True, at present we do not quite know how to go beyond ordinality. Log-rolling and vote-trading may capture some of the cardinal aspects of the preferences, but at some cost.[8] Yet even should the conceptual and technical obstacles to intra- and inter-individual comparison of preference intensity be overcome,[9] many objections to the social choice approach would remain. I shall discuss two sets of objections, both related to the assumption of given preferences. I shall argue, first, that the preferences people choose to express may not be a good guide to what they really prefer; and secondly that what they really prefer may in any case be a fragile foundation for social choice.

In actual fact, preferences are never 'given', in the sense of being directly observable. If they are to serve as inputs to the social choice process, they must somehow be *expressed* by the individuals. The expression of preferences is an action, which presumably is guided by these very same preferences.[10] It is then far from obvious that the individually rational action is to express these preferences as they are. Some methods for aggregating preferences are such that it may pay the individual to express false preferences, i.e. the outcome may in some cases be better according to his real preferences if he chooses not to express them truthfully. The condition for strategy-proofness for social choice mechanisms was designed expressly to exclude this possibility. It turns out, however, that the systems in which honesty always pays

[7]Cf. C. d'Aspremont and L. Gevers, 'Equity and the information basis of collective choice,' *Review of Economic Studies*, 1977, 44: 199–210.

[8]W. Riker and P. Ordeshook, *An Introduction to Positive Political Theory* (Englewood Cliffs, N.J.: Prentice Hall, 1973), p. 112–13.

[9]Cf. the contributions of Donald Davidson and Allan Gibbard in *Foundations of Social Choice Theory*.

[10]Presumably, but not obviously, since the agent might have several preference orderings and rely on higher-order preferences to express, as suggested for instance by A. Sen, 'Liberty, unanimity and rights', *Economica*, 1976, 43: 217–45.

are rather unattractive in other respects.[11] We then have to face the possibility that even if we require that the social preferences be Pareto-optimal with respect to the expressed preferences, they might not be so with respect to the real ones. Strategy-proofness and collective rationality, therefore, stand and fall together. Since it appears that the first must fall, so must the second. It then becomes very difficult indeed to defend the idea that the outcome of the social choice mechanism represents the common good, since there is a chance that everybody might prefer some other outcome.

Amos Tversky has pointed to another reason why choices — or expressed preferences — cannot be assumed to represent the real preferences in all cases.[12] According to his 'concealed preference hypothesis', choices often conceal rather than reveal underlying preferences. This is especially so in two sorts of cases. First, there are the cases of anticipated regret associated with a risky decision. Consider the following example (from Tversky):

> On her twelfth birthday, Judy was offered a choice between spending the weekend with her aunt in the city (C), or having a party for all her friends. The party could take place either in the garden (GP) or inside the house (HP). A garden party would be much more enjoyable, but there is always the possibility of rain, in which case an inside party would be more sensible. In evaluating the consequences of the three options, Judy notes that the weather condition does not have a significant effect on C. If she chooses the party, however, the situation is different. A garden party will be a lot of fun if the weather is good, but quite disastrous if it rains, in which case an inside party will be acceptable. The trouble is that Judy expects to have a lot of regret if the party is to be held inside and the weather is very nice.
>
> Now, let us suppose that for some reason it is no longer possible to have an outside party. In this situation, there is no longer any regret associated with holding an inside party in good weather because (in this case) Judy has no other place for holding the party. Hence, the elimination of an available course of action (holding the party outside) removes the regret associated with an inside party, and increases its overall utility. It stands to reason, in this case, that if Judy was indifferent between C and HP, in the presence of GP, she will prefer HP to C when GP is eliminated.

What we observe here is the violation of condition (8) above, the so-called 'independence of irrelevant alternatives'. The expressed pref-

[11]P. Pattanaik, *Strategy and Group Choice* (Amsterdam: North-Holland, 1978) offers a survey of the known results. The only strategy-proof mechanisms for social choice turn out to be the dictatorial one (the dictator has no incentive to misrepresent his preferences) and the randomizing one of getting the probability that a given option will be chosen equal to the proportion of voters that have it as their first choice.

[12]A. Tversky, 'Choice, preferences and welfare: some psychological observations', paper presented at a colloquium on 'Foundations of social choice theory', Ustaoset (Norway), 1981.

erences depend causally on the set of alternatives. We may assume that the real preferences, defined over the set of possible outcomes, remain constant, contrary to the case to be discussed below. Yet the preferences over the *pairs* (choice, outcome) depend on the set of available choices, because the 'costs of responsibility' differentially associated with various such pairs depend on what else one 'could have done'. Although Judy could not have escaped her predicament by deliberately making it physically impossible to have an outside party,[13] she might well have welcomed an event outside her control with the same consequence.

The second class of cases in which Tversky would want to distinguish the expressed preferences from the real preferences concerns decisions that are unpleasant rather than risky. For instance, 'society may prefer to save the life of one person rather than another, and yet be unable to make this choice'. In fact, losing both lives through inaction may be preferred to losing only one life by deliberate action. Such examples are closely related to the problems involved in act utilitarianism versus outcome utilitarianism.[14] One may well judge that it would be a good thing if state A came about, and yet not want to be the person by whose agency it comes about. The reasons for not wanting to be that person may be quite respectable, or they may not. The latter would be the case if one were afraid of being blamed by the relatives of the person who was deliberately allowed to die, or if one simply confused the causal and the moral notions of responsibility. In such cases the expressed preferences might lead to a choice that in a clear sense goes against the real preferences of the people concerned.

A second, perhaps more basic, difficulty is that the real preferences themselves might well depend causally on the feasible set. One instance is graphically provided by the fable of the fox and the sour grapes.[15] For the 'ordinal utilitarian', as Arrow for instance calls himself,[16] there would be no welfare loss if the fox were excluded from consumption of the grapes, since he thought them sour anyway. But of course the cause of his holding them to be sour was his conviction that he would in any case be excluded from consuming them, and then it is difficult to justify the allocation by invoking his preferences. Con-

[13]Cf. J. Elster (*Ulysses and the Sirens* (Cambridge: Cambridge University Press, 1979, Ch II)) or T. Schelling 'The intimate contest for self-command', *The Public Interest*, 1980, 60: 94–118) for the idea of deliberately restricting one's feasible set to make certain undesirable behaviour impossible at a later time. The reason this does not work here is that the regret would not be eliminated.

[14]Cf. for instance B. Williams ('A critique of utilitarianism', in J. J. C. Smart and B. A. O. Williams, *Utilitarianism: For and Against* (Cambridge: Cambridge University Press, 1973, pp. 77–150)) or A. Sen 'Utilitarianism and welfarism', *Journal of Philosophy*, 1979, 76: 463–88.

[15]Cf. J. Elster *Sour Grapes* (Cambridge: Cambridge University Press, 1983, Chap. III) for a discussion of this issue.

[16]K. Arrow, 'Some ordinal-utilitarian notes on Rawls's theory of justice', *Journal of Philosophy*, 1973, 70: 245–63.

versely, the phenomenon of 'counter-adaptive preferences'—the grass is always greener on the other side of the fence, and the forbidden fruit always sweeter—is also baffling for the social choice theorist, since it implies that such preferences, if respected, would not be satisfied— and yet the whole point of respecting them would be to give them a chance of satisfaction.

Adaptive and counter-adaptive preferences are only special cases of a more general class of desires, those which fail to satisfy some substantive criterion for acceptable preferences, as opposed to the purely formal criterion of transitivity. I shall discuss these under two headings: autonomy and morality.

Autonomy characterizes the way in which preferences are shaped rather than their actual content. Unfortunately I find myself unable to give a positive characterization of autonomous preferences, so I shall have to rely on two indirect approaches. First, autonomy is for desires what judgment is for belief. The notion of judgment is also difficult to define formally, but at least we know that there are persons who have this quality to a higher degree than others: people who are able to take account of vast and diffuse evidence that more or less clearly bears on the problem at hand, in such a way that no element is given undue importance. In such people the process of belief formation is not disturbed by defective cognitive processing, nor distorted by wishful thinking and the like. Similarly, autonomous preferences are those that have not been shaped by irrelevant causal processes—a singularly unhelpful explanation. To improve somewhat on it, consider, secondly, a short list of such irrelevant causal processes. They include adaptive and counter-adaptive preferences, conformity and anti-conformity, the obsession with novelty and the equally unreasonable resistance to novelty. In other words, preferences may be shaped by adaptation to what is possible, to what other people do or to what one has been doing in the past—or they may be shaped by the desire to differ as much as possible from these. In all of these cases the source of preference change is not in the person, but outside him—detracting from his autonomy.

Morality, it goes without saying, is if anything even more controversial. (Within the Kantian tradition it would also be questioned whether it can be distinguished at all from autonomy.) Preferences are moral or immoral by virtue of their content, not by virtue of the way in which they have been shaped. Fairly uncontroversial examples of unethical preferences are spiteful and sadistic desires, and arguably also the desire for positional goods, i.e. goods such that it is logically impossible for more than a few to possess them.[17] The desire for an income twice the average can lead to less welfare for everybody, so that such prefer-

---

[17]F. Hirsh, *Social Limits to Growth* (Cambridge: Harvard University Press, 1976).

ences fail to pass the Kantian generalization test.[18] Also they are closely linked to spite, since one way of getting more than others is to take care that they get less—indeed this may often be a more efficient method than trying to excel.[19]

To see how the lack of autonomy may be distinguished from the lack of moral worth, let me use *conformity* as a technical term for a desire caused by a drive to be like other people, and *conformism* for a desire to be like other people, with anti-conformity and anti-conformism similarly defined. Conformity implies that other people's desires enter into the causation of my own, conformism that they enter irreducibly into the description of the object of my desires. Conformity may bring about conformism, but it may also lead to anti-conformism, as in Theodore Zeldin's comment that among the French peasantry 'prestige is to a great extent obtained from conformity with traditions (so that the son of a non-conformist might be expected to be one too)'.[20] Clearly, conformity may bring about desires that are morally laudable, yet lacking in autonomy. Conversely, I do not see how one could rule out on *a priori* grounds the possibility of autonomous spite, although I would welcome a proof that autonomy is incompatible not only with anti-conformity, but also with anti-conformism.

We can now state the objection to the political view underlying social choice theory. It is, basically, that it embodies a confusion between the kind of behaviour that is appropriate in the market place and that which is appropriate in the forum. The notion of consumer sovereignty is acceptable because, and to the extent that, the consumer chooses between courses of action that differ only in the way they affect him. In political choice situations, however, the citizen is asked to express his preference over states that also differ in the way in which they affect other people. This means that there is no similar justification for the corresponding notion of the citizen's sovereignty, since other people may legitimately object to social choice governed by preferences that are defective in some of the ways I have mentioned. A social choice mechanism is capable of resolving the market failures that would result from unbridled consumer sovereignty, but as a way of redistributing welfare it is hopelessly inadequate. If people affected each other only by tripping over each other's feet, or by dumping their

---

[18]T. Haavelmo, 'Some observations on welfare and economic growth', in W. A. Eltis, M. Scott and N. Wolfe (eds.) *Induction, Growth and Trade: Essays in Honour of Sir Roy Harrod* (Oxford: Oxford University Press, 1970) offers a model in which everybody may suffer a loss of welfare by trying to keep up with the neighbours.

[19]One may take the achievements of others as a parameter and one's own as the control variable, or conversely try to manipulate the achievements of others so that they fall short of one's own. The first of these ways of realizing positional goods is clearly less objectionable than the second, but still less pure than the non-comparative desire for a certain standard of excellence.

[20]T. Zeldin, *France 1848–1945*, Vol. 1 (Oxford: Oxford University Press, 1973) p. 143.

garbage into one another's backyards, a social choice mechanism might cope. But the task of politics is not only to eliminate inefficiency, but also to create justice—a goal to which the aggregation of prepolitical preferences is a quite incongruous means.

This suggests that the principles of the forum must differ from those of the market. A long-standing tradition from the Greek *polis* onwards suggests that politics must be an open and public activity, as distinct from the isolated and private expression of preferences that occurs in buying and selling. In the following sections I look at two different conceptions of public politics, increasingly removed from the market theory of politics. Before I go on to this, however, I should briefly consider an objection that the social choice theorist might well make to what has just been said. He could argue that the only alternative to the aggregation of given preferences is some kind of censorship or paternalism. He might agree that spiteful and adaptive preferences are undesirable, but he would add that any institutional mechanism for eliminating them would be misused and harnessed to the private purposes of power-seeking individuals. Any remedy, in fact, would be worse than the disease. This objection assumes (i) that the only alternative to aggregation of given preferences is censorship, and (ii) that censorship is always objectionable. Robert Goodin[20a] challenges the second assumption, by arguing that laundering or filtering of preferences by self-censorship is an acceptable alternative to aggregation. I shall now discuss a challenge to the first assumption, viz. the idea of a *transformation* of preferences through public and rational discussion.

II

Today this view is especially associated with the writings of Jürgen Habermas on 'the ethics of discourse' and 'the ideal speech situation'. As mentioned above, I shall present a somewhat stylized version of his views, although I hope they bear some resemblance to the original.[21] The core of the theory, then, is that rather than aggregating or filtering preferences, the political system should be set up with a view to changing them by public debate and confrontation. The input to the social choice mechanism would then not be the raw, quite possibly selfish or irrational, preferences that operate in the market, but informed and other-regarding preferences. Or rather, there would not be any need for an aggregating mechanism, since a rational discussion would tend to produce unanimous preferences. When the private and idiosyncratic

[20a]R. Goodin, "Laundering Preferences", in J. Elster and A. Hylland, *Foundations of Social Choice Theory* (Cambridge: Cambridge University Press, 1985) pp. 82–101.
[21]I rely mainly on J. Habermas 'Diskursethik—notizen zu einem Begrundingsprogram.' Mimeographed, 1982.

wants have been shaped and purged in public discussion about the public good, uniquely determined rational desires would emerge. Not optimal compromise, but unanimous agreement is the goal of politics on this view.

There appear to be two main premises underlying this theory. The first is that there are certain arguments that simply cannot be stated publicly. In a political debate it is pragmatically impossible to argue that a given solution should be chosen just because it is good for oneself. By the very act of engaging in a public debate — by arguing rather than bargaining — one has ruled out the possibility of invoking such reasons.[22] To engage in discussion can in fact be seen as one kind of self-censorship, a pre-commitment to the idea of rational decision. Now, it might well be thought that this conclusion is too strong. The first argument only shows that in public debate one has to pay some lip-service to the common good. An additional premise states that over time one will in fact come to be swayed by considerations about the common good. One cannot indefinitely praise the common good 'du bout des lèvres, for — as argued by Pascal in the context of the wager — one will end up having the preferences that initially one was faking.[23] This is a psychological, not a conceptual premise. To explain why going through the motions of rational discussion should tend to bring about the real thing, one might argue that people tend to bring what they mean into line with what they say in order to reduce dissonance, but this is a dangerous argument to employ in the present context. Dissonance reduction does not tend to generate autonomous preferences. Rather one would have to invoke the power of reason to break down prejudice and selfishness. By speaking with the voice of reason, one is also exposing oneself to reason.

To sum up, the conceptual impossibility of expressing selfish arguments in a debate about the public good, and the psychological difficulty of expressing other-regarding preferences without ultimately coming to acquire them, jointly bring it about that public discussion tends to promote the common good. The *volonté générale*, then, will not simply be the Pareto-optimal realization of given (or expressed) preferences,[24] but the outcome of preferences that are themselves shaped by a concern for the common good. For instance, by mere aggregation of given preferences one would be able to take account of some negative externalities, but not of those affecting future generations. A social choice mechanism might prevent persons now living

[22]K. Midgaard, 'On the significance of language and a richer concept of rationality', in L. Lewin and E. Vedung (eds.) *Politics as Rational Action* (Dordrecht: Reidel, 1980) pp. 83–97.

[23]For Pascal's argument, cf. Elster (1979, Chap. II, 3).

[24]As suggested by W. Runciman and A. Sen 'Games, justice and the general will,' *Mind*, 1965, 74: 554–62.

from dumping their garbage into one another's backyards, but not from dumping it on the future. Moreover, considerations of distributive justice within the Pareto constraint would now have a more solid foundation, especially as one would also be able to avoid the problem of strategy-proofness. By one stroke one would achieve more rational preferences, as well as the guarantee that they will in fact be expressed.

I now want to set out a series of objections — seven altogether — to the view stated above. I should explain that the goal of this criticism is not to demolish the theory, but to locate some points that need to be fortified. I am, in fact, largely in sympathy with the fundamental tenets of the view, yet fear that it might be dismissed as Utopian, both in the sense of ignoring the problem of getting from here to there, and in the sense of neglecting some elementary facts of human psychology.

The *first objection* involves a reconsideration of the issues of paternalism. Would it not, in fact, be unwarranted interference to impose on the citizens the obligation to participate in political discussion? One might answer that there is a link between the right to vote and the obligation to participate in discussion, just as rights and duties are correlative in other cases. To acquire the right to vote, one has to perform certain civic duties that go beyond pushing the voting button on the television set. There would appear to be two different ideas underlying this answer. First, only those should have the right to vote who are sufficiently *concerned* about politics to be willing to devote some of their resources — time in particular — to it. Secondly, one should try to favour *informed* preferences as inputs to the voting process. The first argument favours participation and discussion as a sign of interest, but does not give it an instrumental value in itself. It would do just as well, for the purpose of this argument, to demand that people should pay for the right to vote. The second argument favours discussion as a means to improvement — it will not only select the right people, but actually make them more qualified to participate.

These arguments might have some validity in a near-ideal world, in which the concern for politics was evenly distributed across all relevant dimensions, but in the context of contemporary politics they miss the point. The people who survive a high threshold for participation are disproportionately found in a privileged part of the population. At best this could lead to paternalism, at worst the high ideals of rational discussion could create a self-elected elite whose members spend time on politics because they want power, not out of concern for the issues. As in other cases, to be discussed later, the best can be the enemy of the good. I am not saying that it is impossible to modify the ideal in a way that allows both for rational discussion and for low-profile participation, only that any institutional design must respect the trade-off between the two.

My *second objection* is that even assuming unlimited time for discussion, unanimous and rational agreement might not necessarily ensue. Could there not be legitimate and unresolvable differences of opinions over the nature of the common good? Could there not even be a plurality of ultimate values?

I am not going to discuss this objection, since it is in any case preempted by the *third objection*. Since there are in fact always time constraints on discussions — often the stronger the more important the issues — unanimity will rarely emerge. For any constellation of preferences short of unanimity, however, one would need a social choice mechanism to aggregate them. One can discuss only for so long, and then one has to make a decision, even if strong differences of opinion should remain. This objection, then, goes to show that the transformation of preferences can never do more than supplement the aggregation of preferences, never replace it altogether.

This much would no doubt be granted by most proponents of the theory. True, they would say, even if the ideal speech situation can never be fully realized, it will nevertheless improve the outcome of the political process if one goes some way towards it. The *fourth objection* questions the validity of this reply. In some cases a little discussion can be a dangerous thing, worse in fact than no discussion at all, viz. if it makes some but not all persons align themselves on the common good. The following story provides an illustration:

> Once upon a time two boys found a cake. One of them said, 'Splendid! I will eat the cake.' The other one said, 'No, that is not fair! We found the cake together, and we should share and share alike, half for you and half for me.' The first boy said, 'No, I should have the whole cake!' Along came an adult who said, 'Gentlemen, you shouldn't fight about this: you should *compromise*. Give him three quarters of the cake.'[25]

What creates the difficulty here is that the first boy's preferences are allowed to count twice in the social choice mechanism suggested by the adult: once in his expression of them and then again in the other boy's internalized ethic of sharing. And one can argue that the outcome is socially inferior to that which would have emerged had they both stuck to their selfish preferences. When Adam Smith wrote that he had never known much good done by those who affected to trade for the public good, he may only have had in mind the harm that can be done by *unilateral* attempts to act morally. The categorical imperative itself may be badly served by people acting unilaterally on it.[26] Also, an inferior outcome may result if discussion brings about partial adherence to morality in all participants rather than full adherence in some and none in others, as in the story of the two boys. Thus Serge Kolm argues that

---

[25]R. Smullyan *This Book Needs No Title* (Englewood Cliffs, NJ: Prentice Hall, 1980) p. 56.

[26]J. Sobel '"Everyone", consequences and generalization arguments', *Inquiry*, 1967, 10: 373–404.

economies with moderately altruistic agents tend to work less well than economies where either everybody is selfish or everybody is altruistic.[27]

A *fifth objection* is to question the implicit assumption that the body politic as a whole is better or wiser than the sum of its parts. Could it not rather be the case that people are made more, not less, selfish and irrational by interacting politically? The cognitive analogy suggests that the rationality of beliefs may be positively as well as negatively affected by interaction. On the one hand there is what Irving Janis has called 'group-think', i.e. mutually reinforcing bias.[28] On the other hand there certainly are many ways in which people can, and do, pool their opinions and supplement each other to arrive at a better estimate.[29] Similarly autonomy and morality could be enhanced as well as undermined by interaction. Against the pessimistic view of Reinhold Niebuhr that individuals in a group show more unrestrained egoism than in their personal relationships,[30] we may set Hannah Arendt's optimistic view:

> American faith was not all based on a semireligious faith in human nature, but on the contrary, on the possibility of checking human nature in its singularity, by virtue of human bonds and mutual promises. The hope for man in his singularity lay in the fact that not man but men inhabit the earth and form a world between them. It is human worldliness that will save men from the pitfalls of human nature.[31]

Niebuhr's argument suggests an aristocratic disdain of the *mass*, which transforms individually decent people — to use a characteristically condescending phrase — into an unthinking horde. While rejecting this as a general view, one should equally avoid the other extreme, suggested by Arendt. Neither the Greek nor the American assemblies were the paradigms of discursive reason that she makes them out to be. The Greeks were well aware that they might be tempted by demagogues, and in fact took extensive precautions against this tendency.[32] The American town surely has not always been the incarnation of collective freedom, since on occasion it could also serve as the springboard for witch hunts. The mere decision to engage in rational discussion does not ensure that the transactions will in fact be conducted rationally,

[27]S.-C. Kolm 'Altruisme et efficacites', *Social Science Information*, 1981, 20: 293–354.

[28]I. Janis, *Victims of Group-Think* (Boston: Houghton Mifflin, 1972).

[29]Cf. R. Hogarth 'Methods for aggregating opinions', in H. Jungermann and G. de Zeeuw (eds.) *Decision Making and Change in Human Affairs* (Dordrecht: Reidel, 1977, pp. 231–56) and K. Lehrer 'Consensus and comparison. A theory of social rationality', in C. A. Hooker, J. J. Leach and E. F. McClennen (eds.) *Foundations and Applications of Decision of Theory*. Vol. 1: *Theoretical Foundations* (Dordrecht: Reidel, 1978) pp. 283–310.

[30]R. Niebuhr *Moral Man and Immoral Society* (New York: Scribner's, 1932) p. 11.

[31]H. Arendt *On Revolution* (Harmondsworth: Pelican Books, 1973) p. 174.

[32]M. Finley, 'The freedom of the citizen in the Greek world', in M. Finley (ed.) *Democracy: Ancient and Modern* (London: Chatto and Windus, 1973); see also Elster (1979, Chap. II.8).

since much depends on the structure and the framework of the proceedings. The random errors of selfish and private preferences may to
some extent cancel each other out and thus be less to be feared than the
massive and coordinated errors that may arise through group-think. On
the other hand, it would be excessively stupid to rely on mutually
compensating vices to bring about public benefits as a general rule. I
am not arguing against the need for public discussion, only for the need
to take the question of institutional and constitutional design very
seriously.

A *sixth objection* is that unanimity, were it to be realized, might easily
be due to conformity rather than to rational agreement. I would in fact
tend to have more confidence in the outcome of a democratic decision
if there was a minority that voted against it, than if it was unanimous. I
am not here referring to people expressing the majority preferences
against their real ones, since I am assuming that something like the
secret ballot would prevent this. I have in mind that people may come
to change their real preferences, as a result of seeing which way the
majority goes. Social psychology has amply shown the strength of this
bandwagon effect,[33] which in political theory is also known as the
'chameleon' problem.[34] It will not do to argue that the majority to
which the conformist adapts his view is likely to pass the test of rationality even if his adherence to it does not, since the majority could well
be made up of conformists each of whom would have broken out had
there been a minority he could have espoused.

To bring the point home, consider a parallel case of non-autonomous
preference formation. We are tempted to say that a man is free if he can
get or do whatever it is that he wants to get or do. But then we are
immediately faced with the objection that perhaps he only wants what
he can get, as the result of some such mechanism as 'sour grapes'.[35] We
may then add that, other things being equal, the person is freer the
more things he wants to do which he is not free to do, since these show
that his wants are not in general shaped by adaptation to his possibilities. Clearly, there is an air of paradox over the statement that a man's
freedom is greater the more of his desires he is not free to realize, but
on reflection the paradox embodies a valid argument. Similarly, it is
possible to dissolve the air of paradox attached to the view that a
collective decision is more trustworthy if it is less than unanimous.

My *seventh objection* amounts to a denial of the view that the need to
couch one's argument in terms of the common good will purge the

---

[33]S. Asch, 'Studies of independence and conformity: A. A minority of one against a
unanimous majority', *Psychology Monographs*, 1956, 70, is a classic study.

[34]See A. Goldman 'Toward a theory of social power', *Philosophical Studies*, 1972, 23:
221–68, for discussion and further references.

[35]I. Berlin *Two Concepts of Liberty* (Oxford: Oxford University Press, 1969) p. xxxviii;
cf. also Elster *Sour Grapes*, Chap. III.3.

desires of all selfish arguments. There are in general many ways of realizing the common good, if by that phrase we now only mean some arrangement that is Pareto-superior to uncoordinated individual decisions. Each such arrangement will, in addition to promoting the general interest, bring an extra premium to some specific group, which will then have a strong interest in that particular arrangement.[36] The group may then come to prefer the arrangement because of that premium, although it will argue for it in terms of the common good. Typically the arrangement will be justified by a causal theory — an account, say, of how the economy works — that shows it to be not only *a* way, but the only way of promoting the common good. The economic theories underlying the early Reagan administration provide an example. I am not imputing insincerity to the proponents of these views, but there may well be an element of wishful thinking. Since social scientists disagree so strongly among themselves as to how societies work, what could be more human than to pick on a theory that uniquely justifies the arrangement from which one stands to profit? The opposition between general interest and special interests is too simplistic, since the private benefits may causally determine the way in which one conceives of the common good.

These objections have been concerned to bring out two main ideas. First, one cannot assume that one will in fact approach the good society by acting as if one had already arrived there. The fallacy inherent in this 'approximation assumption'[37] was exposed a long time ago in the economic 'theory of the second best':

> It is *not* true that a situation in which more, but not all, of the optimum conditions are fulfilled is necessarily, or is even likely to be, superior to a situation in which fewer are fulfilled. It follows, therefore, that in a situation in which there exist many constraints which prevent the fulfilment of the Paretian optimum conditions, the removal of any one constraint may affect welfare or efficiency either by raising it, by lowering it or by leaving it unchanged.[38]

The ethical analogue is not the familiar idea that some moral obligations may be suspended when other people act non-morally.[39] Rather it is that the nature of the moral obligation is changed in a non-moral environment. When others act non-morally, there may be an obligation to deviate not only from what they do, but also from the behaviour that

---

[37]A. Margalit, 'Ideals and second bests', in S. Fox (ed.) *Philosophy of Education* (Jerusalem: Van Leer Foundation, 1983) pp. 77–90.

[38]R. Lipsey and K. Lancaster 'The general theory of the second-best', *Review of Economic Studies*, 1956–7, 24: p. 12.

[39]This is the point emphasised in D. Lyons *Forms and Limits of Utilitarianism* (Oxford: Oxford University Press, 1965).

would have been optimal if adopted by everybody.[40] In particular, a little discussion, like a little rationality or a little socialism, may be a dangerous thing.[41] If, as suggested by Habermas, free and rational discussion will only be possible in a society that has abolished political and economic domination, it is by no means obvious that abolition can be brought about by rational argumentation. I do not want to suggest that it could occur by force—since the use of force to end the use of force is open to obvious objections. Yet something like irony, eloquence or propaganda might be needed, involving less respect for the interlocutor than what would prevail in the ideal speech situation.

As will be clear from these remarks, there is a strong tension between two ways of looking at the relation between political ends and means. On the one hand, the means should partake of the nature of the ends, since otherwise the use of unsuitable means might tend to corrupt the end. On the other hand, there are dangers involved in choosing means immediately derived from the goal to be realized, since in a non-ideal situation these might take us away from the end rather than towards it. A delicate balance will have to be struck between these two, opposing considerations. It is in fact an open question whether there exists a ridge along which we can move to the good society, and if so whether it is like a knife-edge or more like a plateau.

The second general idea that emerges from the discussion is that even in the good society, should we hit upon it, the process of rational discussion could be fragile, and vulnerable to adaptive preferences, conformity, wishful thinking and the like. To ensure stability and robustness there is a need for structures—political institutions or constitutions—that could easily reintroduce an element of domination. We would in fact be confronted, at the political level, with a perennial dilemma of individual behaviour. How is it possible to ensure at the same time that one is bound by rules that protect one from irrational or unethical behaviour—and that these rules do not turn into prisons from which it is not possible to break out even when it would be rational to do so?[42]

---

[40]Cf. B. Hansson 'An analysis of some deontic logics', *Nous*, 1970, 3: 373–98; as well as D. Føllesdal and R. Hilpinen 'Deontic logic: an introduction' in R. Hilpinen (ed.) *Deontic Logic: Introductory and Systematic Readings* (Dordrecht: Reidel, 1971) pp. 1–35, for discussions of 'conditional obligations' within the framework of deontic logic. It does not appear, however, that the framework can easily accommodate the kind of dilemma I am concerned with here.

[41]Cf. for instance S.-C. Kolm *La transition socialiste* (Paris: Editions du Cerf, 1977) concerning the dangers of a piecemeal introduction of socialism—also mentioned by Margalit (1983) as an objection to Popper's strategy for piecemeal social engineering.

[41]Cf. for instance S.-C. Kolm *La transition socialiste* (Paris: Editions du Cerf, 1977) concerning the dangers of a piecemeal introduction of socialism—also mentioned by Margalit (1983) as an objection to Popper's strategy for piecemeal social engineering.

[42]Cf. G. Ainslie 'A behavioral economic approach to the defense mechanisms', *Social Science Information* 1982, 21: 735–80 and Elster (1979, Chap. II.9).

III

It is clear from Habermas's theory, I believe, that rational political discussion has an *object* in terms of which it makes sense.[43] Politics is concerned with substantive decision-making, and is to that extent instrumental. True, the idea of instrumental politics might also be taken in a more narrow sense, as implying that the political process is one in which individuals pursue their selfish interests, but more broadly understood it implies only that political action is primarily a means to a non-political end, only secondarily, if at all, an end in itself. In this section I shall consider theories that suggest a reversal of this priority, and that find the main point of politics in the educative or otherwise beneficial effects on the participants. And I shall try to show that this view tends to be internally incoherent, or self-defeating. The benefits of participation are by-products of political activity. Moreover, they are *essentially* by-products, in the sense that any attempt to turn them into the main purpose of such activity would make them evaporate.[44] It can indeed be highly satisfactory to engage in political work, but only on the condition that the work is defined by a serious purpose which goes beyond that of achieving this satisfaction. If that condition is not fulfilled, we get a narcissistic view of politics — corresponding to various consciousness-raising activities familiar from the last decade or so.

My concern, however, is with political theory rather than with political activism. I shall argue that certain types of arguments for political institutions and constitutions are self-defeating, since they justify the arrangement in question by effects that are essentially by-products. Here an initial and important distinction must be drawn between the task of justifying a constitution *ex ante* and that of evaluating it *ex post* and at a distance. I argue below that Tocqueville, when assessing the American democracy, praised it for consequences that are indeed by-products. In his case, this made perfectly good sense as an analytical attitude adopted after the fact and at some distance from the system he was examining. The incoherence arises when one invokes the same arguments before the fact, in public discussion. Although the constitution-makers may secretly have such side effects in mind, they cannot coherently invoke them in public.

Kant proposed a *transcendental formula of public right*: 'All actions affecting the rights of other human beings are wrong if their maxim is not compatible with their being made public.'[45] Since Kant's illustra-

---

[43]Indeed, Habermas (1982) is largely concerned with maxims for *action*, not with the evaluation of states of affairs.

[44]Cf. J. Elster *Explaining Technical Change* (Cambridge: Cambridge University Press, 1983, Chap. III) for a discussion of the notion that some psychological or social states are essentially by-products of actions undertaken for some other purpose.

[45]I. Kant *Perpetual Peace* in H. Reiss (ed.) *Kant's Political Writings* (Cambridge: Cambridge University Press, 1795) p. 126.

tions of the principle are obscure, let me turn instead to John Rawls, who imposes a similar condition of publicity as a constraint on what the parties can choose in the original position.[46] He argues, moreover, that this condition tends to favour his own conception of justice, as compared to that of the utilitarians.[47] If utilitarian principles of justice were openly adopted, they would entail some loss of self-esteem, since people would feel that they were not fully being treated as ends in themselves. Other things being equal, this would also lead to a loss in average utility. It is then conceivable that public adoption of Rawls's two principles of justice would bring about a higher average utility than public adoption of utilitarianism, although a lower average than under a secret utilitarian constitution introduced from above. The latter possibility, however, is ruled out by the publicity constraint. A utilitarian could not then advocate Rawls's two principles on utilitarian grounds, although he might well applaud them on such grounds. The fact that the two principles maximize utility would essentially be a by-product, and if chosen on the grounds that they are utility-maximizing they would no longer be so Utilitarianism, therefore, is self-defeating in Kant's sense: 'it essentially lacks openness'.[48]

Derek Parfit has raised a similar objection to act consequentialism (AC) and suggested how it could be met:

> This gives to all one common aim: the best possible outcome. If we try to achieve this, we may often fail. Even when we succeed, the fact that we are disposed to try might make the outcome worse. AC might thus be indirectly self-defeating. What does this show? A consequentialist might say: 'It shows that AC should be only one part of our moral theory. It should be the part that covers successful acts. When we are certain to succeed, we should aim for the best possible outcome. Our wider theory should be this: we should have the aim and dispositions having which would make the outcome best. This wider theory would not be self-defeating. So the objection has been met.'[49]

Yet there is an ambiguity in the word 'should' in the penultimate sentence, since it is not clear whether we are told that it is good to have certain aims and dispositions, or that we should aim at having them. The latter answer immediately raises the problem that having certain aims and dispositions — i.e. being a certain kind of person — is essentially a by-product. When instrumental rationality is self-defeating, we cannot decide on instrumentalist grounds to take leave of it — no more than we can fall asleep by deciding not to try to fall asleep. Although

[46]J. Rawls *A Theory of Justice* (Cambridge: Harvard University Press, 1971) p. 133.

[47]Rawls *A Theory of Justice*, pp. 177ff, esp. 181.

[48]Williams 'Critique of Utilitarianism', p. 123.

[49]D. Parfit, 'Prudence, morality and the prisoner's dilemma', *Proceedings of the British Academy* (Oxford: Oxford University Press, 1981) p. 554.

spontaneity may be highly valuable on utilitarian grounds, 'you cannot both genuinely possess this kind of quality and also reassure yourself that while it is free and creative and uncalculative, it is also acting for the best'.[50]

Tocqueville, in a seeming paradox, suggested that democracies are less suited than aristocracies to deal with long-term planning, and yet are superior in the long-run to the latter. The paradox dissolves once it is seen that the first statement involves time at the level of the actors, the second at the level of the observer. On the one hand, 'a democracy finds it difficult to coordinate the details of a great undertaking and to fix on some plan and carry it through with determination in spite of obstacles. It has little capacity for combining measures in secret and waiting patiently for the result'.[51] On the other hand, 'in the long run government by democracy should increase the real forces of a society, but it cannot immediately assemble at one point and at a given time, forces as great as those at the disposal of an aristocratic government'.[52] The latter view is further elaborated in a passage from the chapter on 'The Real Advantages Derived by American Society from Democratic Government':

> That constantly renewed agitation introduced by democratic govern-
> ment into political life passes, then, into civil society. Perhaps, taking
> everything into consideration, that is the greatest advantage of demo-
> cratic government, and I praise it much more on account of what it
> causes to be done than for what it does. It is incontestable that the
> people often manage public affairs very badly, but their concern ther-
> ewith is bound to extend their mental horizon and to shake them out
> of the rut of ordinary routine . . . Democracy does not provide a
> people with the most skillful of governments, but it does that which
> the most skillful government often cannot do: it spreads throughout
> the body social a restless activity, superabundant force, and energy
> never found elsewhere, which, however little favoured by circum-
> stances, can do wonders. Those are its true advantages.[53]

The advantages of democracies, in other words, are mainly and essentially by-products. The avowed aim of democracy is to be a good system
of government, but Tocqueville argues that it is inferior in this respect
to aristocracy, viewed purely as a decision-making apparatus. Yet the
very activity of governing democratically has as a by-product a certain
energy and restlessness that benefits industry and generates prosperity.
Assuming the soundness of this observation, could it ever serve as a
public justification for introducing democracy in a nation that had not
yet acquired it? The question is somewhat more complex than one

[50]Williams, p. 131); also Elster (*Sour Grapes*, Chap. II.3).
[51]A. Tocqueville, *Democracy in America* (New York: Anchor Books, 1969) p. 229.
[52]Tocqueville, p. 224.
[53]Tocqueville, pp. 243–4.

might be led to think from what I have said so far, since the quality of the decisions is not the only consideration that is relevant for the choice of a political system. The argument from *justice* could also be decisive. Yet the following conclusion seems inescapable: if the system has no inherent advantage in terms of justice or efficiency, one cannot coherently and publicly advocate its introduction because of the side effects that would follow in its wake. There must be a *point* in democracy as such. If people are motivated by such inherent advantages to throw themselves into the system, other benefits may ensue — but the latter cannot by themselves be the motivating force. If the democratic method is introduced in a society solely because of the side effects on economic prosperity, and no one believes in it on any other ground, it will not produce them.

Tocqueville, however, did not argue that political activity is an end in itself. The justification for democracy is found in its effects, although not in the intended ones, as the strictly instrumental view would have it. More to the point is Tocqueville's argument for the jury system: 'I do not know whether a jury is useful to the litigants, but I am sure that it is very good for those who have to decide the case. I regard it as one of the most effective means of popular education at society's disposal.'[54] This is still an instrumental view, but the gap between the means and the end is smaller. Tocqueville never argued that the effect of democracy was to make politicians prosperous, only that it was conducive to general prosperity. By contrast, the justification of the jury system is found in the effect on the jurors themselves. And, as above, that effect would be spoilt if they believed that the impact on their own civic spirit was the main point of the proceedings.

John Stuart Mill not only applauded but advocated democracy on the ground of such educative effects on the participants. In current discussion he stands out both as an opponent of the purely instrumental view of politics, that of his father James Mill,[55] and as a forerunner of the theory of participatory democracy.[56] In his theory the gap between means and ends in politics is even narrower, since he saw political activity not only as a means to self-improvement, but also as a source of satisfaction and thus a good in itself. As noted by Albert Hirschman, this implies that 'the benefit of collective action for an individual is not the difference between the hoped-for result and the effort furnished by

[54]Tocqueville, p. 275.

[55]Cf. A. Ryan 'Two concepts of politics and democracy: James and John Stuart Mill', in M. Fleisher (ed.) *Machiavelli and the Nature of Political Thought* (London: Croom Helm, 1972) corresponds in part to the distinction between the first and the second of the theories discussed here, in part to the distinction between the first and the third, as he does not clearly separate the public conception of politics from the non-instrumental one.

[56]C. Pateman *Participation and Democratic Theory* (Cambridge: Cambridge University Press, 1970) p. 29.

him or her, but the *sum* of these two magnitudes'.[57] Yet this very way of paraphrasing Mill's view also points to a difficulty. Could it really be the case that participation would yield a benefit even when the hoped-for results are nil, as suggested by Hirschman's formula? Is it not rather true that the effort is itself a function of the hoped-for result, so that in the end the latter is the only independent variable? When Mill refers, critically, to the limitations of Bentham, whose philosophy 'can teach the means of organising and regulating the merely *business* part of the social arrangement',[58] he seems to be putting the cart before the horse. The non-business part of politics may be the more valuable, but the value is contingent on the importance of the business part.

For a fully developed version of the non-instrumental theory of politics, we may go to the work of Hannah Arendt. Writing about the distinction between the private and the public realm in ancient Greece, she argues that:

> Without mastering the necessities of life in the household, neither life nor the 'good life' is possible, but politics is never for the sake of life. As far as the members of the *polis* are concerned, household life exists for the sake of the 'good life' in the *polis*.[59]
>
> The public realm . . . was reserved for individuality; it was the only place where men could show who they really and inexchangeably were. It was for the sake of this chance, and out of love for a body politic that it made it possible to them all, that each was more or less willing to share in the burden of jurisdiction, defence and administration of public affairs.[60]

Against this we may set the view of Greek politics found in the work of M. I. Finley. Asking why the Athenian people claimed the right of every citizen to speak and make proposals in the Assembly, yet left its exercise to a few, he finds that 'one part of the answer is that the *demos* recognised the instrumental role of political rights and were more concerned in the end with the substantive decisions, were content with their power to select, dismiss and punish their political leaders'.[61] Elsewhere he writes, even more explicitly: 'Then, as now, politics was instrumental for most people, not an interest or an end in itself.'[62] Contrary to what Arendt suggests, the possession or the possibility of exercising a political right may be more important than the actual exercise. Moreover, even the exercise derives its value from the decisions to be taken. Writing about the American town assemblies, Arendt

[57]A. Hirschman *Shifting Involvements* (Princeton: Princeton University Press, 1982) p. 29.
[58]J. Mill 'Bentham', in J. S. Mill *Utilitarianism* (London: Fontana Books, 1962) p. 105.
[59]H. Arendt *The Human Condition* (Chicago: University of Chicago Press, 1958) p. 37.
[60]Arendt *The Human Condition* p. 41.
[61]Finley, 'Politics', p. 83.
[62]M. Finley 'Politics', in M. I. Finley (ed.) *The Legacy of Greece* (Oxford: Oxford University Press, 1981) p. 31.

argues that the citizens participated 'neither exclusively because of duty nor, and even less, to serve their own interests but most of all because they enjoyed the discussions, the deliberations, and the making of decisions'.[63] This, while not putting the cart before the horse, at least places them alongside each other. Although discussion and deliberation in other contexts may be independent sources of enjoyment, the satisfaction one derives from *political* discussion is parasitic on decision-making. Political debate is about what to *do* — not about what ought to be the case. It is defined by this practical purpose, not by its subject-matter.

Politics in this respect is on a par with other activities such as art, science, athletics or chess. To engage in them may be deeply satisfactory, if you have an independently defined goal such as 'getting it right' or 'beating the opposition'. A chess player who asserted that he played not to win, but for the sheer elegance of the game, would be in narcissistic bad faith — since there is no such thing as an elegant way of losing, only elegant and inelegant ways of winning. When the artist comes to believe that the process and not the end result is his real purpose, and that defects and irregularities are valuable as reminders of the struggle of creation, he similarly forfeits any claim to our interest. The same holds for E. P. Thompson, who, when asked whether he really believed that a certain rally in Trafalgar Square would have any impact at all, answered: 'That's not really the point, is it? The point is, it shows that democracy's alive . . . A rally like that gives us self-respect. Chartism was terribly good for the Chartists, although they never got the Charter.'[64] Surely, the Chartists, if asked whether they thought they would ever get the Charter, would not have answered: 'That's not really the point, is it?' It was because they believed they might get the Charter that they engaged in the struggle for it with the seriousness of purpose that also brought them self-respect as a side effect.[65]

IV

I have been discussing three views concerning the relation between economics and politics, between the market and the forum. One extreme is 'the economic theory of democracy', most outrageously stated by Schumpeter, but in essence also underlying social choice theory. It is a market theory of politics, in the sense that the act of voting is a private act similar to that of buying and selling. I cannot accept, there-

[63]Arendt *On Revolution*, p. 119.

[64]*Sunday Times*, 2 November 1980.

[65]Cf. also B. Barry 'Comment', in S. Benn *et al.* (eds.) *Political Participation* (Canberra: Australian National University Press, 1978) p. 47.

fore, Alan Ryan's argument that 'On any possible view of the distinction between private and public life, voting is an element in one's public life.'[66] The very distinction between the secret and the open ballot shows that there is room for a private–public distinction within politics. The economic theory of democracy, therefore, rests on the idea that the forum should be like the market, in its purpose as well as in its mode of functioning. The purpose is defined in economic terms, and the mode of functioning is that of aggregating individual decisions.

At the other extreme there is the view that the forum should be completely divorced from the market, in purpose as well as in institutional arrangement. The forum should be more than the distributive totality of individuals queuing up for the election booth. Citizenship is a quality that can only be realized in public, i.e. in a collective joined for a common purpose. This purpose, moreover, is not to facilitate life in the material sense. The political process is an end in itself, a good or even the supreme good for those who participate in it. It may be applauded because of the educative effects on the participants, but the benefits do not cease once the education has been completed. On the contrary, the education of the citizen leads to a preference for public life as an end in itself. Politics on this view is not *about* anything. It is the agonistic display of excellence,[67] or the collective display of solidarity, divorced from decision-making and the exercise of influence on events.

In between these extremes is the view I find most attractive. One can argue that the forum should differ from the market in its mode of functioning, yet be concerned with decisions that ultimately deal with economic matters. Even higher-order political decisions concern lower-level rules that are directly related to economic matters. Hence constitutional arguments about how laws can be made and changed, constantly invoke the impact of legal stability and change on economic affairs. It is the concern with substantive decisions that lends the urgency to political debates. The ever-present constraint of *time* creates a need for focus and concentration that cannot be assimilated to the leisurely style of philosophical argument in which it may be better to travel hopefully than to arrive. Yet within these constraints arguments form the core of the political process. If thus defined as public in nature, and instrumental in purpose, politics assumes what I believe to be its proper place in society.

[66]Ryan 'Two Concepts of Policy and Democracy', p. 105.
[67]P. Veyne *Le pain et le cirque* (Paris: Seuil, 1976) makes a brilliant statement of this non-instrumental attitude among the elite of the Ancient World.

11

JAMES M. BUCHANAN

Politics without Romance:
A Sketch of Positive Public Choice Theory
and Its Normative Implications

IN THIS ESSAY, I propose to summarize the emergence and the content of the "theory of public choice," or, alternatively, the economic theory of politics, or "the new political economy."[1] This area of research has become important only in the decades after World War II. Indeed in Europe and Japan, the theory has come to command the attention of scholars only within the 1970s; developments in America stem from the 1950s and 1960s. As I hope that my remarks here will suggest, the theory of public choice is not without antecedents, and especially in the European thought of the eighteenth and nineteenth centuries. Ecclesiastes tells us that there is nothing new under the sun, and in a genuine sense, such a claim is surely correct, and especially in the so-called social sciences. (I am reminded of this every week when I see my mathematically inclined younger colleagues in economics rediscovering almost every wheel that older economists have ever talked about.) In terms of its impact on the realm of prevailing ideas, however, "public choice" is *new*, and this subdiscipline that falls halfway between economics and political science has turned around the thinking of many persons. If I am allowed to use Thomas Kuhn's overly used word here, we can, I think, say that a new *paradigm* has been substituted for an old

[1]For an earlier, and differently organized, discussion, see J. Buchanan, 'From private preferences to public philosophy: the development of public choice'', in A. Selden (ed.) *The Economics of Politics* (London: Institute of Economics, 1978). For a more technical survey, see D. Mueller, "Public Choice: A Survey," *Journal of Economic Literature*, 1976, 14(2): 395–433.

one. Or, to go somewhat further back, and to use Nietzsche's metaphor, we now look at some aspects of our world, and specifically our world of politics, through a different window.

My primary title for this essay, "Politics without Romance," was chosen for its descriptive accuracy. Public choice theory has been the avenue through which a romantic and illusory set of notions about the workings of governments and the behavior of persons who govern has been replaced by a set of notions that embody more skepticism about what governments can do and what governors will do, notions that are surely more consistent with the political reality that we may all observe about us. I have often said that public choice offers a "theory of governmental failure" that is fully comparable to the "theory of market failure" that emerged from the theoretical welfare economics of the 1930s and 1940s. In that earlier effort, the system of private markets was shown to "fail" in certain respects when tested against the idealized criteria for efficiency in resource allocation and distribution. In the later effort, in public choice, government or political organization is shown to "fail" in certain respects when tested for the satisfaction of idealized criteria for efficiency and equity. What has happened is that today we find few informed scholars who would try to test markets against idealized models. The private sector–public sector decision that each community must make is now more likely to be discussed in more meaningful terms, with organizational arrangements analyzed by comparisons between realistically modeled alternatives.

It seems to be nothing more than simple and obvious wisdom to compare social institutions as they might be expected actually to operate rather than to compare romantic models of how such institutions might be hoped to operate. But such simple and obvious wisdom was lost to the informed consciousness of Western man for more than a century. Nor is such wisdom today by any means universally accepted. The socialist mystique to the effect that the state, that politics, somehow works its way toward some transcendent "public good" is with us yet, in many guises, as we must surely acknowledge. And, even among those who reject such mystique, there are many who unceasingly search for the ideal that will resolve the dilemma of politics.

Especially at this early point, however, I do not want to appear to place too much emphasis on the normative implications of public choice theory. These implications can stand on their own, and they can be allowed to emerge as they will or will not from the positive analysis. The *theory* of public choice, as such, is or can be a wholly positive theory, wholly scientific and *wertfrei* in the standard meanings of these terms. The implications for the comparative evaluation of institutions, noted above, have to do with methods of making such comparisons, not with specific results. I do not want to commit the naturalistic fallacy, and I make no claim that public choice theory, any more than economic theory, can tell a community of persons what they "should" choose to do.

Definition

Let me now be somewhat more concrete and try to define "public choice theory" more directly. Such a definition can perhaps best be clarified by reference to economic theory, if only because the latter is more familiar. What is economic theory? It is a body of analysis that offers an understanding, an explanation, of the complex exchange process that we call "an economy." It is a body of analysis that allows us to relate the behavior of individual participants in market activity, as buyers, sellers, investors, producers, entrepreneurs, to the results that are attained for the whole community, results that are not within the purposes or the knowledge of the separate participants themselves (I should note here that Austria has a very proud and important heritage in the development of economic theory as I have here defined it, and I may say in passing that one of the most exciting and most encouraging developments within economics in the United States today is the observed resurgence of interest in "Austrian economics," and notably as among young research scholars.)

Public choice theory essentially takes the tools and methods of approach that have been developed to quite sophisticated analytical levels in economic theory and applies these tools and methods to the political or governmental sector, to politics, to the public economy. As with economic theory, the analysis attempts to relate the behavior of individual actors in the governmental sector, that is, the behavior of persons in their various capacities as voters, as candidates for office, as elected representatives, as leaders or members of political parties, as bureaucrats (all of these are "public choice" roles) to the composite of outcomes that we observe or might observe. Public choice theory attempts to offer an understanding, an explanation, of the complex institutional interactions that go on within the political sector. I emphasize the word *complex* here, since the appropriate contrast to be made is with the approach that models government as some sort of monolith, with a being of its own, somehow separate and apart from the individuals who actually participate in the process.

Methodological Individualism

As my definition suggests, public choice theory is methodologically individualistic, in the same sense that economic theory is. The basic units are choosing, acting, behaving persons rather than organic units such as parties, provinces, or nations. Indeed, yet another label for the subject matter here is "An Individualistic Theory of Politics."

There is no formal connection between the methodological individualism that describes formal public choice theory and the motivations that are attributed to persons as they behave in their various public choice capacities or roles listed above. It would be possible to construct a fully consistent and methodologically individualistic theory of politics on the romantic assumption that all persons in their political roles seek only to further their own conceptions of some "common good," and with utter and total disregard for their own more narrowly defined self-interest. Such a theory would not escape problems of reconciling differing persons' differing conceptions of just what defines "common good." But testable propositions might emerge from such a theory, and empirical work might be commenced to test these propositions.

But most of the scholars who have been instrumental in developing public choice theory have themselves been trained initially as economists. There has been, therefore, a tendency for these scholars to bring with them models of man that have been found useful within economic theory, models that have been used to develop empirically testable and empirically corroborated hypotheses. These models embody the presumption that persons seek to maximize their own utilities, and that their own narrowly defined economic well-being is an important component of these utilities. At this point, however, I do not want to enter into either a defense of or an attack on the usefulness of *homo economicus*, either in economics or in any theory of politics. I would say only, as I have many times before, that the burden of proof should rest with those who suggest that wholly different models of man apply in the political and the economic realms of behavior. Logical consistency suggests that, at least initially, we examine the implications of using the *same* models in different settings.

As I have already noted, we commence with individuals as utility maximizers. And, for present purposes, we do not need to specify just what arguments are contained in a person's utility function. We can, at this stage, allow for saints as well as sinners. In one sense, we can simply define a person in terms of his set of preferences, his utility function. This function defines or describes a set of possible trade-offs among alternatives for potential choice, whether the latter be those between apples and oranges at the fruit stand or between peace and war for the nation.

Once we begin analysis in terms of preference or utility functions, we are led almost immediately to inquire about possible differences among persons. Since there seems to be no self-evident reason why separate persons should exhibit the same preferences, it seems best to commence with the presumption that preferences may differ. Within economic theory, such differences present no problem. Indeed, quite the opposite. If one person places a relatively higher value on apples as compared with oranges than another person, an exchange opportunity is presented. Both persons can gain utility by trade. Indeed this trading to mutual advantage is what economic theory is all about, no matter how esoteric its modern practitioners may make it seem to be in its detail.

Political Exchange

By any comparison with politics, economic theory is *simple*. The process of "political exchange" is necessarily more complex than that of economic exchange through orderly markets, and for two quite separate reasons. In the first place, basic "political exchange," the conceptual contract under which the constitutional order is itself established, must precede any meaningful economic interaction. Orderly trade in private goods and services can take place only within a defined legal structure that establishes individuals' rights of ownership and control of resources, that enforces private contracts, and that places limits on the exercise of governmental powers. In the second place, even within a well-defined and functioning legal order, "political exchange" necessarily involves *all* members of the relevant community rather than the two trading partners that characterize economic exchange.[2]

The two levels of "political exchange" provide a somewhat natural classification for two related but separate areas of inquiry, both of which fall within the corpus of public choice. The first area of inquiry may be called an "economic theory of constitutions."[3] This theory has historical antecedents in the theory of social contract, and it also has modern philosophical generalization in the work of *Rawls*.[4] The second area of inquiry involves the "theory of political institutions" as these might be predicted to work within a constitutional-legal structure. The subject matter incorporates theories of voting and voting rules, theories of electoral and party competition, and theories of bureaucracy.[5]

---

[2]For a development of the distinction between political exchange at the constitutional and the postconstitutional levels, see J. Buchanan, *The Limits of Liberty* (Chicago: University of Chicago Press, 1975).

[3]The development of such a theory was the primary purpose of the book that I wrote jointly with Tullock, *The Calculus of Consent* (Ann Arbor: University of Michigan Press, 1962).

[4]J. Rawls, *A Theory of Justice* (Cambridge: Harvard University Press, 1971).

[5]In modern public choice theory, the theory of voting rules commences with D. Black, *Theory of Committees and Elections* (Cambridge: Cambridge University Press, 1958). The theory of electoral or party competition stems largely from the work of A. Downs, *An Economic Theory of Democracy* (New York: Harper & Row, 1957). The theory of bureaucracy in its modern sense was first developed in G. Tullock, *The Politics of Bureaucracy* (Washington, DC: Public Affairs Press, 1965).

The Economic Theory of Constitutions

As I have stated, this aspect of modern public choice theory is closely related to an important strand of ideas in traditional political theory or political philosophy, namely, the theory of the social contract or compact. The whole discussion here is directly relevant to the classic set of issues involving the *legitimacy* of political order. What gives legitimacy to governments, or to governors? What rights can some men possess to rule over other men?

At some basic philosophical level, the individualist must reject the notion that any such "rights of governance" exist. In this sense, I have often called myself a philosophical anarchist. Nonetheless, we are obligated to look squarely at the alternative social order that anarchy would represent, and without the romantic blinders that putative anarchists have always worn, then and now. And we look to Thomas Hobbes, whose seventeenth-century vision becomes very appealing to those of us who live in the late twentieth century. Hobbes described the life of persons in a society without government, without laws, as "solitary, poor, nasty, brutish, and short." In this Hobbesian perspective, any person in such a jungle would value security to life and property so highly that any contract with a sovereign government would seem highly beneficial. The person would agree to abide by the laws laid down by the sovereign, even if he recognizes that there were essentially no limits that could be placed on the sovereign's use of these laws for its own exploitative purposes.

Montesquieu, John Locke, and the American Founding Fathers were more optimistic than Hobbes in their conception of constitutional contract as potentially binding on the activities of government. And I think that a reading of history will, to an extent at least, bear out their conception. Governments have been limited by constitutions, and part of the Western heritage to this day reflects the eighteenth-century wisdom that imposed some limits on governmental powers. But the nineteenth- and twentieth-century fallacy in political thought was embodied in the presumption that electoral requirements were in themselves sufficient to hold government's Leviathan-like proclivities in check, the presumption that, so long as there were constitutional guarantees for free and periodic elections, the range and extent of governmental action would be controlled. Only in the middle of this century have we come to recognize that such electoral constraints do not keep governments within the implied "contract" through which they might have been established, the "contract" which alone can give governments any claim to legitimacy in the eyes of citizens.

The theory of constitutions that makes up a central part of public choice represents, in part, a return to the eighteenth- as opposed to the nineteenth- or twentieth-century perspective. The theory raises questions about how governments may be constrained, and about how governments should be constrained. What should governments be allowed to do? What is the appropriate sphere of political action? How large a share of national product should be available for political disposition? What sort of political decision structures should be adopted at the constitutional stage? Under what conditions and to what extent should individuals be franchised?

These questions, and many others like them, clearly depend for answers on some positive, predictive analysis of how different political institutions will operate if, in fact, they are constitutionally authorized. An informed, and meaningful, theory of constitutions cannot be constructed until and unless there exists some theory of the operation of alternative political rules.

Postconstitutional Politics

In a postconstitutional setting, with a defined legal order, there will remain opportunities for mutually advantageous "political exchanges." That is to say, after the conceptualized constitutional "contract" has established what has been variously called the "protective," "minimal," or "night-watchman" state, there are still likely to be efficiency-enhancing complex trades among all persons in the community. The "productive state" may emerge to provide "public goods," goods that are nonexcludable as among separate beneficiaries and that may be more cheaply produced jointly than separately.

How should the complex political exchanges be organized so as to insure that all beneficiaries secure net gains in the process? Voluntaristic trade akin to the pairwise matching of buyers and sellers that characterizes private-goods market exchange may not be possible. A role for governmental action is suggested, but how are government decisions to be made and by whom? By what rules? And how might various rules be predicted to work?

The theory here, as it has developed, has involved two distinct types of questions. First, it has attempted to look at how differing individual preferences over joint outcomes are reconciled, or might be reconciled. That is, how do groups of persons reach collective decisions under differing procedural rules? This type of theory has not been concerned with government, as such. In effect, it is a theory of *demand* for government goods and services without any accompanying theory of *supply*. The second, and more recent, development has addressed the quite different set of questions relating to the behavior of persons who are themselves charged with powers of governance, with supplying the goods and services that might be demanded by the citizenry. It will be useful to summarize the strands of postconstitutional political analysis separately.

Theory of Voting Rules

We may commence with the work of *Black*, who asked the simple question: How do committees reach decisions under simple majority voting rules? Building on only bits and pieces of precursory work by Condorcet, Lewis Caroll, and a few others, *Black* was led to analyze the properties of majority voting, and he discovered the problem of the majority cycle, the problem that has occupied perhaps an undue amount of attention in public choice theory. There may exist situations where no single one of the possible alternatives for choice can command majority support over all other alternatives, despite the consistency of the preference sets of all members of the choosing group. In such a cyclical majority setting, there is no stable group decision attainable by majority rule; the group cannot make up its collective mind; it cannot decide.

Simultaneously with *Black*, and for a different purpose, *Arrow*[6] was examining the desirable properties of a "social welfare function," and he was attempting to determine whether such a function could ever be constructed from a set of individual orderings. He reached the conclusion that no such function satisfying minimally acceptable properties could be found, and for basically the same reasons that *Black* developed more closely in connection with majority voting rules. *Arrow*'s work is not narrowly within what we might call the "public choice tradition," since he was, and is, concerned not with how institutions work but the logical structure of collective or social choice. Nonetheless, it was *Arrow*'s work that exerted a major influence on the thinking of social scientists; his work was taken to have demonstrated that government cannot work, if work here is defined in terms of the standard economist's criteria for consistency in choice. Collectivities in which individual preferences differ cannot, à la *Black*, make up their collective or group mind. And, à la *Arrow*, such groups cannot be assigned an ordering that will array all possible outcomes that is itself both consistent and reflective of individual orderings. Since the 1950s, since *Arrow* and *Black*, social choice theorists have explored in exhaustive logical and mathematical detail possible ways and means of escaping from the implications of the *Arrow* impossibility theorem, but they have had little or no success. "Social choice theory" has itself become a major growth industry, with an equilibrium not yet in sight.

Let me return to the work of *Black*, who, when confronted with the prospect of majority rule cycles, discovered that under certain configurations of preferences such cycles would not arise. If the alternatives for collective choice can be arrayed in such a fashion that individual orderings over these alternatives are single-peaked, for all voters in the

[6]K. Arrow, *Social Choice and Individual Values* (New York: John Wiley, 1951).

group, there will be a unique majority outcome, one that will defeat any other outcome in a series of pairwise majority votes. This outcome or option will be that one which best satisfies or which is most preferred by the voter who is *median* among all voters, with respect to preferences over the options. The conditions required for single-peakedness are plausibly applicable in situations where the alternatives for collective choice are reducible to quantitative variations along a single dimension, for example, proposed amounts of public spending on a given public service. Consider a school board or committee of three members, one of whom prefers high spending on education, one of whom prefers medium spending, and the third of whom prefers low spending. So long as the high spender prefers medium to low spending, and so long as the low spender prefers medium to high spending, majority voting within the three-member committee will produce a stable medium spending outcome.

This tendency of majority voting rules to produce determinate outcomes that correspond to the preferences of the median voter under certain conditions has led to many studies, both analytical and empirical, notably in public finance applications of public choice, and particularly with reference to the budgetary decisions made in local governments. Median-voter models break down, however, even with simple budgetary allocation problems, when more than one dimension is introduced. If voters, or members of a committee, consider simultaneously several issues or dimensions, such as, say, spending on education and spending on police, the cyclical majority problem returns. And, related to this return, the multiplicity of dimensions allows for vote trading and "logrolling," the analysis of which has been important in public choice theory from its inception.

As I have already noted, the theory of voting and voting rules sketched here in summary is not a theory of government or of politics at all. It is, instead, a theory or set of theories about how groups of persons reach some decision or choice on what might be *demanded*, by the group, from some supplying agent or agency. Implicitly, the analysis proceeds on the presumption that the goods or services demanded are supplied passively and that the motivations of suppliers may be neglected. It is as if all collective decisions are somehow analogous to the decision made by a group meeting in a closed room about the setting for the thermostat, the presumption being that, once a joint decision is made, the heating or cooling system will respond automatically and passively to the demands placed on it.

REPRESENTATION AND ELECTORAL COMPETITION

Once we so much as move beyond the simple committee or town-meeting setting, however, something other than the passive response of suppliers must be reckoned with in any theory of politics that can pretend to model reality. Even if we take only the single step from town-meeting democracy to representative democracy, we must introduce the possible divergence between the interests of the representative or agent who is elected or appointed to act for the group and the interests of the group members themselves.

It is at this point that electoral competition, as an institution, plays a role that has some similarities with that played by market competition in the economy. In the latter, the principle of consumer sovereignty prevails if sellers are sufficiently competitive. At the idealized limit, no single seller can exercise any power over buyers. But to what extent does a system of electoral competition generate comparable results? To what extent is voter sovereignty analogous to consumer sovereignty? There are major differences that should be recognized, despite the underlying similarities. Persons or parties that seek to represent the interests of voters compete for approval or favor much in the manner as the sellers of products in imperfectly competitive markets for private goods and services. But politics differs categorically from markets in that, in political competition, there are mutually exclusive sets of losers and winners. Only one candidate or party wins; all others lose. Only one party is the governing party. One way of stating the basic difference here is to say that, in economic exchange, decisions are made at the margin, in terms of more or less, whereas in politics, decisions are made among mutually exclusive alternatives, in terms of all-or-none prospects. The voter may be disappointed when his candidate or party or policy proposal loses in a sense that is not experienced in market exchange.

At best electoral competition places limits on the exercise of discretionary power on the part of those who are successful in securing office. Reelection prospects tend to keep the self-interests of politicians within reasonable range of those of the median voter, but there is nothing to channel outcomes toward the needs of the nonmedian voting groups.

THEORY OF BUREAUCRACY

Even if we ignore the possible divergencies between the interests of legislative representatives, as elected agents of the voters, and those interests of the voters themselves, we remain without an effective model of government because we have not accounted for the behavior of those persons who actually *supply* the goods and services that are provided via governmental auspices. Voters elect members of legislatures or parliaments. Members of legislatures, through coalitions or through parties, make selections among various policy alternatives or options. But the implementation of policy, the actual process of government, remains with persons who hold positions in the bureaucracy.

How do these persons behave? How are the conflicts between their own interests and those of the voters reconciled?

Recent developments in public choice theory have demonstrated the limits of legislative control over the discretionary powers of the bureaucracy. Modern government is complex and many-sided, so much so that it would be impossible for legislatures to make more than a tiny fraction of all genuine policy decisions. Discretionary power must be granted to bureaucrats over wide ranges of decision. Further, the bureaucracy can manipulate the agenda for legislative action for the purpose of securing outcomes favorable to its own interests. The bureaucracy can play off one set of constituents against others, insuring that budgets rise much beyond plausible efficiency limits.

Increasingly, public choice scholars have started to model governments in monopoly rather than competitive terms. Electoral competition has come more and more to be viewed as competition among prospective monopolists, all of whom are bidding for an exclusive franchise, with profit maximizing assumed to characterize the behavior of the successful bidder. Governments are viewed as exploiters of the citizenry, rather than the means through which the citizenry secures for itself goods and services that can best be provided jointly or collectively. Both the modern analysis and the observed empirical record suggests that governments have, indeed, got out of hand.

Can Leviathan Be Limited?

The rapidly accumulating developments in the theory of public choice — ranging from sophisticated analyses of schemes for amalgamating individual preferences into consistent collective outcomes, through the many models that demonstrate with convincing logic how political rules and institutions fail to work as their idealizations might promise, and finally to the array of empirical studies that corroborate the basic economic model of politics — have all been influential in modifying the way that modern man views government and political process. The romance is gone, perhaps never to be regained. The socialist paradise is lost. Politicians and bureaucrats are seen as ordinary persons much like the rest of us, and "politics" is viewed as a set of arrangements, a game if you will, in which many players with quite disparate objectives interact so as to generate a set of outcomes that may not be either internally consistent or efficient by any standards.

I do not want to claim, or to be taken to claim, too much for the contribution of public choice theory in turning attitudes around here, in being responsible for the paradigm shift. For social scientists, for scholars and intellectuals, the availability of an alternative model of political process probably has been of some considerable importance. But for members of the general public, the simple observation of failure on the part of the governments to deliver on their promises, these failures have been much more important in modifying attitudes than any set of ideas or any ideology.

I noted earlier that the fallacy of nineteenth- and twentieth-century political thought lay in an implicit faith that electoral constraints would alone be sufficient to hold the Leviathan-like proclivities of government in check. The experience in Western nations since World War II has exposed this fallacy for what it is. And we are now seeking to reimpose constitutional limits on government over and beyond those exercised through democratic electoral constraints. At least we are trying to do so in the United States. Beyond minimal efforts, I am not sure that there is a comparable movement at work in Europe. It seems to me highly doubtful that this objective can be successfully accomplished. Having come to command shares in national income or product that were undreamt of, even in the most roseate of the early democratic socialist predictions, modern governmental bureaucracies will not relinquish their relative positions in society without struggle.

Nonetheless, the effort is being made and will be made. In America, 1978 was the year of Proposition 13, when the voters of California turned back, by a two to one margin, the growth of government spending and taxing. This event sent political shock waves throughout the Western world. The United States is now (1979) inundated with various proposals, at all levels of government, designed to limit the expansion of governmental powers. "Bridling the passions of the sovereign" —this eighteenth-century slogan has resurfaced to command political respectability.

I have indicated that developments in public choice theory may have been in some small way influential in generating this shift in attitudes toward bureaucracies, politicians, and government. But the question remains as to what contribution public choice theory might make in the face of the developing distrust of traditional political institutions. It is here that the economic theory of constitutions, discussed earlier as a part of public choice analysis, becomes relatively the most important area of emphasis. Western societies face a task of *reconstruction*; basic political institutions must be reexamined and rebuilt so as to keep governments as well as citizens within limits of tolerance. But we are approaching a period when critical diagnosis is not enough. Criticism alone can generate chaos, whether this be in the form of gradual breakdown or in the form of violent disruption. The reconstructive reform in our institutions can be accomplished without revolution of either the left or right, but this path toward the future requires that the public come to understand the limits of change as well as the value. Zealotry in the cause of antipolitics, antigovernment, anti-institutions movements can result in a drift toward anarchistic terror, the jungle against which Hobbes warned us all. We must indeed keep the "miracle" of social order clearly in our mind as we seek ways and means of reforming arrangements that seem to have got out of hand. I think that public choice theory offers an analytical setting that allows us to discuss genuine reconstruction in our constitutions that may be made without major social costs.

12

F. A. HAYEK

Competition as a Discovery Procedure

1

IT IS DIFFICULT to defend economists against the charge that for some 40 to 50 years they have been discussing competition on assumptions that, *if* they were true of the real world, would make it wholly uninteresting and useless. If anyone really knew all about what economic theory calls the *data*, competition would indeed be a very wasteful method of securing adjustment to these facts. It is thus not surprising that some people have been led to the conclusion that we can either wholly dispense with the market, or that its results should be used only as a first step towards securing an output of goods and services which we can then manipulate, correct, or redistribute in any manner we wish. Others, who seem to derive their conception of competition solely from modern textbooks, have not unnaturally concluded that competition does not exist.

Against this, it is salutary to remember that, *wherever* the use of competition can be rationally justified, it is on the ground that we do *not* know in advance the facts that determine the actions of competitors. In sports or in examinations, no less than in the award of government contracts or of prizes for poetry, it would clearly be pointless to arrange for competition, if we were certain beforehand who would do best. As indicated in the title of this lecture, I propose to consider competition as a procedure for the discovery of such facts as, without resort to it, would not be known to anyone, or at least would not be utilised.[1]

This may at first appear so obvious and incontestable as hardly to deserve attention. Yet, some interesting consequences that are not so obvious immediately follow from the explicit formulation of the above apparent truism. One is that competition is valuable *only* because, and so far as, its results are unpredictable and on the whole different from those which anyone has, or could have, deliberately aimed at. Further, that the generally beneficial effects of competition must include disappointing or defeating some particular expectations or intentions.

Closely connected with this is an interesting methodological consequence. It goes far to account for the discredit into which the microeconomic approach to theory has fallen. Although this theory seems to me to be the only one capable of explaining the role of competition, it is no longer understood, even by some professed economists. It is therefore worthwhile to say at the outset a few words about the methodological peculiarity of any theory of competition, because it has made its conclusions suspect to many of those who habitually apply an over-simplified test to decide what they are willing to accept as scientific. The necessary consequence of the reason why we use competition is that, *in those cases in which it is interesting*, the validity of the theory can never be tested empirically. We can test it on conceptual models, and we might conceivably test it in artificially created real situations, where the facts which competition is intended to discover are already known to the observer. But in such cases it is of no practical value, so that to carry out the experiment would hardly be worth the expense. If we do not know the facts we hope to discover by means of competition, we can never ascertain how effective it has been in discovering those facts that might be discovered. All we can hope to find out is that, on the whole, societies which rely for this purpose on competition have achieved their aims more successfully than others. This is a conclusion which the history of civilisation seems eminently to have confirmed.

The peculiarity of competition — which it has in common with scientific method — is that its performance cannot be tested in particular instances where it is significant, but is shown only by the fact that the market will prevail in comparison with any alternative arrangements. The advantages of accepted scientific procedures can never be proved scientifically, but only demonstrated by the common experience that,

---

[1]Since I wrote this my attention has been drawn to a paper by Leopold Von Wiese on 'Die Konkurrenz, vorwiegend in soziologisch-systematischer Betrachtung', *Verhandlungen des 6. Deutschen Soziologentages*, 1929, where, on p. 27, he discusses the 'experimental' nature of competition.

on the whole, they are better adapted to delivering the goods than alternative approaches.[2]

The difference between economic competition and the successful procedures of science consists in the fact that the former is a method of discovering particular facts relevant to the achievement of specific, temporary purposes, while science aims at the discovery of what are sometimes called 'general facts', which are regularities of events. Science concerns itself with unique, particular facts only to the extent that they help to confirm or refute theories. Because these refer to general, permanent features of the world, the discoveries of science have ample time to prove their value. In contrast, the benefits of particular facts, whose usefulness competition in the market discovers, are in a great measure transitory. So far as the theory of scientific method is concerned, it would be as easy to discredit it on the ground that it does not lead to testable predictions about what science will discover, as it is to discredit the theory of the market on the ground that it fails to predict particular results the market will achieve. This, in the nature of the case, the theory of competition cannot do in any situation in which it is sensible to employ it. As we shall see, its capacity to predict is necessarily limited to predicting the kind of pattern, or the abstract character of the order that will form itself, but does not extend to the prediction of particular facts.[3]

2

Having relieved myself of this pet concern, I shall return to the central subject of this lecture, by pointing out that economic theory sometimes appears at the outset to bar its way to a true appreciation of the character of the process of competition, because it starts from the assumption of a 'given' supply of scarce goods. But which goods are scarce goods, or which things are goods, and how scarce or valuable they are — these are precisely the things which competition has to discover. Provisional results from the market process at each stage alone tell individuals what to look for. Utilisation of knowledge widely dispersed in a society with extensive division of labour cannot rest on individuals knowing all the particular uses to which well-known things in their individual environment might be put. Prices direct their attention to what is worth finding out about market offers for various things

[2]Cf. the interesting studies of the late Michael Polanyi in *The Logic of Liberty*, London, 1951, which show how he has been led from the study of scientific method to the study of competition in economic affairs; and see also K. R. Popper, *The Logic of Scientific Discovery*, London, 1959.

[3]On the nature of 'pattern prediction' see my essay on 'The theory of complex phenomena' in *Studies in Philosophy, Politics and Economics*, London and Chicago, 1967.

and services. This means that the, in some respects always unique, combinations of individual knowledge and skills, which the market enables them to use, will not merely, or even in the first instance, be such knowledge of facts as they could list and communicate if some authority asked them to do so. The knowledge of which I speak consists rather of a capacity to find out particular circumstances, which becomes effective only if possessors of this knowledge are informed by the market which kinds of things or services are wanted, and how urgently they are wanted.[4]

This must suffice to indicate what kind of knowledge I am referring to when I call competition a discovery procedure. Much would have to be added to clothe the bare bones of this abstract statement with concrete flesh, so as to show its full practical importance. But I must be content with thus briefly indicating the absurdity of the usual procedure of starting the analysis with a situation in which all the facts are supposed to be known. This is a *state* of affairs which economic theory curiously calls 'perfect competition'. It leaves no room whatever for the *activity* called competition, which is presumed to have already done its task. However, I must hurry on to examine a question, on which there exists even more confusion—namely, the meaning of the contention that the market adjusts activities spontaneously to the facts it discovers —or the question of the purpose for which it uses this information.

The prevailing confusion here is largely due to mistakenly treating the order which the market produces as an 'economy' in the strict sense of the word, and judging results of the market process by criteria which are appropriate only to such a single organised community serving a given hierarchy of ends. But such a hierarchy of ends is not relevant to the complex structure composed of countless individual economic arrangements. The latter, unfortunately, we also describe by the same word 'economy', although it is something fundamentally different, and must be judged by different standards. An economy, in the strict sense of the word, is an organisation or arrangement in which someone deliberately allocates resources to a unitary order of ends. Spontaneous order produced by the market is nothing of the kind; and in important respects it does not behave like an economy proper. In particular, such spontaneous order differs because it does *not* ensure that what general opinion regards as more important needs are always satisfied before the less important ones. This is the chief reason why people object to it. Indeed, the whole of socialism is nothing but a demand that the market order (or catallaxy, as I like to call it, to prevent confusion with an

---

[4]Cf. Samuel Johnson in J. Boswell, *Life of Samuel Johnson*, L. F. Powell's revision of G. B. Hill's edition, Oxford, 1934, vol. II, p. 365 (18 April 1775): 'Knowledge is of two kinds. We know a subject ourselves, or we know where we can find information about it.'

economy proper)[5] should be turned into an economy in the strict sense, in which a common scale of importance determines which of the various needs are to be satisfied, and which are not to be satisfied.

The trouble with this socialist aim is a double one. As is true of every deliberate organisation, only the knowledge of the organiser can enter into the design of the economy proper, and all the members of such an economy, conceived as a deliberate organisation, must be guided in their actions by the unitary hierarchy of ends which it serves. On the other hand, advantages of the spontaneous order of the market, or the catallaxy, are correspondingly two. Knowledge that is used in it is that of all its members. Ends that it serves are the separate ends of those individuals, in all their variety and contrariness.

Out of this fact arise certain intellectual difficulties which worry not only socialists, but all economists who want to assess the accomplishments of the market order; because, if the market order does not serve a definite order of ends, indeed if, like any spontaneously formed order, it cannot legitimately be said to *have* particular ends, it is also not possible to express the value of the results as a sum of its particular individual products. What, then, do we mean when we claim that the market order produces in some sense a maximum or optimum?

The fact is, that, though the existence of a spontaneous order not made for a particular purpose cannot be properly said to have a purpose, it may yet be highly conducive to the achievement of many different individual purposes not known as a whole to any single person, or relatively small group of persons. Indeed, rational action is possible only in a fairly orderly world. Therefore it clearly makes sense to try to produce conditions under which the chances for any individual taken at random to achieve his ends as effectively as possible will be very high — even if it cannot be predicted which particular aims will be favoured, and which not.

As we have seen, the results of a discovery procedure are in their nature unpredictable; and all we can expect from the adoption of an effective discovery procedure is to improve the chances for unknown people. The only common aim which we can pursue by the choice of this technique of ordering social affairs is the general kind of pattern, or the abstract character, of the order that will form itself.

3

Economists usually ascribe the order which competition produces as an equilibrium — a somewhat unfortunate term, because such an equi-

---

[5]For a fuller discussion see now my *Law, Legislation and Liberty*, vol. II, *The Mirage of Social Justice*, London and Chicago, 1976, pp. 107–20.

librium presupposes that the facts have already all been discovered and competition therefore has ceased. The concept of an 'order' which, at least for the discussion of problems of economic policy, I prefer to that of equilibrium, has the advantage that we can meaningfully speak about an order being approached to various degrees, and that order can be preserved throughout a process of change. While an economic equilibrium never really exists, there is some justification for asserting that the kind of order of which our theory describes an ideal type, is approached in a high degree.

This order manifests itself in the first instance in the circumstance that the expectations of transactions to be effected with other members of society, on which the plans of all the several economic subjects are based, can be mostly realised. This mutual adjustment of individual plans is brought about by what, since the physical sciences have also begun to concern themselves with spontaneous orders, or 'self-organising systems', we have learnt to call 'negative feedback'. Indeed, as intelligent biologists acknowledge, 'long before Claude Bernard, Clerk Maxwell, Walter B. Cannon, or Norbert Wiener developed cybernetics, Adam Smith has just as clearly used the idea in *The Wealth of Nations*. The "invisible hand" that regulated prices to a nicety is clearly this idea. In a free market, says Smith in effect, prices are regulated by negative feedback.'[6]

We shall see that the fact that a high degree of coincidence of expectations is brought about by the systematic disappointment of some kind of expectations is of crucial importance for an understanding of the functioning of the market order. But to bring about a mutual adjustment of individual plans is not all that the market achieves. It also secures that whatever is being produced will be produced by people who can do so more cheaply than (or at least as cheaply as) anybody who does not produce it (and cannot devote his energies to produce something else comparatively even more cheaply), and that each product is sold at a price lower than that at which anybody who in fact does not produce it could supply it. This, of course, does not exclude that some may make considerable profits over their costs if these costs are much lower than those of the next efficient potential producer. But it does mean that of the combination of commodities that is in fact produced, as much will be produced as we know to bring about by any known method. It will of course not be as much as we might produce if all the knowledge anybody possessed or can acquire were commanded by some one agency, and fed into a computer (the cost of finding out would, however, be considerable). Yet we do injustice to the achievement of the market if we judge it, as it were, from above, by comparing

[6]G. Hardin, *Nature and Man's Fate* (1951), Mentor ed. 1961, p. 54.

it with an ideal standard which we have no known way of achieving. If we judge it, as we ought to, from below, that is, if the comparison in this case is made against what we could achieve by any other method —especially against what would be produced if competition were prevented, so that only those to whom some authority had conferred the right to produce or sell particular things were allowed to do so. All we need to consider is how difficult it is in a competitive system to discover ways of supplying to consumers better or cheaper goods than they already get. Where such unused opportunities seem to exist we usually find that they remain undeveloped because their use is either prevented by the power of authority (including the enforcement of patent privileges), or by some private misuse of power which the law ought to prohibit.

It must not be forgotten that in this respect the market only brings about an approach towards some point on that n-dimensional surface, by which pure economic theory represents the horizon of all possibilities to which the production of any one proportional combination of commodities and services could conceivably be carried. The market leaves the particular combination of goods, and its distribution among individuals, largely to unforeseeable circumstances—and, in this sense, to accident. It is, as Adam Smith already understood,[7] as if we had agreed to play a game, partly of skill and partly of chance. This competitive game, at the price of leaving the share of each individual in some measure to accident, ensures that the real equivalent of whatever his share turns out to be, is as large as we know how to make it. The game is, to use up-to-date language, not a zero-sum game, but one through which, by playing it according to the rules, the pool to be shared is enlarged, leaving individual shares in the pool in a great measure to chance. A mind knowing all the facts could select any point he liked on the surface and distribute this product in the manner he thought right. But the only point on, or tolerably near, the horizon of possibilities which we know how to reach is the one at which we shall arrive if we leave its determination to the market. The so-called 'maximum' which we thus reach naturally cannot be defined as a sum of particular things, but only in terms of the chances it offers to unknown people to get as large a real equivalent as possible for their relative shares, which will be determined partly by accident. Simply because its results cannot be assessed in terms of a single scale of values, as is the case in an economy proper, it is very misleading to assess the results of a catallaxy as if it were an economy.

---

[7]Adam Smith, *The Theory of Moral Sentiments*, London, 1759, part VI, chapter 2, penultimate paragraph, and part VII, section II, chapter 1.

4

Misinterpretation of the market order as an economy that can and ought to satisfy different needs in a certain order of priority, shows itself particularly in the efforts of policy to correct prices and incomes in the interest of what is called 'social justice'. Whatever meaning social philosophers have attached to this concept, in the practice of economic policy it has almost always meant one thing, and one thing only: the protection of certain groups against the necessity to descend from the absolute or relative material position which they have for some time enjoyed. Yet this is not a principle on which it is possible to act generally without destroying the foundations of the market order. Not only continuous increase, but in certain circumstances even mere maintenance of the existing level of incomes, depends on adaptation to unforeseen changes. This necessarily involves the relative, and perhaps even the absolute, share of some having to be reduced, although they are in no way responsible for the reduction.

The point to keep constantly in mind is that *all* economic adjustment is made necessary by unforeseen changes; and the whole reason for employing the price mechanism is to tell individuals that what they are doing, or can do, has for some reason for which they are not responsible become less or more demanded. Adaptation of the whole order of activities to changed circumstances rests on the remuneration derived from different activities being changed, without regard to the merits or faults of those affected.

The term 'incentives' is often used in this connection with somewhat misleading connotations, as if the main problem were to induce people to exert themselves sufficiently. However, the chief guidance which prices offer is not so much how to act, but *what to do*. In a continuously changing world even mere maintenance of a given level of wealth requires incessant changes in the direction of the efforts of some, which will be brought about only if the remuneration of some activities is increased and that of others decreased. With these adjustments, which under relatively stable conditions are needed merely to maintain the income stream, no 'surplus' is available which can be used to compensate those against whom prices turn. Only in a rapidly growing system can we hope to avoid absolute declines in the position of some groups.

Modern economists seem in this connection often to overlook that even the relative stability shown by many of those aggregates which macro-economics treats as data, is itself the result of a micro-economic process, of which changes in relative prices are an essential part. It is only thanks to the market mechanism that someone else is induced to step in and fill the gap caused by the failure of anyone to fulfil the expectations of his partners. Indeed, all those aggregate demand and supply curves with which we like to operate are not really objectively given facts, but results of the process of competition going on all the time. Nor can we hope to learn from statistical information what changes in prices or incomes are necessary in order to bring about adjustments to the inevitable changes.

The chief point, however, is that in a democratic society it would be wholly impossible by commands to bring about changes which are not felt to be just, and the necessity of which could never be clearly demonstrated. Deliberate regulation in such a political system must always aim at securing prices which appear to be just. This means in practice preservation of the traditional structure of incomes and prices. An economic system in which each gets what others think he deserves would necessarily be a highly inefficient system—quite apart from its being also an intolerably oppressive system. Every 'incomes policy' is therefore more likely to prevent than to facilitate those changes in the price and income structures that are required to adapt the system to new circumstances.

It is one of the paradoxes of the present world that the communist countries are probably freer from the incubus of 'social justice', and more willing to let those bear the burden against whom developments turn, than are the 'capitalist' countries. For some Western countries at least the position seems hopeless, precisely because the ideology dominating their politics makes changes impossible that are necessary for the position of the working class to rise sufficiently fast to lead to the disappearance of this ideology.

5

If even in highly developed economic systems competition is important as a process of exploration in which prospectors search for unused opportunities that, when discovered, can also be used by others, this is to an even greater extent true of underdeveloped societies. My first attention has been deliberately given to problems of preserving an efficient order for conditions in which most resources and techniques are generally known, and constant adaptations of activities are made necessary only by inevitably minor changes, in order to maintain a given level of incomes. I will not consider here the undoubted role competition plays in the advance of technological knowledge. But I do want to point out how much more important it must be in countries where the chief task is to discover yet unknown opportunities of a society in which in the past competition has not been active. It may not be altogether absurd, although largely erroneous, to believe that we can foresee and control the structure of society which further technological advance will produce in already highly developed countries. But it is simply fantastic to believe that we can determine in advance the social structure in a country where the chief problem still is to discover what material and human resources are available, or that for such a country we can predict the particular consequences of any measures we may take.

Apart from the fact that there is in such countries so much more to be discovered, there is still another reason why the greatest freedom of competition seems to be even more important there than in more advanced countries. This is that required changes in habits and customs will be brought about only if the few willing and able to experiment with new methods can make it necessary for the many to follow them, and at the same time to show them the way. The required discovery process will be impeded or prevented, if the many are able to keep the few to the traditional ways. Of course, it is one of the chief reasons for the dislike of competition that it not only shows how things can be done more effectively, but also confronts those who depend for their incomes on the market with the alternative of imitating the more successful or losing some or all of their income. Competition produces in this way a kind of impersonal compulsion which makes it necessary for numerous individuals to adjust their way of life in a manner that no deliberate instructions or commands could bring about. Central direction in the service of so-called 'social justice' may be a luxury rich nations can afford, perhaps for a long time, without too great an impairment of their incomes. But it is certainly not a method by which poor countries can accelerate their adaptation to rapidly changing circumstances, on which their growth depends.

Perhaps it deserves mention in this connection that possibilities of growth are likely to be greater the more extensive are a country's yet unused opportunities. Strange though this may seem at first sight, a high rate of growth is more often than not evidence that opportunities have been neglected in the past. Thus, a high rate of growth can sometimes testify to bad policies of the past rather than good policies of the present. Consequently it is unreasonable to expect in already highly developed countries as high a rate of growth as can for some time be achieved in countries where effective utilisation of resources was previously long prevented by legal and institutional obstacles.

From all I have seen of the world the proportion of private persons who are prepared to try new possibilities, if they appear to them to promise better conditions, and if they are not prevented by the pressure of their fellows, is much the same everywhere. The much lamented absence of a spirit of enterprise in many of the new countries is not an unalterable characteristic of the individual inhabitants, but the consequence of restraints which existing customs and institutions place upon them. This is why it would be fatal in such societies for the collective will to be allowed to direct the efforts of individuals, instead of governmental power being confined to protecting individuals against the pressures of society. Such protection for private initiatives and enterprise can only ever be achieved through the institution of private property and the whole aggregate of libertarian institutions of law.

BIBLIOGRAPHY

POLITICAL THEORY IS a vast subject and it is impossible to provide a comprehensive bibliography. I offer instead a selective bibliography of further readings on the themes associated with the different sections of the Introduction, in particular the themes represented by the articles reprinted here. No reading appears more than once.*

1. Introduction: Nature of Political Theory/Justice

Arthur, J. and W. H. Shaw, eds. (1978) *Justice and Economic Distribution* (Englewood Cliffs: Prentice-Hall).

Barry, B. (1965) *Political Argument* (London: Routledge & Kegan Paul).

Barry, N. P. (1981) *An Introduction to Modern Political Theory* (London: Macmillan).

Benn, S. I. and R. S. Peters (1959) *Social Principles and the Democratic State* (London: Allen & Unwin).

Brown, A. (1986) *Modern Political Philosophy* (Harmondsworth: Penguin).

Campbell, T. (1988) *Justice* (London: Macmillan).

de Crespigny, A. and K. Minogue, eds. (1976) *Contemporary Political Philosophers* (London: Methuen).

Feinberg, J. (1973) *Social Philosophy* (Englewood Cliffs, N.J.: Prentice-Hall).

Graham, K., ed. (1982) *Contemporary Political Philosophy* (Cambridge: Cambridge University Press).

Hamlin, A. and P. Pettit, eds. (1989) *The Good Polity* (Oxford: Blackwell).

Kamenka, E. and A. E. Tay, eds. (1979) *Justice* (London: Edward Arnold).

*I am grateful to Frances Redrup for her help in assembling this bibliography.

Laslett, P. et al., eds. (1969–1979) *Philosophy, Politics and Society* (series I–V) (Oxford: Blackwell).
Miller, D. (1976) *Social Justice* (Oxford: Oxford University Press).
Miller, D. and L. Siedentop, eds. (1983) *The Nature of Political Theory* (Oxford: Oxford University Press).
Pettit, P. (1980) *Judging Justice* (London: Routledge & Kegan Paul).
Quinton, A., ed. (1967) *Political Philosophy* (Oxford: Oxford University Press).
Raphael, D. D. (1976) *Problems of Political Philosophy* (London: Macmillan).
Sen, A. (1979) *Collective Choice and Social Welfare* (San Francisco: Holden-Day).
Walzer, M., ed. (1989) 'The State of Political Theory,' *Dissent* (Special Issue).
Weale, A. (1983) *Political Theory and Social Policy* (London: Macmillan).

2. The Desirable

A. CONSEQUENTIALISM VS. NONCONSEQUENTIALISM

Braithwaite, J. and P. Pettit (1990) *Not Just Deserts: A Republican Theory of Criminal Justice* (Oxford: Oxford University Press).
Brandt, R. B. (1979) *A Theory of the Good and the Right* (Oxford: Oxford University Press).
Foot, P. (1978) *Virtues and Vices* (Los Angeles: University of California Press).
Lyons, D. (1965) *The Forms and Limits of Utilitarianism* (Oxford: Oxford University Press).
Parfit, D. (1984) *Reasons and Persons* (Oxford: Oxford University Press).
Regan, D. (1980) *Utilitarianism and Cooperation* (Oxford: Oxford University Press).
Scheffler, S., ed. (1988) *Consequentialism and Its Critics* (Oxford: Oxford University Press).
Scheffler, S. (1982) *The Rejection of Consequentialism* (Oxford: Oxford University Press).
Slote, M. (1985) *Common-Sense Morality and Consequentialism* (London: Routledge & Kegan Paul).
Slote, M. (1989) *Beyond Optimizing* (Cambridge, Mass.: Harvard University Press).

B. RIGHTS

Becker, L. (1977) *Property Rights* (London: Routledge)
Campbell, T. (1983) *The Left and Rights* (London: Routledge).
Dworkin, R. (1977) *Taking Rights Seriously* (London: Duckworth).
Feinberg, J. (1980) *Rights, Justice, and the Bonds of Liberty* (Princeton: Princeton University Press).
Finnis, J. (1980) *Natural Law and Natural Rights* (Oxford: Oxford University Press).
Gewirth, A. (1980) *Reason and Morality* (Chicago: University of Chicago Press).
Kamenka, E. and A. E. S. Tay, eds. (1978) *Human Rights* (London: Edward Arnold).
Melden, A. I. (1959) *Rights and Right Conduct* (Oxford: Blackwell).
Nagel, R. (1974) *Anarchy, State, and Utopia* (New York: Basic Books).
Pennock, J. R. and J. W. Chapman, eds. (1981) *Human Rights: Nomos XXIII* (New York: New York University Press).

Tuck, R. (1979) *Natural Rights Theories: Their Origin and Development* (Cambridge: Cambridge University Press).
Waldron, J., ed. (1984) *Theories of Rights* (Oxford: Oxford University Press).
Waldron, J., ed. (1987) *Nonsense on Stilts* (London: Methuen).
White, A. R. (1984) *Rights* (Oxford: Oxford University Press).

C. LIBERTY

Benn, S. (1989) *A Theory of Freedom* (Cambridge: Cambridge University Press).
Berlin, I. (1967) *Four Essays on Liberty* (Oxford: Oxford University Press).
Dworkin, R. (1988) *The Theory and Practice of Autonomy* (Cambridge: Cambridge University Press).
Flathman, R. E. (1987) *The Philosophy and Politics of Freedom* (Chicago: University of Chicago Press).
Goodin, R. (1988) *Reasons for Welfare* (Princeton: Princeton University Press).
Honderich, T., ed. (1973) *Essays on Freedom of Actions* (London: Routledge & Kegan Paul).
Lindley, R. (1986) *Autonomy* (London: Macmillan).
Oppenheim, F. (1961) *Dimensions of Freedom* (New York: St. Martins Press).
Phillips Griffiths, A., ed. (1983) *Of Liberty* (Cambridge: Cambridge University Press).
Pelczyinski, Z. and J. Gray, eds. (1984) *Conceptions of Liberty in Political Philosophy* (London: Athbone Press).
Raz, J. (1980) *The Morality of Freedom* (Oxford: Oxford University Press).
Ryan, A., ed. (1979) *The Idea of Freedom* (Oxford: Oxford University Press).
Taylor, M. (1982) *Community, Anarchy and Liberty* (Cambridge: Cambridge University Press).
Young, R. (1986) *Personal Autonomy* (London: St. Martins).

D. DEMOCRACY

Barber, B. (1984) *Strong Democracy* (Berkeley: University of California Press).
Barry, B. (1970) *Economists, Sociologists and Democracy* (Chicago: University of Chicago Press).
Burnheim, J. (1985) *Is Democracy Possible?* (Oxford: Polity Press).
Cohen, J. and J. Rogers (1983) *On Democracy* (Harmondsworth: Penguin).
Cunningham, F. (1987) *Democratic Theory and Socialism* (Cambridge: Cambridge University Press).
Dahl, R. (1956) *A Preface to Democratic Theory* (Chicago: University of Chicago Press).
Downs, A. (1957) *An Economic Theory of Democracy* (New York: Harper).
Green, P. (1985) *Retrieving Democracy* (Totowa, N.J.: Rowman & Allenheld).
Habermas, J. (1973) *Legitimation Crisis* (Boston: Bascon).
Hirschman, A. O. (1970) *Exit, Voice and Loyalty* (Cambridge, Mass.: Harvard University Press).
Lively, J. (1975) *Democracy* (Oxford: Blackwell).
Macpherson, C. B. (1973) *Democratic Theory* (Oxford: Oxford University Press).
Macpherson, C. B. (1977) *The Life and Times of Liberal Democracy* (Oxford: Oxford University Press).
Mausbridge, J. (1980) *Beyond Adversarial Democracy* (New York: Basic Books).
Nelson, W. N. (1980) *On Justifying Democracy* (London: Routledge).

Pateman, C. (1970) *Participation and Democratic Theory* (Cambridge: Cambridge University Press).
Pennock, J. R. (1979) *Democratic Political Theory* (Princeton: Princeton University Press).
Riker, W. (1982) *Liberalism against Populism* (San Francisco: Freeman).
Schumpeter, J. (1954) *Capitalism, Socialism and Democracy*, 4th ed. (London: Allen & Unwin).
Singer, P. (1973) *Democracy and Disobedience* (Oxford: Oxford University Press).

E. UTILITY

(see also Consequentialism vs. Nonconsequentialism section)

Frey, R. G., ed. (1984) *Utility and Rights* (Minneapolis: University of Minnesota Press).
Griffin, J. (1986) *Well-Being* (Oxford: Oxford University Press).
Hodgson, D. H. (1967) *The Consequences of Utilitarianism* (Oxford: Oxford University Press).
Miller, H. and W. Williams, eds. (1982) *The Limits of Utilitarianism* (Minneapolis: University of Minnesota Press).
Quinton, A. (1973) *Utilitarian Ethics* (London: Macmillan).
Sen, A. and B. Williams, eds. (1982) *Utilitarianism and Beyond* (Cambridge: Cambridge University Press).
Smart, J. J. C. and B. Williams (1973) *Utilitarianism: For and Against* (Cambridge: Cambridge University Press).
Von Wright, G. H. (1963) *The Varieties of Goodness* (London: Routledge).

F. POVERTY AND RELATED MATTERS

Braybrooke, D. (1987) *Meeting Needs* (Princeton: Princeton University Press).
Goodin, R. (1985) *Protecting the Vulnerable* (Chicago: University of Chicago Press).
Grabb, E. G. (1984) *Social Inequality* (Toronto: Holt, Rinehart & Winston).
Gutman, A. (1980) *Liberal Equality* (Cambridge: Cambridge University Press).
Ignatieff, R. (1984) *The Needs of Strangers* (London: Chatto & Windus).
Leiss, W. (1976) *The Limits of Satisfaction* (Toronto: University of Toronto Press).
Miller, D. (1989) *Market, State and Community* (Oxford: Oxford University Press).
O'Neill, D. (1986) *Faces of Hunger* (London: Allen & Unwin).
Rae, D. et al. (1981) *Equalities* (Cambridge, Mass.: Harvard University Press).
Reeve, A., ed. (1987) *Modern Theories of Exploitation* (London: Sage).
Roemer, J. (1982) *A General Theory of Exploitation and Class* (Cambridge, Mass.: Harvard University Press).
Roemer, J. (1988) *Free to Lose* (London: Radius).
Sen, A. (1973) *On Economic Inequality* (Oxford: Oxford University Press).
Sen, A. (1981) *Poverty and Famines* (Oxford: Oxford University Press).
Springborg, P. (1981) *The Problem of Human Needs and the Critique of Civilization* (London: Allen & Unwin).
Tawney, R. H. (1964) *Equality* (London: Allen & Unwin).
Wiggins, D. (1987) *Needs, Values, Truth* (Oxford: Basil Blackwell).

G. Feminist Critiques

Clark, L. and L. Lange (1979) *The Sexism of Social and Political Thought* (Toronto: University of Toronto Press).

Daly, M. (1984) *Pure Lust: Elemental Feminist Philosophy* (Boston: Beacon Press).

Eisenstein, Z. R. (1981) *The Radical Future of Liberal Feminism* (New York: Longman).

Elshtain, J. B. (1981) *Public Man, Private Woman* (Princeton: Princeton University Press).

Gilligan, C. (1982) *In a Different Voice* (Cambridge, Mass.: Harvard University Press).

Grimshaw, J. (1986) *Philosophy and Feminist Thinking* (Minneapolis: University of Minnesota Press).

Harding, S. and M. B. Hintikka, eds. (1983) *Discovering Reality* (Dordrecht: Reidel).

Kittay, E. F. and D. T. Meyers, eds. (1987) *Women and Moral Theory* (Totowa, N.J.: Rowman & Littlefield).

Lerner, G. (1986) *The Creation of Patriarchy* (New York, Oxford University Press).

Lloyd, G. (1984) *The Man of Reason* (Minneapolis: University of Minnesota Press).

Noddings, N. (1984) *Caring: A Feminine Approach to Ethics and Moral Education* (Los Angeles: University of California Press).

O'Brien, M. (1981) *The Politics of Reproduction* (London: Routledge).

Okin, S. (1979) *Women in Western Political Thought* (Princeton: Princeton University Press).

Pateman, C. and E. Gross, eds. (1987) *Feminist Challenges: Social and Political Theory* (Boston: Northeastern University Press).

Pateman, C. (1988) *The Sexual Contract* (Oxford: Polity Press).

Pateman, C. (1988) *The Disorder of Women* (Oxford: Polity Press).

Pitkin, H. (1984) *Fortune Is a Woman* (Berkeley: University of California Press).

Radcliffe, R. J. (1980) *The Sceptical Feminist* (London: Routledge & Kegan Paul).

Siltanen, J. and M. Stenworth, eds. (1984) *Women and the Public Sphere* (London: Hutchinson).

Sunstein, C., ed. (1989) *Symposium on Feminism and Political Theory* (*Ethics*, Special Issue, Vol. 99.)

Stichm, J. H., ed. (1984) *Women's Views of the Political World of Men* (Dobbs Ferry, N.Y.: Transnational Publishers).

Wolgest, E. (1980) *Equality and the Rights of Women* (Ithaca, N.Y.: Cornell University Press).

3. The Eligible

Barry, B. (1973) *The Liberal Theory of Justice* (Oxford: Oxford University Press).

Barry, B. (1989) *A Treatise on Social Justice. Volume 1: Theories of Justice* (London: Harvester-Wheatsheaf).

Buchanan, J. M. and G. Tullock (1965) *The Calculus of Consent* (Ann Arbor: University of Michigan Press).

Daniels, N. (1975) *Reading Rawls* (Oxford: Blackwell).

Gauthier, D. (1986) *Morals by Agreement* (Oxford: Oxford University Press).

Grice, G. R. (1967) *The Grounds of Moral Judgment* (Cambridge: Cambridge University Press).

Hampton, J. (1986) *Hobbes and the Social Contract Tradition* (Cambridge: Cambridge University Press).

Harsanyi, J. (1976) *Essays on Ethics, Social Behaviour and Scientific Explanation* (Dordrecht: Reidel).

Kukathas, C. and P. Pettit (1990) *Rawls: A Theory of Justice and Its Critics* (Oxford: Polity Press).

Lessnoff, M. (1987) *Social Contract* (London: Macmillan).

Rawls, J. (1971) *A Theory of Justice* (Oxford: Oxford University Press).

Richards, D. A. J. (1971) *A Theory of the Reasons for Action* (Oxford: Oxford University Press).

Sandel, M. (1982) *Liberalism and the Limits of Justice* (Cambridge: Cambridge University Press).

Wolff, R. P. (1977) *Understanding Rawls. A Reconstruction and Critique of A Theory of Justice* (Princeton: Princeton University Press).

4. The Feasible

Arrow, K. (1963) *Social Choice and Individual Values*, 2nd ed. (New Haven: Yale University Press).

Arrow, K. (1983) *Collected Papers: Social Choice and Justice* (Cambridge, Mass.: Harvard University Press).

Axelrod, R. (1984) *The Evolution of Cooperation* (New York: Basic Books).

Bonner, B. (1986) *Politics, Economics and Welfare* (Brighton: Wheatsheaf).

Brennan, G. and J. M. Buchanan (1985) *The Reason of Rules* (Cambridge: Cambridge University Press).

Fishkin, J. (1982) *The Limits of Obligation* (New Haven: Yale University Press).

Goodin, R. (1982) *Political Theory and Public Policy* (Chicago: University of Chicago Press).

Hardin, R. (1982) *Collective Action* (Baltimore: Johns Hopkins University Press).

Hardin, R. (1988) *Morality within the Limits of Reason* (Chicago: University of Chicago Press).

Hindess, B. (1987) *Freedom, Equality and the Market* (London: Tavistock).

McLean, I. (1987) *Public Choice* (Oxford: Blackwell).

Olson, M. (1971) *The Logic of Collective Action* (Cambridge, Mass.: Harvard University Press).

Sen, A. (1987) *On Ethics and Economics* (Oxford: Blackwell).

Sen, A. (1984) *Choice, Welfare and Measurements* (Oxford: Blackwell).

Sugden, R. (1986) *The Economics of Rights, Cooperation and Welfare* (Oxford: Blackwell).

Taylor, M. (1987) *The Possibility of Cooperation* (Cambridge: Cambridge University Press).

5. Conclusion: Individualism

Brennan, G. and C. Walsh, eds. (1989) *Rationality, Individualism and Public Policy* (Canberra: Centre for Federal Financial Relations, Australian National University).

Gaus, G. F. (1983) *The Modern Liberal Theory of Man* (New York: St. Martin's Press).

Heller, T. C., M. Sosna and D. E. Welbery (1986) *Reconstructing Individualism* (Stanford: Stanford University Press).

Kymlicka, W. (1989) *Liberalism, Community and Culture* (Oxford: Oxford University Press).

Larmore, C. (1987) *Patterns of Moral Complexity* (Cambridge: Cambridge University Press).

Lukes, S. (1973) *Individualism* (Oxford: Blackwell).

MacIntyre, A. (1986) *After Virtue. A Study in Moral Theory*, 2nd ed. (London: Duckworth).

Pettit, P. (forthcoming) *The Common Mind: From Folk Psychology to Social and Political Theory* (Oxford: Oxford University Press).

Sandel, M., ed. (1984) *Liberalism and Its Critics* (Oxford: Blackwell).

Taylor, C. (1985) *Philosophical Papers*, 2 vols. (Cambridge: Cambridge University Press).

Walzer, M. (1983) *Spheres of Justice* (Oxford: Blackwell).